The **Essential Guide** for Ca

C000181114

Fra nce

NEW EDITION

200
things for the car enthusiast to see and do!

VELOCE PUBLISHING
THE PUBLISHER OF FINE AUTOMOTIVE BOOKS

Julian Parish

General

1½-litre GP Racing 1961-1965 (Whitelock)
AC Two-litre Saloons & Buckland Sportscars (Archibald)
Alfa Romeo 155/156/147 Competition Touring Cars (Collins)
Alfa Romeo Giulia Coupé GT & GTA (Tipler)
Alfa Romeo Montreal – The dream car that came true (Taylor)
Alfa Romeo Montreal – The Essential Companion (Classic Reprint of 500 copies) (Taylor)
Alfa Tipo 33 (McDonough & Collins)
Alpine & Renault – The Development of the Revolutionary Turbo F1 Car 1968 to 1979 (Smith)
Alpine & Renault – The Sports Prototypes 1963 to 1969 (Smith)
Alpine & Renault – The Sports Prototypes 1973 to 1978 (Smith)
Anatomy of the Classic Mini (Huthert & Ely)
Anatomy of the Works Minis (Moylan)
Armstrong-Siddeley (Smith)
Art Deco and British Car Design (Down)
Autodrome (Collins & Ireland)
Autodrome 2 (Collins & Ireland)
Automotive A-Z, Lane's Dictionary of Automotive Terms (Lane)
Automotive Mascots (Kay & Springate)
Bahamas Speed Weeks, The (O'Neil)
Bentley Continental, Corniche and Azure (Bennett)
Bentley MkVI, Rolls-Royce Silver Wraith, Dawn & Cloud/Bentley R & S-Series (Nutland)
Bluebird CN7 (Stevens)
BMC Competitions Department Secrets (Turner, Chambers & Browning)
BMW 5-Series (Cranswick)
BMW Z-Cars (Taylor)
BMW Boxer Twins 1970-1995 Bible, The (Falloon)
BMW Cafe Racers (Cloesen)
BMW Custom Motorcycles – Choppers, Cruisers, Bobbers, Trikes & Quads (Cloesen)
BMW – The Power of M (Vivian)
Bonjour – Is this Italy? (Turner)
British 250cc Racing Motorcycles (Pereira)
British at Indianapolis, The (Wagstaff)
British Café Racers (Cloesen)
British Cars, The Complete Catalogue of, 1895-1975 (Culshaw & Horrobin)
British Custom Motorcycles – The Brit Chop – choppers, cruisers, bobbers & trikes (Cloesen)
BRM – A Mechanic's Tale (Salmon)
BRM V16 (Ludvigsen)
BSA Bantam Bible, The (Henshaw)
BSA Motorcycles – the final evolution (Jones)
Bugatti Type 40 (Price)
Bugatti 46/50 Updated Edition (Price & Arbey)
Bugatti T44 & T49 (Price & Arbey)
Bugatti 57 2nd Edition (Price)
Bugatti Type 57 Grand Prix – A Celebration (Tomlinson)
Caravan, Improve & Modify Your (Porter)
Caravans, The Illustrated History 1919-1959 (Jenkinson)
Caravans, The Illustrated History From 1960 (Jenkinson)
Carrera Panamericana, La (Tipler)
Car-tastrophes – 80 automotive atrocities from the past 20 years (Honest John, Fowler)
Chrysler 300 – America's Most Powerful Car 2nd Edition (Ackerson)
Chrysler PT Cruiser (Ackerson)
Citroën DS (Bobbitt)
Classic British Car Electrical Systems (Astley)
Cobra – The Real Thing! (Legate)
Competition Car Aerodynamics 3rd Edition (McBeath)
Competition Car Composites A Practical Handbook (Revised 2nd Edition) (McBeath)
Concept Cars, How to illustrate and design (Dewey)
Cortina – Ford's Bestseller (Robson)
Cosworth - The Search for Power (6th edition) (Robson)
Coventry Climax Racing Engines (Hammill)
Daily Mirror 1970 World Cup Rally 40, The (Robson)
Daimler SP250 New Edition (Long)
Datsun Fairlady Roadster to 280ZX – The Z-Car Story (Long)
Dino – The V6 Ferrari (Long)
Dodge Challenger & Plymouth Barracuda (Grist)
Dodge Charger – Enduring Thunder (Ackerson)
Dodge Dynamite! (Grist)
Dorset from the Sea – The Jurassic Coast from Lyme Regis to Old Harry Rocks photographed from its best viewpoint (also Souvenir Edition) (Belasco)
Draw & Paint Cars – How to (Gardiner)
Drive on the Wild Side, A – 20 Extreme Driving Adventures From Around the World (Weaver)
Ducati 750 Bible, The (Falloon)
Ducati 750 SS 'round-case' 1974, The Book of the (Falloon)
Ducati 860, 900 and Mille Bible, The (Falloon)
Ducati Monster Bible (New Updated & Revised Edition), The (Falloon)
Ducati 916 (updated edition) (Falloon)
Dune Buggy, Building A – The Essential Manual (Shakespeare)
Dune Buggy Files (Hale)
Dune Buggy Handbook (Hale)
East German Motor Vehicles in Pictures (Suhr/Weinreich)
Fast Ladies – Female Racing Drivers 1888 to 1970 (Bouzanquet)
Fate of the Sleeping Beauties, The (op de Weegh/Hottendorff/op de Weegh)
Ferrari 288 GTO, The Book of the (Sackey)
Ferrari 333 SP (O'Neil)
Fiat & Abarth 124 Spider & Coupé (Tipler)
Fiat & Abarth 500 & 600 – 2nd Edition (Bobbitt)
Fiats, Great Small (Ward)
Fine Art of the Motorcycle Engine, The (Peirce)
Ford Cleveland 335-Series V8 engine 1970 to 1982 – The Essential Source Book (Hammill)
Ford F100/F150 Pick-up 1948-1996 (Ackerson)
Ford F150 Pick-up 1997-2005 (Ackerson)
Ford GT – Then, and Now (Streather)
Ford GT40 (Legate)
Ford Midsize Muscle – Fairlane, Torino & Ranchero (Cranswick)
Ford Model Y (Roberts)
Ford Small Block V8 Racing Engines 1962-1970 – The Essential Source Book (Hammill)
Ford Thunderbird From 1954, The Book of the (Long)
Formula 5000 Motor Racing, Back then ... and back now (Lawson)
Forza Minardi! (Vigar)
France: the essential guide for car enthusiasts – 200 things for the car enthusiast to see and do (Parish)
From Crystal Palace to Red Square – A Hapless Biker's Road to Russia (Turner)
Funky Mopeds (Skelton)
Grand Prix Ferrari – The Years of Enzo Ferrari's Power, 1948-1980 (Pritchard)
Grand Prix Ford – DFV-powered Formula 1 Cars (Robson)
GT – The World's Best GT Cars 1953-73 (Dawson)
Hillclimbing & Sprinting – The Essential Manual (Short & Wilkinson)
Honda NSX (Long)
Inside the Rolls-Royce & Bentley Styling Department – 1971 to 2001 (Hull)
Intermeccanica – The Story of the Prancing Bull (McCredie & Reisner)
Italian Cafe Racers (Cloesen)
Italian Custom Motorcycles (Cloesen)
Jaguar, The Rise of (Price)
Jaguar XJ 220 – The Inside Story (Moreton)
Jaguar XJ-S, The Book of the (Long)
Japanese Custom Motorcycles – The Nippon Chop – Chopper, Cruiser, Bobber, Trikes and Quads (Cloesen)
Jeep CJ (Ackerson)
Jeep Wrangler (Ackerson)
The Jowett Jupiter - The car that leaped to fame (Nankivell)
Karmann-Ghia Coupé & Convertible (Bobbitt)
Kawasaki Triples Bible, The (Walker)
Kawasaki Z1 Story, The (Sheehan)
Kris Meeke – Intercontinental Rally Challenge Champion (McBride)
Lamborghini Miura Bible, The (Sackey)
Lamborghini Urraco, The Book of the (Landsem)
Lambretta Bible, The (Davies)
Lancia 037 (Collins)
Lancia Delta HF Integrale (Blaettel & Wagner)
Land Rover Series III Reborn (Porter)
Land Rover, The Half-ton Military (Cook)
Laverda Twins & Triples Bible 1968-1986 (Falloon)
Lea-Francis Story, The (Price)
Le Mans Panoramic (Ireland)
Lexus Story, The (Long)
Little book of microcars, the (Quellin)
Little book of smart, the – New Edition (Jackson)
Little book of trikes, the (Quellin)
Lola – The Illustrated History (1957-1977) (Starkey)
Lola – All the Sports Racing & Single-seater Racing Cars 1978-1997 (Starkey)
Lola T70 – The Racing History & Individual Chassis Record – 4th Edition (Starkey)
Lotus 18 Colin Chapman's U-turn (Whitelock)
Lotus 49 (Oliver)
Marketingmobiles, The Wonderful Wacky World of (Hale)
Maserati 250F In Focus (Pritchard)
Mazda MX-5/Miata 1.6 Enthusiast's Workshop Manual (Grainger & Shoemark)
Mazda MX-5/Miata 1.8 Enthusiast's Workshop Manual (Grainger & Shoemark)
Mazda MX-5 Miata, The book of the – The 'Mk1' NA-series 1988 to 1997 (Long)
Mazda MX-5 Miata Roadster (Long)
Mazda Rotary-engined Cars (Cranswick)
Maximum Mini (Booij)
Meet the English (Bowie)
Mercedes-Benz SL – R230 series 2001 to 2011 (Long)
Mercedes-Benz SL – W113-series 1963-1971 (Long)
Mercedes-Benz SL & SLC – 107-series 1971-1989 (Long)
Mercedes-Benz SLK – R170 series 1996-2004 (Long)
Mercedes-Benz SLK – R171 series 2004-2011 (Long)
Mercedes-Benz W123-series – All models 1976 to 1986 (Long)
Mercedes G-Wagen (Long)
MGA (Price Williams)
MGB & MGB GT– Expert Guide (Auto-doc Series) (Williams)
MGB Electrical Systems Updated & Revised Edition (Astley)
Micro Caravans (Jenkinson)
Micro Trucks (Mort)
Microcars at Large! (Quellin)
Mini Cooper – The Real Thing! (Tipler)
Mini Minor to Asia Minor (West)
Mitsubishi Lancer Evo, The Road Car & WRC Story (Long)
Montlhéry, The Story of the Paris Autodrome (Boddy)
Morgan Maverick (Lawrence)
Morgan 3 Wheeler – back to the future!, The (Dron)
Morris Minor, 60 Years on the Road (Newell)
Moto Guzzi Sport & Le Mans Bible, The (Falloon)
Motor Movies – The Posters! (Veysey)
Motor Racing – Reflections of a Lost Era (Carter)
Motor Racing – The Pursuit of Victory 1930-1962 (Carter)
Motor Racing – The Pursuit of Victory 1963-1972 (Wyatt/Sears)
Motor Racing Heroes – The Stories of 100 Greats (Newman)
Motorcycle Apprentice (Cakebread)
Motorcycle GP Racing in the 1960s (Pereira)
Motorcycle Road & Racing Chassis Designs (Noakes)
Motorhomes, The Illustrated History (Jenkinson)
Motorsport In colour, 1950s (Wainwright)
MV Agusta Fours, The book of the classic (Falloon)
N.A.R.T. – A concise history of the North American Racing Team 1957 to 1983 (O'Neil)
Nissan 300ZX & 350Z – The Z-Car Story (Long)
Nissan GT-R Supercar: Born to race (Gorodji)
Northeast American Sports Car Races 1950-1959 (O'Neil)
The Norton Commando Bible – All models 1968 to 1978 (Henshaw)
Nothing Runs – Misadventures in the Classic, Collectable & Exotic Car Biz (Slutsky)
Off-Road Giants! (Volume 1) – Heroes of 1960s Motorcycle Sport (Westlake)
Off-Road Giants! (Volume 2) – Heroes of 1960s Motorcycle Sport (Westlake)
Off-Road Giants! (volume 3) – Heroes of 1960s Motorcycle Sport (Westlake)
Pass the Theory and Practical Driving Tests (Gibson & Hoole)
Peking to Paris 2007 (Young)
Pontiac Firebird – New 3rd Edition (Cranswick)
Porsche Boxster (Long)
Porsche 356 (2nd Edition) (Long)
Porsche 908 (Födisch, Neßhöver, Roßbach, Schwarz & Roßbach)
Porsche 911 Carrera – The Last of the Evolution (Corlett)
Porsche 911R, RS & RSR, 4th Edition (Starkey)
Porsche 911, The Book of the (Long)
Porsche 911 – The Definitive History 2004-2012 (Long)
Porsche – The Racing 914s (Smith)
Porsche 911SC 'Super Carrera' – The Essential Companion (Streather)
Porsche 914 & 914-6: The Definitive History of the Road & Competition Cars (Long)
Porsche 924 (Long)
The Porsche 924 Carreras – evolution to excellence (Smith)
Porsche 928 (Long)
Porsche 944 (Long)
Porsche 964, 993 & 996 Data Plate Code Breaker (Streather)
Porsche 993 'King Of Porsche' – The Essential Companion (Streather)
Porsche 996 'Supreme Porsche' – The Essential Companion (Streather)
Porsche 997 2004-2012 – Porsche Excellence (Streather)
Porsche Racing Cars – 1953 to 1975 (Long)
Porsche Racing Cars – 1976 to 2005 (Long)
Porsche – The Rally Story (Meredith)
Porsche: Three Generations of Genius (Meredith)
Preston Tucker & Others (Linde)
RAC Rally Action! (Gardiner)
RACING COLOURS – MOTOR RACING COMPOSITIONS 1908-2009 (Newman)
Racing Line – British motorcycle racing in the golden age of the big single (Guntrip)
Rallye Sport Fords: The Inside Story (Moreton)
Renewable Energy Home Handbook, The (Porter)
Roads with a View – England's greatest views and how to find them by road (Corfield)
Rolls-Royce Silver Shadow/Bentley T Series Corniche & Camargue – Revised & Enlarged Edition (Bobbitt)
Rolls-Royce Silver Spirit, Silver Spur & Bentley Mulsanne 2nd Edition (Bobbitt)
Rootes Cars of the 50s, 60s & 70s – Hillman, Humber, Singer, Sunbeam & Talbot (Rowe)
Rover P4 (Bobbitt)
Runways & Racers (O'Neil)
Russian Motor Vehicles – Soviet Limousines 1930-2003 (Kelly)
Russian Motor Vehicles – The Czarist Period 1784 to 1917 (Kelly)
RX-7 – Mazda's Rotary Engine Sportscar (Updated & Revised New Edition) (Long)
Scooters & Microcars, The A-Z of Popular (Dan)
Scooter Lifestyle (Grainger)
SCOOTER MANIA! – Recollections of the Isle of Man International Scooter Rally (Jackson)
Singer Story: Cars, Commercial Vehicles, Bicycles & Motorcycle (Atkinson)
Sleeping Beauties USA – abandoned classic cars & trucks (Marek)
SM – Citroën's Maserati-engined Supercar (Long & Claverol)
Speedway – Auto racing's ghost tracks (Collins & Ireland)
Sprite Caravans, The Story of (Jenkinson)
Standard Motor Company, The Book of the (Robson)
Steve Hole's Kit Car Cornucopia – Cars, Companies, Stories, Facts & Figures: the UK's kit car scene since 1949 (Hole)
Subaru Impreza: The Road Car And WRC Story (Long)
Supercar, How to Build your own (Thompson)
Tales from the Toolbox (Oliver)
Tatra – The Legacy of Hans Ledwinka, Updated & Enlarged Collector's Edition of 1500 copies (Margolius & Henry)
Taxi! The Story of the 'London' Taxicab (Bobbitt)
To Boldly Go – twenty six vehicle designs that dared to be different (Hull)
Toleman Story, The (Hilton)
Toyota Celica & Supra, The Book of Toyota's Sports Coupés (Long)
Toyota MR2 Coupés & Spyders (Long)
Triumph Bonneville Bible (59-83) (Henshaw)
Triumph Bonneville!, Save the – The inside story of the Meriden Workers' Co-op (Rosamond)
Triumph Motorcycles & the Meriden Factory (Hancox)
Triumph Speed Twin & Thunderbird Bible (Woolridge)
Triumph Tiger Cub Bible (Estall)
Triumph Trophy Bible (Woolridge)
Triumph TR6 (Kimberley)
TT Talking – The TT's most exciting era – As seen by Manx Radio TT's lead commentator 2004-2012 (Lambert)
Two Summers – The Mercedes-Benz W196R Racing Car (Ackerson)
TWR Story, The – Group A (Hughes & Scott)
Unraced (Collins)
Velocette Motorcycles – MSS to Thruxton – New Third Edition (Burris)
Vespa – The Story of a Cult Classic in Pictures (Uhlig)
Vincent Motorcycles: The Untold Story since 1946 (Guyony & Parker)
Volkswagen Bus Book, The (Bobbitt)
Volkswagen Bus or Van to Camper, How to Convert (Porter)
Volkswagens of the World (Glen)
VW Beetle Cabriolet – The full story of the convertible Beetle (Bobbitt)
VW Beetle – The Car of the 20th Century (Copping)
VW Bus – 40 Years of Splitties, Bays & Wedges (Copping)
VW Bus Book, The (Bobbitt)
VW Golf: Five Generations of Fun (Copping & Cservenka)
VW – The Air-cooled Era (Copping)
VW T5 Camper Conversion Manual (Porter)
VW Campers (Copping)
Volkswagen Type 3, The book of the – Concept, Design, International Production Models & Development (Glen)
You & Your Jaguar XK8/XKR – Buying, Enjoying, Maintaining, Modifying – New Edition (Thorley)
Which Oil? – Choosing the right oils & greases for your antique, vintage, veteran, classic or collector car (Michell)
Works Minis, The Last (Purves & Brenchley)
Works Rally Mechanic (Moylan)

For updates to the content of this guide and the latest information on motoring events in France, please visit **www.driveguide.guru/france**
For any questions or suggestions for changes, email **driveguide.guru@gmail.com**

First published April 2017 by Veloce Publishing Limited, Veloce House, Parkway Farm Business Park, Middle Farm Way, Poundbury, Dorchester DT1 3AR, England. Fax 01305 268864 / e-mail info@veloce.co.uk / web www.veloce.co.uk or www.velocebooks.com. ISBN: 978-1-787110-57-1 UPC: 6-36847-01057-7 © 2017 Julian Parish and Veloce Publishing. All rights reserved. With the exception of quoting brief passages for the purpose of review, no part of this publication may be recorded, reproduced or transmitted by any means, including photocopying, without the written permission of Veloce Publishing Ltd. Throughout this book logos, model names and designations, etc, have been used for the purposes of identification, illustration and decoration. Such names are the property of the trademark holder as this is not an official publication. Readers with ideas for automotive books, or books on other transport or related hobby subjects, are invited to write to the editorial director of Veloce Publishing at the above address. British Library Cataloguing in Publication Data – A catalogue record for this book is available from the British Library. Typesetting, design and page make-up all by Veloce Publishing Ltd. Printed in India by Replika Press.

Contents

Cover image courtesy Julian Parish.

Introduction

France is the world's most popular destination for tourists. If you're reading this guide, there's a good chance you've already been there ... perhaps many times.

Sometimes, it seems hard to be a car-lover in France today: access to the centre of major cities is increasingly restricted for older cars and there are speed cameras everywhere. The terrorist attacks since 2015 have imposed stringent new security requirements on many event organisers, while local authorities everywhere face ever greater pressure on their budgets.

Despite all this, many French people have a real passion for cars, and there is a wealth of things for the enthusiast to see and do. A survey carried out by the French historic vehicle federation, the FFVE, in 2015 documented 6500 events taking place each year, or the equivalent of one in each 'département' every week of the year.

For nearly twenty years I have had the good fortune to live in France, and to discover many of these places and events with fellow car club members. Some, like Rétromobile in Paris or the Cité de l'Automobile in Mulhouse, need little introduction. As I talked with friends back in England, however, I realised that many of these attractions – often in areas popular with holidaymakers – were little known, and that it was hard to find information about them, especially in English. In fact, there didn't seem to be a guide like this in English, or even in French. And so the idea for this guide was born.

France for car enthusiasts

The entries in this guide are split into five sections: Museums, Shows & Tours, Market Place, Motorsport and Circuits. France has fewer grand collections sponsored by its major manufacturers than neighbouring Germany, but many of its provincial museums have exceptional collections and are unjustly overlooked. If you are willing to accept the patina of use and gentle decay, and are intrigued by the quirky and unusual, there are some real surprises in store!

Car clubs are the lifeblood of the classic car movement in France, with a huge number of informal meetings taking place every weekend. As a new generation of enthusiasts emerges, there's an increasing range of activities for admirers of upcoming classics or 'Youngtimers.' If your preference is for prewar racers or older classics, you still have plenty of choice, from touring rallies to lavish concours d'élégance. You'll find suggestions on combining visits to motoring shows and museums with wine-tastings, Michelin-starred restaurants and even a flower show!

Many historic cars change hands between club members, and there are fewer professional classic car dealers in France than in the UK. Auctions help fill that gap, and you'll find details of the main auction houses in the Market Place sections of the guide, along with information on specialists in automobilia and on parts fairs across the country.

For lovers of motorsport, the Grand Prix de Monaco, Le Mans 24 Hours race and Monte Carlo Rally ensure that France's heritage is unrivalled. Alongside these modern-day sporting fixtures, there are many historic revival events which allow competitors to re-live the experience of classic rallies and of Grands Prix held on city streets or racetracks.

The last section in each chapter of this guide presents a selection of circuits. As well as organising driving courses in the latest sports cars or hosting events, nearly all of these hold regular track days or can be booked by clubs.

New edition

This edition of the guide has been comprehensively updated. It includes nearly a dozen completely new entries, including major attractions such as the Conservatoire de la Monoplace Française at Magny-Cours, the Classic Festival at Nogaro and Les Grandes Heures Automobiles at Montlhéry. Other entries – like those for Chantilly Arts & Élégance or the old circuit at Reims-Gueux – have been rewritten and extended. Altogether, there are more than 140 all-new images. And throughout the guide, the Practical Information boxes and QR codes have been revised.

Whether you take part or visit them as a spectator, I hope you will enjoy discovering these places and events as much as I have done in researching this guide. Bonne route!

Julian Parish
Montfort-l'Amaury, France

Enjoying the French countryside during the Rallye de Paris. (Courtesy Rallystory)

Using the guide

With so much to see and do, this guide provides plenty of signposts to help you find your way around!

This guide is divided into five main chapters, each covering a large region of France. Each is colour-coded (**①**) and opens with a regional overview map (**②**), so that you can locate places on your journey across the country, or near your destination; a 'minimap' (**③**) shows the area covered by that chapter. Each entry is pinpointed on the map (**④**), and is also colour-coded, to match the section in which it appears; its page number is listed in the map key (**⑤**).

Chapters

Paris & the Ile-de-France ⊕
Western France ⊕
Southern France ⊕
Central France & The Alps ⊕
North-East France ⊕

All of the main chapters carry colour-coded top bars.

Southern France ⊕

Italy

Spain

Contents

106

Map markers

Map markers show where each entry is located and are colour-coded to denote the section it falls in.

The Grand Prix de Pau Historique 2003 / The...

Each chapter is divided into five sections, each carrying a colour-coded tab at the page edge and a unique symbol in the top corner (**⑥** and **⑦**, opposite page). The number of entries in each section varies by region; Paris & the Ile-de-France, for example, has relatively few Motorsport events, but lots of Market Place entries, covering automobilia as well

Sections

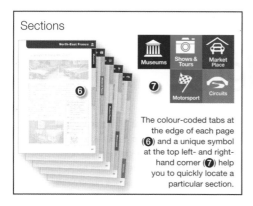

The colour-coded tabs at the edge of each page (**6**) and a unique symbol at the top left- and right-hand corner (**7**) help you to quickly locate a particular section.

as cars. Most entries are presented in alphabetical order, but the country's biggest attractions, such as Rétromobile or Le Mans Classic, appear on a double-page spread at the start of that section.

Each entry follows a consistent format, with the text and photographs providing a snapshot of the place or event, its history and how to enjoy it, whether as a participant or as a visitor.

A 'Practical information' box (**8**) provides details including opening times, the organiser's website, and, whenever possible, a contact number and e-mail. Street address and GPS coordinates are given for each entry, together with public transport information, when this is convenient. For smartphones and tablets, scanning the QR code (**9**) will take you to the entry's websites. For circuit entries, there's a track diagram, too (**10**).

At the end of the guide, *Driving in France* and *Event calendar* chapters provide tips on driving and an overview of the year's events, with *Further reading* suggestions and a comprehensive *Index* completing the guide.

Online extras

You'll find a wealth of additional information and extras, including a calendar for this year's exact dates for each event and a downloadable POI (Points of Interest) file for popular satnav devices, on the guide website at www.driveguide.guru.

When, where and how ...

Practical information

⊘ = Opening information

⌂ = Address

Ⓜ = Metro line

🚌 = Bus services

🚆 = Train services

🚋 = Tram lines

🖼 = GPS Satnav coordinates

🌐 = Website

📞 = Telephone number

✉ = Email

Every entry in this guide features a Practical information box which provides a wealth of details – from when an attraction is open and its address, to public transport links, GPS coordinates for Satnavs, and website and contact details – there's even a QR code (**9**) which you can scan with your mobile phone or tablet device to visit the entry's website.

Circuit diagrams

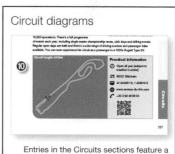

Entries in the Circuits sections feature a track diagram (**10**) showing the Start/Finish line, track length and travel direction.

Note: Every effort has been made to check all the information in this guide carefully, but changes will inevitably occur, for which the author and publisher cannot be held responsible. **Please check with the venue/organiser before travelling, especially if you want to see a specific car or exhibit, and to check current prices.**

Merci!

Without the hard work and dedication of thousands of enthusiasts in France – many of them unpaid volunteers – the places and events described in this book would simply not exist, and this guide could never have been written. As I travelled around France to research this book, I was overwhelmed by the generosity of the people I met, who took me around their collections and invited me to their events. They provided me with a wealth of documents and illustrations, of which I can reproduce only a fraction here. Sadly, there is too little space to list all of them on this page, but I would especially like to thank the following people who helped me with my research:

Anne Quémy (Automédon and Vincennes en anciennes), Yannick Yvin (Automobile Club de l'Ouest), Jean-Louis Chêne (Circuit Historique de Laon), Julien Laurent (Circuit de Serre Chevalier), Richard Keller (Cité de l'Automobile), Marc-André Biehler & Catherine Oudoul (Citroën), Stéphane Auvrignon (Classic British Welcome), Domitie Myter (Classic Days and Classic Heritage), Rémi Depoix (Festival Automobile International), Patrick Rollet (FIVA and Rallye International du Pays de Fougères), Franz Hummel (Les Grandes Heures Automobiles), Jean-Claude Fillon (Grand Prix Historique de Bressuire), Loïc Monnier (Le Manoir de l'Automobile), Colin Murrell (MG Owners' Club), Hervé Boutelier (Musée Automobile de Laon), Valentin & Magaly Giron (FFVE and Musée Automobile de Vendée), Thierry Dubois (www.nationale7. com), Henri Suzeau (Peter Auto), Christian Abed & Stéphane Giraud (Rallystory), Elodie Chauderlot (Rétromobile), Denis Huille (UTAC) and Viviane Zaniroli (Zaniroli Classic Events).

Claude Bohère and Thierry Réaubourg, both seasoned motoring journalists, were invaluable to me in reviewing my plans.

I must also express my gratitude to the many friends who provided advice and encouragement as I worked on this project, and in particular Marie Augereau, Pete Bennett, Nick & Jean Bonthrone, Richard Bready, Nic & Joc Ridley and Barry Tomalin.

Finally, I am immensely grateful to the fantastic team at Veloce Publishing, especially Rod Grainger and Kevin Atkins, who produced this new edition with their customary professionalism and enthusiasm.

A toutes et à tous, je vous dis "Merci!"

Paris & the Ile-de-France

With 47 million visitors to the Greater Paris area each year, the 'City of Light' needs little introduction.

Simply reached by air or high-speed train, it's easy to take in some of its many motoring attractions during a holiday or business trip. France's capital city is home to Rétromobile, the country's biggest classic car show, and to the world's most visited motor show, the Mondial de l'Automobile.

Paris is a great city to explore on foot: why not take a walk down the Champs-Élysées, originally home to the country's first car showrooms, and look at the manufacturers' displays, or visit France's leading gallery of motoring art and specialist bookshops?

Outside the capital, the biggest highlight is the famous banked track at Montlhéry, which hosts several events for lovers of historic cars, from the Vintage Revival through to the Youngtimers' Festival,

The start of the Tour Auto, in the magnificent setting of the Grand Palais. (Courtesy Richard Bord) / Participants in the summer Traversée de Paris at the place de la Concorde.

9

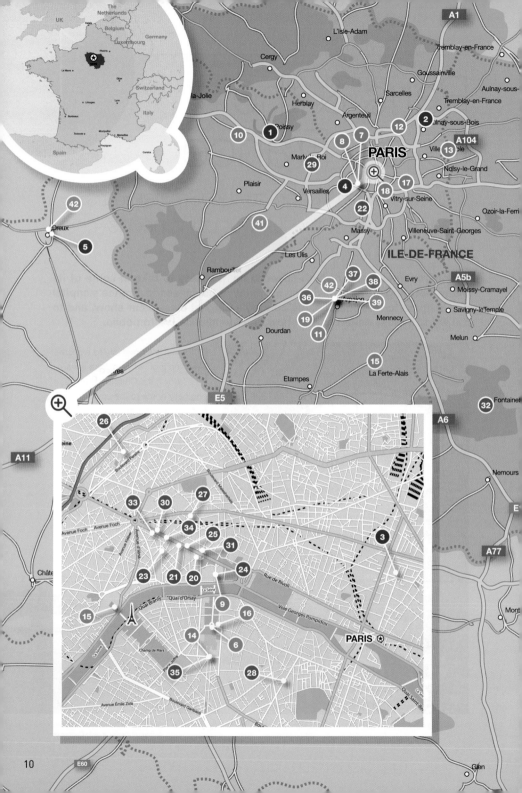

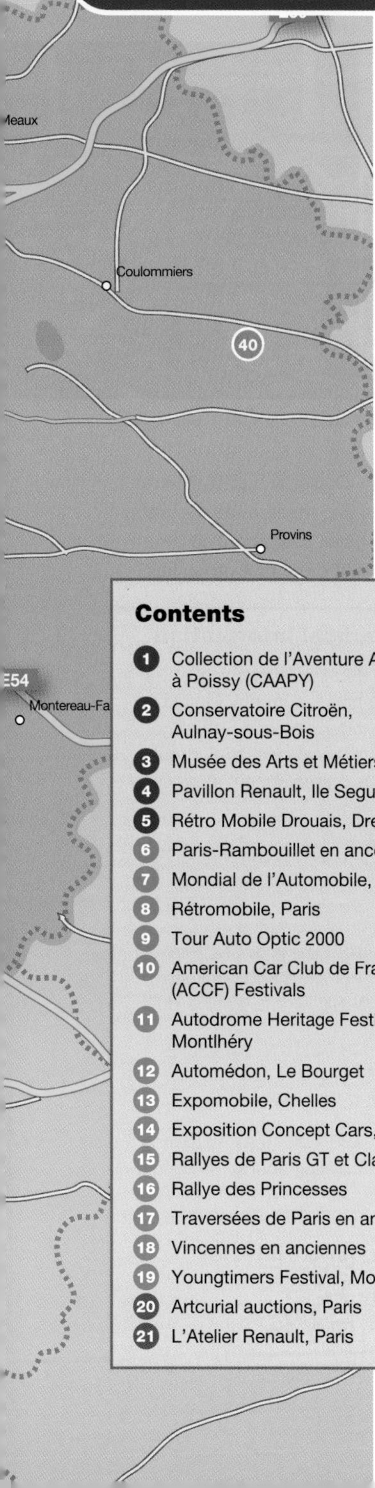
Coulommiers
40
Provins
E54

for cars from the '70s to '90s. There are many more events throughout the year within an hour's drive of Paris. You'll find details of all these, and many less well-known attractions, in the following pages.

Rétromobile, the grandest classic car show in France. (Courtesy Comexposium)

Contents

Museums

Shows & Tours

Market Place

Motorsport

Circuits

L'Aventure Automobile à Poissy (CAAPY)

Overview of the Talbot area of the museum. (Courtesy L'Aventure Automobile à Poissy-CAAPY) / Simca 5 display, with cutaway chassis and period advertising

Few car factories have had such a varied past as that at Poissy. Originally built by Ford in the 1930s, it was taken over by Simca in 1954, who expanded and modernised the plant. During the 1960s, Simca was progressively taken over by Chrysler, itself acquired by Peugeot in 1978. After briefly re-launching the Talbot brand in the 1980s, the PSA group has continued to develop the site, which now produces such small cars as the Peugeot 208 and DS3.

This diverse history is reflected in the museum. Opened in 2002 and run by enthusiasts with support from Peugeot, it houses 70 cars from the different manufacturers whose cars were built there. Beginning with a Ford F472A from 1946, there is a fine display of Simca models from the '50s and '60s. Highlights include a Simca 9 Figoni and a 936 minicar prototype, together with an imposing Vedette Présidence. The Talbot years are represented by a Talbot Sunbeam Lotus, rallied by Guy Fréquelin and Jean Todt, and a now rare Tagora saloon. Contemporary accessories and publicity materials complete the displays, together with an exhibit showing a Peugeot 309 being built.

Practical information

🕐 Restricted opening hours, currently Monday afternoon and Saturday only (see website); groups by appointment at other times

🏠 212, boulevard Pelletier, 78955 Carrières-sous-Poissy

🚆 RER line A or SNCF to Poissy, then 15-minute walk

🖥 48.94217 N, 2.03852 E

🌐 www.caapy.net

📞 +33 1 30 19 41 15 (during opening hours)

✉ caapy@peugeot.com

Simca Chambord with period photograph in front of the château at ... Chambord.

Museums

Conservatoire Citroën, Aulnay-sous-Bois

Citroën's 2CV family (Ami, Dyane and Méhari) with period advertising poster by André François. (Courtesy Citroën Communication/ N Zwickel) / Citroën BX4TC rally cars and RE-2 helicopter. (Courtesy Citroën Communication/Jérôme Lejeune)

For any Citroën enthusiast, this collection should be at the top of the list of places to see in France. Although the factory at Aulnay closed in 2013 after 40 years' production, Citroën has committed to keeping this site open. Its Heritage staff personally lead tours of the collection (in English and French), so you'll need to book in advance.

Originally opened in 2001, the Conservatoire brings together some 400 cars from the manufacturer's sites around Paris and in Rennes, and also from Spain and Portugal. Citroën's factory at Slough, west of London, is remembered with British-built 2CV and Traction Avant models. Many of the cars were taken straight from the production lines, but there are some extraordinary prototypes and one-offs, too, such as the 1982 Visa Lotus, effectively a Lotus Esprit Turbo powertrain under a modified Visa body. An RE-2 helicopter from 1975 marks Citroën's take on personal transportation of the future, as well as an attempt to diversify its business.

The Conservatoire also houses Citroën's extensive archives, and visitors can buy thematic dossiers for nearly 20 different models, as well as a personalised document set for every Citroën car built from 1919-90.

Practical information

🕐 Open by appointment only – book in advance

🏠 Boulevard André Citroën, 93601 Aulnay-sous-Bois. Use Visitors' entrance, gate 1

🗺 48.961151 N, 2.488276 E

🌐 www.citroen.fr/univers-citroen/citroen-heritage/conservatoire-citroen.html

📞 +33 1 56 50 80 22

✉ conservatoire@citroen.com

Citroën Traction Avant and early 2CV models. (Courtesy Citroën Communication/N Zwickel)

Museums

Shows & Tours

Market Place

Motorsport

Circuits

Musée des Arts et Métiers, Paris

Established by the Abbé Grégoire in 1794 – and completely renovated in 2000 – the Musée des Arts et Métiers is Paris' oldest scientific museum. It displays more than 3000 inventions, with highlights including the Lumière brothers' first camera and Foucault's famous pendulum. The exhibits are set out in seven thematic areas, including mechanics and transport, with audioguides and a free mobile app to help you make the most of your visit.

A replica of Leyat's Hélica, seen here on the track at Montlhéry.

The museum's transport section is grouped into three parts, covering steam-powered transport from 1750 to 1850, mass transportation from 1850 to 1950, and individual transport from 1950 onwards. The museum is best known for Cugnot's 1770 steam-driven dray, the world's first self-propelled vehicle, and for Leyat's curious propeller-driven Hélica from the early 1920s.

Make sure you don't miss the additional transport display in the former church: a multi-level metal structure which seems strangely out of place in this historic setting. As well as the Hélica, you'll find Amédée Bollée's L'Obéissante steamer from 1873, a splendid 1935 Hispano-Suiza K6 coupé de ville and, rather incongruously, a 1983 Renault RE40 F1 car driven by Alain Prost. There is also a huge engine built in 1892 by Rudolf Diesel himself.

The main entrance to the museum.

Practical information

🕐 Open Tuesday-Sunday 10am-6pm and Thursday evenings until 9.30pm; closed 1 May & 25 December

🏠 60, rue Réaumur, 75003 Paris

Ⓜ Lines 3 & 11, Arts et Métiers

🚌 Lines 20, 38, 39 & 47

🖼 48.865842 N, 2.355481 E

🌐 www.arts-et-metiers.net

📞 +33 1 53 01 82 00

Museums

Shows & Tours

Market Place

Motorsport

Circuits

Pavillon Renault, Ile Seguin

Renault's temporary pavilion. / Little now remains of Renault's industrial past.

For nearly a hundred years the area of Boulogne-Billancourt, to the west of Paris, was at the heart of Renault's car production. The first cars were built on the Ile Seguin in 1929, but the site reached its peak after the Second World War, producing the 4CV and Renault 4 models. 10,000 workers were employed there, turning out over 1100 cars per day. It was also the scene of historic workers' demonstrations during the Front Populaire in 1936, and again in 1968. In 1992, however, the factory closed as Renault moved its manufacturing away from Paris.

Today, the site has found a new vocation: a major development plan is under way, and by 2018 the Ile Seguin will be home to shops, offices and centres for contemporary art and music. Its industrial heritage will be celebrated in a permanent exhibition, but, since 2012, you can visit the temporary Pavillon Renault. Informative displays chart the rise and eventual decline of Renault's factory and its contribution to the region's social and industrial history, with one of the cars built there also on show. Just opposite the pavilion is Renault's test centre for its latest electric cars, such as the Zoë and Twizy.

Practical information

🕐 Open Wednesday to Sunday afternoons only (see website for more details)

🏠 Ile Seguin, 92100 Boulogne-Billancourt

🚋 T2: Brimborion, then take footbridge to island

🖼 48.823823 N, 2.233292 E

🌐 www.otbb.org/pavillon-sur-lile-seguin/

📞 +33 1 47 61 91 70

✉ contact@otbb.org

Celebrating the Renault 4, seventies-style.

Rétro Mobile Drouais, Dreux

Outside the museum on National Heritage Day. / The pride of the museum, a Facel Vega HK 500, built in Dreux.

80km (50 miles) due west from Paris, Dreux's main connection to automotive history is through the luxury sports cars built here by Facel Vega from 1939-64, in a factory a stone's throw away from the town's car museum. Don't be put off by its location in a former abattoir, the museum is run by a friendly and enthusiastic association. With 20 cars plus some cycles and motorbikes, it's one of the smallest museums in this guide, but well worth a stop if you're heading to Chartres or Normandy. If you can, allow an hour for the interesting guided tour by one of the volunteers.

The exhibits cover the period from 1885 to 1965, and there's a good selection of pre-1940 cars. Many of the cars have a strong local connection: as well as a 1960 Facel Vega HK500 displayed with information about how the cars were built, take a look at the 1929 Peugeot 201 T Camionnette, and 1930 Delahaye ambulance, both used in the town. French marques predominate and include some rare models, such as a 1922 Sidea PL, and a post-war La Licorne 164 LR Coach.

Practical information

🕐 Open first Sunday afternoon each month, and for the 'Journées du patrimoine' weekend in September

🏠 95, rue du Commandant Beaurepaire, 28100 Dreux

🗺 48.742875 N, 1.376016 E

🌐 www.tourisme28.com/notre-selection/235245-dreux-musee-retro-mobile-drouais

📞 +33 2 37 43 01 15

From a veteran De Dion Bouton to a late-model La Licorne.

Paris-Rambouillet en ancêtre

Panhard-Levassor next to a De Dion-Bouton outside the château at Rambouillet / 1902 De Dion-Bouton vis-à-vis with tiller steering riding through the grounds of the château.

Enthusiasts rarely get the chance to see the earliest veteran cars take to the road, but this run – which is held every two years – is one of the best opportunities. Its origins go right back to the dawn of motoring in 1898, when the first race was held between Paris and Rambouillet; the following year, it would be won by the brothers Louis and Marcel Renault.

Today, three clubs – Renaissance Auto, the delightfully named Teuf-Teuf and Les Bielles de Jadis – jointly organise this commemorative event, starting from the Invalides in central Paris and covering 70km (43 miles) to the château in Rambouillet. Along the way, there are stops at historic sites such as the Château de Versailles and the Abbaye des Vaux-de-Cernay, as well as a steep climb up to Saint-Cloud, which really puts the 60 or so cars to the test.

Reserved for cars at least 100 years old, French makes predominate: De Dion-Bouton and Renault of course, but Grégoire, Delaunay-Belleville and Richard Brasier too. There are plenty of foreign participants though, with a large contingent of British entrants. The cars remain on display at Rambouillet in the afternoon, giving visitors a chance to chat with their owners.

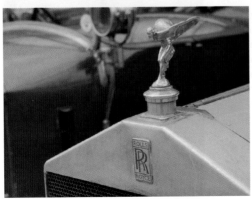

Early 'red-letter' Rolls-Royce.

Practical information

🕐 Held biennially in June (even years)

🏠 Starts from Place des Invalides, 75007 Paris

Ⓜ Line 13, Invalides

🖼 48.858360 N, 2.312910 E

🌐 www.renaissanceauto.org

📞 + 33 1 34 85 60 66

✉ renaissanceauto@orange.fr

Mondial de l'Automobile, Paris

Hall 1 is always crowded, as here, at the Peugeot stand.
(Courtesy Mondial de l'Automobile)

Although attendance was down for its last edition, the Mondial de l'Automobile remains the world's most visited motor show, with over a million visitors in 2016. For two weeks in October every other year (alternating with Frankfurt), the eight halls of the capital's largest exhibition centre are given over to the world's newest cars. Although it competes with shows in the US and China, as well as Frankfurt and Geneva, many manufacturers continue to display design concepts here; highlights in 2016 included design studies from Citroën, BMW and Mercedes. Electric cars are increasingly important as well, with a dedicated test track outside the halls.

The Mondial de l'Automobile isn't just about the latest technology though. The show

Striking model shows off the new RCF coupé from Lexus.

The 'Love Bug' in the special exhibition on Cars and the Cinema.

itself has a long history, going back to 1898. From 1901-61 it took place under the splendid glass dome of the Grand Palais, before moving here in 1962. Since 1992, the history of motoring has been celebrated each year in a special exhibition, normally in Hall 8. For each show a different theme is chosen: in 2016 Cars and the Cinema, and before that, fascinating displays of car advertising, vehicles from French museums, or cars and fashion. Don't miss this: it's a real treat! For 2016 the organisers invited Coys of London to hold an auction of classic cars during the show, but this met with mixed results, so may not be continued in future years.

Parking can be hard, but the Porte de Versailles is well served by public transport. The weekends are generally very crowded; if you can, try to visit mid-week, or wrangle an invitation to the VIP evening at the start of the show.

Practical information

🕐 October, biennially (even years)

🏠 Paris Expo, Porte de Versailles, 75015 Paris

Ⓜ Line 12, Porte de Versailles or line 8, Balard

🚌 Lines 39 & 80

🚊 Lines T2 & T3, Porte de Versailles

🗺 48.832322 N, 2.28773 E

🌐 www.mondial-automobile.com

Mercedes Generation EQ concept prefigures electric cars of the future.

19

Rétromobile, Paris

Rétromobile traditionally marks the start of the French classic car season, and what a start! Together with Techno Classica Essen in Germany, Rétromobile is one of the most stylish events in Europe. 80% of its more than 100,000 visitors return every year, so if you haven't visited it yet, be sure to add it to your 'Must do' list. Rétromobile started in 1976 as an autojumble and has grown alongside the classic car movement in France. The organisers continue to innovate, expanding into additional halls and adding displays of recent classics and a 'craftsmen's village.'

The major car manufacturers invest heavily in this show, with large displays backed by the French manufacturers, Mercedes, BMW, Jaguar and others. Whether they're in the organisers' central exhibit or on the stands of leading European dealers, you can see some of the rarest and most magnificent cars from the last century. Group B rally cars,

Top European dealers come to Paris to sell historic racers. (Courtesy Comexposium)

the designs of Philippe Charbonneaux or the cars of the Indian Maharajahs have been among the highlights of recent years. The show also hosts the most important auction of historic cars to take place in France, often setting new records. You can rely on Rétromobile to uncover some

Artcurial's prestigious auction takes place within the exhibition hall. (Courtesy Comexposium)

Enormous Pathé Marconi bus in the special feature dedicated to Philippe Charbonneaux's designs.

of motoring's eccentricities, such as the bizarre rhomboid cars shown in 2016 or little known amphibious or electric vehicles.

Rétromobile makes space, too, for more popular models, plus 100 clubs and many specialist traders exhibits. The show provides an exceptional opportunity to look at motoring art, including paintings, photographs and sculptures. It isn't the cheapest place to buy parts or automobilia though; if you're coming back to Paris, Automédon (page 26) is a less expensive option.

Practical information

🕐 Early February every year

🏠 Paris Expo, Porte de Versailles, 75015 Paris

Ⓜ Line 12, station Porte de Versailles or line 8, station Balard

🚋 Lines T2 & T3, Porte de Versailles

🚌 Lines 39 & 80

📷 48.832322 N, 2.28773 E

🌐 www.retromobile.com

Parts galore! (Courtesy Comexposium)

Tour Auto Optic 2000

Originally created by the Automobile Club de France in 1899, the Tour Auto Optic 2000 is the oldest motor race in the world still organised today. In its heyday from the 1950s to the early '70s, many of the greatest drivers of the period took part, among them Stirling Moss, Phil Hill, and Maurice Trintignant.

In 1992, Patrick Peter revived the tour as an historic event and it has become – in the words of the British journalist Richard Meaden, writing on *The Telegraph* website, "one of the greatest classic car events around," combining "adrenalin, stunning scenery and sumptuous lunches." (Well, this is France, after all!) Starting in Paris, the tour takes more than 200 participants through 2000km (1250 miles) of French countryside, ending at a major coastal destination such as Biarritz, La Rochelle or Marseille. In 2016, the organizers added a night stage in the hills behind Nice and in 2017, for the first time, the event will finish in Brittany.

Ford GT40, a regular entrant in the Tour Auto.

The main hall of the Grand Palais.

The roof of the Grand Palais reflected in the bonnet of an Osca.

Entrants can choose the regularity class, keeping to a fixed average speed, or the competition category, with timed stages on closed roads and races at circuits along the route. Cars are split into four classes, but all must be eligible to have competed in the original races from 1951-82. The event brings out a splendid line-up of Ferraris (no fewer than 36 in some recent years), AC Cobras, Porsches, Jaguars and more. BMW is an official partner of the event and can be relied on to show some of its finest historic models from the event's heyday, such as the 507 or 3.0 CSL.

Taking part costs several thousand euros, but you can join 100,000 fellow enthusiasts and watch the show go by for much less. The tour starts in the fabulous surroundings of the Grand Palais in central Paris, with admission to this – and each day's parc fermé – by buying a copy of the programme. You can also watch the competition sessions at the racetracks, or simply enjoy the cars roar past from the terrace of a village café.

Original rally plaque on a 1953 Sunbeam Alpine.

Practical information

🕐 April every year

🏠 Starts from the Grand Palais, avenue Winston Churchill, 75008 Paris

Ⓜ Lines 1 & 13, Champs-Élysées-Clémenceau

🚌 Lines 42, 73, 83 & 93

🖥 48.866063 N, 2.313826 E

🌐 www.tourauto.com

📞 +33 1 42 59 73 40

1952 Ferrari 225S on the road south of Paris on day one.

Museums

Shows & Tours

Market Place

Motorsport

Circuits

23

American Car Club de France (ACCF) Festivals

Corvette line-up in front of the Château d'Aveny. / Ford Fairlane 500 Skyliner with folding metal hardtop. (Courtesy Christian Lemonchois/ACCF)

American cars have long held a special appeal in France, not just for car enthusiasts but for the general public who enjoy American music and films. Until the energy crisis of 1973/4, American cars were regularly sold in France and cars like the Ford Mustang became famous in films such as *Un homme et une femme* and in motorsport: Johnny Hallyday even drove one in the Monte Carlo Rally. Many more were sold in neighbouring countries such as Belgium and Switzerland. It's no surprise, therefore, to see many American cars at classic car meetings in France.

For many years, the ACCF could claim to be the biggest American car club in Europe. In recent years the club has undergone a big shake-up and is finding its feet again, so check its website for the latest activities. The ACCF organises or takes part in many US car events throughout France, but the biggest is usually the American Car Festival held in the Ile-de-France, often in the grounds of a château. Open to all, this attracts several hundred US cars of all periods, from prewar Cadillacs to the latest Corvettes, and the public can enjoy live music from a rock or country music band.

Practical information

🕐 Normally every September, but date varies; check website for current year

🏠 Different locations within the Ile-de-France, 2016 event at Parc des Expositions, 78361 Mantes-la-Jolie

🖥 48.998897 N, 1.717259 E

🌐 www.accf.com

📞 +33 1 34 75 57 79

✉ contact@accf.com

Different generations of the Ford Mustang, including the author's 1997 GT coupé.

Autodrome Heritage Festival, Montlhéry

A Fiat Balilla harries an MG through the corners. / Waiting patiently for the start.

If your interests include cars from many different periods, this can be a good event at which to get to know the old Autodrome at Montlhéry. Although overtaken now by Les Grandes Heures Automobiles (page 51), it attracts a good range of cars of all periods, from vintage racers through to recent classics. There's plenty to see and do over the weekend, which culminates in a final parade of all the participants on Sunday afternoon. If you're coming over with your own classic, you can book to take part in the sessions on the historic banked track or – a less expensive option – take a place in the paddock. The event is open to the public, if you just want to watch the action from the stands, and you can even go around the circuit in a 1958 Renault Galion bus!

The Festival is well supported by clubs and the French manufacturers, and there are special features every year: the 90th anniversary of the Montlhéry track itself in 2014, or birthday celebrations for models such as the Citroën Méhari or Matra Murena. The organizers recently added a small concours d'état, but it is the action on track which makes Montlhéry such a special venue.

Practical information

🕐 June every year

🏠 Autodrome de Linas-Montlhéry, avenue Georges Boillot, 91310 Linas

📷 48.621999 N, 2.247294 E

🌐 parisautoevents.com

📞 +33 1 69 80 17 00

✉ pae@utaceram.com

View from the control tower over the start lane. (Courtesy Paris Auto Events)

Museums

Shows & Tours

Market Place

Motorsport

Circuits

Automédon, Le Bourget

Named after Achilles' charioteer in Greek mythology, this well-established show is a counterpoint to Rétromobile (page 20) for enthusiasts in Paris, and the last major event of the season in the Ile-de-France. Much more informal in style, it attracts 15,000 visitors each year. The exhibition hall at Le Bourget is a rather drab building, but is easy to get to by train or from the A1 autoroute just north of Paris. There's a huge outside parking area for classic cars, too; as many as 2500 come each year, which makes for a second exhibition outdoors! The show is especially popular with owners of American cars.

Automédon is strongly supported by clubs and traders, and there are dedicated areas for 'Youngtimers' and motorbikes, and – new in 2016 – for lorries and historic caravans. In the past couple of years, the centrepiece displays have included some exceptional cars, from Aston Martin's centenary in 2013 to the cars of the Monte Carlo Rally in 2016. For 2017, a celebration of French coachbuilders is planned. You can be sure, too, to find other rarities at the show, from a Citroën SM Mylord to a Bizzarrini GT.

Bizzarrini 5000 GT: part of a display of Italian supercars.

Modern WRC cars featured in a celebration of the Monte Carlo Rally. / Plenty of club and trade stands to visit.

Practical information

🕐 October every year

🏠 Carrefour Charles Lindbergh, 93550 Le Bourget

🚆 RER line B to Le Bourget, then free shuttle

📷 48.9441 N, 2.431852 E

🌐 automedon.fr

📞 +33 1 64 46 52 22

✉ organisation@automedon.fr

Expomobile, Chelles

00,000 ... not the number of visitors to this show, but the number of flowers at the garden centre where it's held! If your partner is more interested in plants than old cars, this could be the perfect afternoon out. Laurent Laplace has created a unique event to celebrate the 'Fête du muguet' (the lily of the valley) every spring. Held in Chelles, in the eastern suburbs of Paris, it's close to Disneyland and the A4 autoroute.

Among the colourful displays of roses, geraniums and petunias, the show presents a varied mix of classic cars, from pre-1900 veterans to recent supercars. The event is well supported by owners' clubs, such as Les Amis de Delage or Vincennes en anciennes.

Chelles is home to the AMTUIR bus museum, which

The Laplace family has run this show for nearly 20 years. (Courtesy Jardinerie Laurent Laplace)

is generally closed to the public, but usually displays a couple of old Paris buses at this show, which is an added bonus. There is a large grassy area behind the garden centre, too, so that visitors can sit down to enjoy some live music or a refreshing drink. Many clubs make it part of their programme, with as many 1100 classic cars coming along on the morning of May 1.

The French Rolls-Royce Drivers' Club is one of those supporting this event. / An early Chevrolet Corvette among the flowers.

Practical information

🕐 Around May 1 holiday every year

🏠 Jardinerie Laplace, 78, route de Montfermeil, 77500 Chelles

🚌 RER line E to Chelles Gournay, then bus 613, stop rue Prudence

🖥 48.889503 N, 2.582506 E

🌐 www.jardinerie-laplace.fr

📞 +33 1 64 21 38 03

✉ laurent.laplace77@orange.fr

Exposition Concept Cars, Paris

Peugeot 908 HY. / BMW 3.0 CSL Hommage R.

A highlight of the week-long International Automobile Festival, which culminates in the annual award for 'The most beautiful car of the year', this show is a rare treat for visitors to the capital.

The Concept Car Show is held in a large marquee in front of the Invalides, where Napoléon is buried. Visiting it at nightfall, when the golden dome is floodlit, is an especially magic moment. The show provides a unique opportunity to see the latest design studies from studios around the world. Many of the cars are the stuff of dreams, like the Touring Disco Volante, the Peugeot Onyx – with its audacious copper panels – or the latest concepts from Giugiaro's Italdesign. Others – like the BMW 3.0 CSL Hommage R – hark back to their manufacturer's heritage. But the show also gives a glimpse of the design direction of mainstream cars closer to production: the Alpine A110-50, Renault's Initiale Paris and Citroën's C-Cactus concepts have all been shown here.

As well as more than 20 concept cars, recent shows have featured motorbikes, motoring art and sculptures. A few days later, the same location hosts the major auction held by RM Sotheby's (page 49).

Citroën C-Cactus concept in front of the Invalides.

Practical information

🕐 End of January/early February each year

🏠 In front of the Invalides dome, place Vauban, 75007 Paris

Ⓜ Line 13, Varenne

🚌 Lines 82 & 92

🖳 48.853881 N, 2.31237 E

🌐 www.festivalautomobile.com

☎ +33 1 40 74 97 97

✉ desk@festivalautomobile.com

Museums

Shows & Tours

Market Place

Motorsport

Circuits

Rallyes de Paris GT et Classic

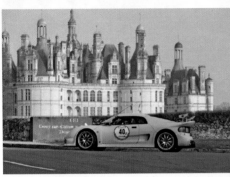

The Rallye de Paris GT in front of the château at Chambord. (Courtesy Rallystory/Philippe Fugier) / The Eiffel Tower, traditional starting point for the Rallye de Paris. (Courtesy Rallystory/ Philippe Fugier)

If you imagine what an ideal classic rally in France might be, you'll probably think of driving along open roads in the countryside, stopping at a château or two and enjoying some fine meals and great wine. Add to that mix a couple of sessions on famous racetracks and you have the formula for the Rallye de Paris.

Created by Hervé Charbonneaux for Parisian enthusiasts more than 20 years ago, the Rallye de Paris has grown into one of the best organised and most stylish events of its kind, attracting participants from all over Europe. The Rallye Classic, for cars up to 1986, is now run in parallel with the Rallye GT, for modern GT and supercars. Held over a spring weekend, it's shorter and less expensive to take part in than the Tour Auto (page 22).

This is not a regularity event, so the road stages follow a set route, but with no time constraints. In recent years participants have driven through Burgundy and the Sologne, savouring meals at the châteaux of Fontainebleau, Meursault, and Pommard. Each day also includes a session at one of France's major circuits, such as Magny-Cours or Dijon-Prenois.

Practical information

🕐 March every year

🏠 Start varies each year (see website)

🌐 www.rallystory.com

📞 +33 1 42 12 07 08

✉ contact@rallystory.com

On the track at Le Mans with the Rallye de Paris Classic. (Courtesy Rallystory/Car Media)

Rallye des Princesses

The joy of the open road. (Courtesy Richard Bord/Zaniroli Classic Events) / Victory! (Courtesy Richard Bord/Zaniroli Classic Events)

The story of the Rallye des Princesses really begins back in 1929, when the Comte de Rohan-Chabot launched a motoring event exclusively for women, the Rallye Paris-Saint Raphaël, which ran until 1974. 26 years later, Viviane Zaniroli created a new rally in the same spirit, the Rallye des Princesses. 80 all-women crews, with their cars divided into Historic and Classic classes, set off each year from Paris to drive to the south of France, finishing five days later in the fashionable resort of Saint-Tropez.

For some of the competitors it's a serious sporting challenge, while others see it more as a chance to get away from it all. For these drivers and their navigators, the pace of the rally can come as a shock: entrants cover 300km (180 miles) or more each day, often on minor roads. The rally is run on strict regularity principles, and the crews are required to match an average speed of between 40-50km/h (25-31mph), according to the age of their car. But the rally's motto is 'Sportswoman by day, Princess by night', and each day ends in some style, with an especially lavish gala dinner on the last day.

Practical information

🕐 June every year

🏠 Starts from Place Vendôme, 75001 Paris

Ⓜ Line 1, Tuileries

🚌 Line 72

📷 48.867491 N, 2.329420 E

🌐 www.zaniroli.com/rallye-des-princesses

📞 +33 4 92 82 20 00

✉ info@zaniroli.com

Each of them a princess! (Courtesy Richard Bord/Zaniroli Classic Events)

Traversées de Paris en anciennes

Summer picnic at Meudon. (Courtesy Vincennes en anciennes) / Stopping to enjoy the view from Montmartre. (Courtesy Vincennes en anciennes)

While local club members often go for a celebratory drive on New Year's Day, Parisian enthusiasts wait a few more days before seeing in the New Year with this Sunday morning drive through the capital. It's not expensive to take part, but you need to register well in advance and your car must be at least 30 years old. Starting at 8am from the Château de Vincennes, 700 vehicles (mainly cars, but also some motorbikes and even tractors) converge on the city, for a 30km (18 miles) route, taking in many of its tourist sights including the Bastille, Montmartre, the Invalides and the Champs-Élysées, with a mid-morning stop at the Place de la Concorde. If you don't have your own classic, you can book a seat on a prewar Paris bus, or just watch the cavalcade go past.

The success of the winter event has prompted the organisers to add a similar event in the summer. The principle is the same, but with the frequent bonus of excellent weather: there are plenty of convertibles joining the parade and participants often dress in period attire. The trip finishes with a huge open-air picnic in the grounds of the observatory at Meudon.

Practical information

🕐 January and late July/ August every year

🏛 Starts from the esplanade in front of the Château de Vincennes

Ⓜ Line 1, Château de Vincennes

🖥 48.840835 N, 2.435611 E

🌐 www. vincennesenanciennes.com

📞 + 33 6 33 80 31 91

✉ inscription@ vincennesenanciennes.com

1917 Ford Model T Torpédo at the place Vendôme. (Courtesy Vincennes en anciennes)

Museums

Shows & Tours

Market Place

Motorsport

Circuits

Vincennes en anciennes

A s well as organising the Traversées de Paris twice a year, the club Vincennes en anciennes, the largest multi-marque club in France, runs an informal get-together – or 'rencard' in French – once a month, in front of the Château de Vincennes. The meeting is open to all enthusiasts, and pride of place is given to a different marque each month.

T-series MG in front of the château.

The gathering at Vincennes is the best-attended of those in the Paris area and is popular even during the quieter winter months. It's a great place to catch up with fellow enthusiasts over a coffee, and sometimes discover some rare models. And if your family or friends aren't interested in cars, they can always visit the château!

Informal meetings like this are a key part of the classic car scene in France. In the Paris area, there are also well-attended meetings run by local clubs near Versailles, and in front of the châteaux at Chantilly (which also has a major equestrian museum) and Thoiry (where there is a zoo as well) – see a pattern developing here? The weekly newspaper *La Vie de l'Auto* gives a comprehensive listing of all upcoming meetings across the country.

Practical information

🕐 The first Sunday morning of each month (check online for latest details)

🏠 The esplanade in front of the Château de Vincennes

Ⓜ Line 1, Château de Vincennes

🗺 48.840835 N, 2.435611 E

🌐 www. vincennesenanciennes. com

✉ organisation@ vincennesenanciennes.com

MG, a popular marque of honour.

Youngtimers Festival, Montlhéry

An immaculate Renault 5 Turbo 2. / Youngtimers magazine, sponsor of the meeting.

When the events team at Montlhéry (page 33) organised its first meeting for recent classics, or 'Youngtimers' as the French say, in 2012, they expected 100 or so cars to show up – and were staggered when 700 owners registered. As a new generation of enthusiasts looks back to their youth, the cars of the '70s, '80s and '90s have become increasingly popular, sometimes to the dismay of owners of older classics. This one-day event, sponsored by *Youngtimers* magazine and open to the public, is the best of the shows in France dedicated to these emerging classics.

Participants can opt to take their cars on the banked track – a popular choice for owners of performance models – or stay in the paddock, where several parts traders also take stands. Everyone gets the chance to join a parade lap at the end of the day. Citroën, Peugeot and Renault are the best represented makes, with models such as the Renault 20/30 celebrating its 40th anniversary during the event. But there are plenty of BMWs, Mercedes and VWs too, as well as rarer marques like Alpina and Venturi.

Looking out on the starting line: an eclectic mix of cars.

Practical information

🕐 April every year

🏠 Autodrome de Linas-Montlhéry, avenue Georges Boillot, 91310 Linas

📷 48.621999 N, 2.247294 E

🌐 parisautoevents.com

📞 +33 1 69 80 17 00

✉ pae@utaceram.com

Artcurial auctions, Paris

1987 Ferrari Testarossa which belonged to the film star Alain Delon – Shalva the dog not included! (Courtesy Artcurial Motorcars) / 1962 Ferrari 250 GT Cabriolet, which sold for €827,000. (Courtesy Artcurial Motorcars)

Of all the French auction houses selling historic cars, Artcurial is the largest and most prestigious. It holds auctions at Rétromobile (page 20) and Le Mans Classic (page 88), as well as at its own salerooms on the Champs-Élysées. So successful are some of its Parisian sales that it has even had to take over a nearby theatre to fit everyone in. Regardless of the venue, however, Artcurial's auctions are a great spectacle to watch: Hervé Poulain, a former driver at Le Mans and originator of the BMW Art Cars, and Matthieu Lamoure really know how to work an audience!

The cars sold by Artcurial include many of the rarest and most valuable models traded in France: racing cars with a sporting pedigree, top flight restorations from workshops such as Lecoq, and cars from private collections built up over decades or owned by famous film stars, sometimes reaching several million euros. But each sale usually features some more accessible cars, often in excellent condition, as well as a large selection of automobilia, including period drawings and mascots. Admission to the pre-sale viewing and auction itself is by catalogue; these are quite expensive, but a fine souvenir to keep.

Practical information

🕐 Regular sales throughout the year (see website for details)

🏠 7, rond-point des Champs-Élysées, 75008 Paris

Ⓜ Lines 1 & 9, Franklin D Roosevelt

🚌 Lines 28, 42, 73, 80, 83 & 93

▦ 48.868708 N, 2.309271 E

🌐 www.artcurial.com

📞 +33 1 42 99 20 73

✉ motorcars@artcurial.com

Viewing the cars before a sale on the Champs-Élysées.

L'Atelier Renault, Paris

Renault has been part of the Champs-Élysées for more than a century and opened its first showroom here in 1910. By then, Paris' most famous avenue was already home to France's annual Salon Automobile (held in the Grand Palais) and the starting point for some of the country's first unofficial motor races. At the outbreak of the First World War no fewer than 17 car manufacturers had showrooms here.

In 1962 Renault transformed its site into Le Pub Renault, combining a display of cars with a bar and restaurant. With the creation of

The façade of L'Atelier Renault, at the time of the launch of the Captur SUV.

L'Atelier Renault in 2000 – modernised again in 2011 – Renault brought the concept right up-to-date. 2.5 million people now visit it every year.

Regularly changing displays feature Renault's sporting achievements or their investments in electric power, whilst Renault Classic often shows cars from the company's historic collections. Meanwhile, a retail section sells a good range of scale models, clothing and other goodies for the Renault and Alpine brands. Computer terminals and a range of books provide information on the company's current range and history. Upstairs, the restaurant and bar is an often-crowded meeting place, popular with cinemagoers as well as car lovers.

Practical information

🕐 Open every day from 10.30am, including evenings

🏠 53, avenue des Champs-Élysées, 75008 Paris

Ⓜ Lines 1 & 9, Franklin D Roosevelt

🚌 Lines 32, 42, 73 & 80

📷 48.870344 N, 2.305486 E

🌐 https://atelier.renault.com

📞 +33 1 76 84 19 19

Alpine A110-50 prototype, seen here at the Avignon Motor Festival.

Auto Passion Café, Paris

Museums

Shows & Tours

Market Place

Motorsport

Circuits

If you're looking for a place to host a club event, or simply enjoy a meal with car-loving friends, this restaurant at the Porte d'Orléans is a natural choice. Options include lunch and dinner every day and brunch at the weekend. It's easily reached by public transport and not far from the Porte de Versailles, where the Mondial de l'Automobile and Rétromobile are held.

The unique ambiance of the Auto Passion Café. (Courtesy Vincent Durand)

The automotive theme is everywhere; from the pictures covering the walls and the displays of scale models, to the full-size cars often on show at the entrance. Even the loos have racing harnesses! With space for 200 guests, the restaurant has areas for different marques, so whether your preference is for Lotus or Ferrari, you can sit next to images of your favourite car.

The motoring refrain continues on the menu: begin with a starter from the '*Grille de depart*,' choose your main course '*A la kart*,' and power through to a dessert from the '*Ligne d'arrivée*.' For kids, there's a special '*Petit pilote*' menu. The food is better than you might expect; the owner Vincent Durand started his career at two of the capital's most prestigious addresses, the Crillon hotel and Lapérouse restaurant.

If you can't run to a new Ferrari, enjoy a glass of champagne! (Courtesy Vincent Durand)

Practical information

🕐 Open 7 days a week, 10am-2am

🏠 197, boulevard Brune, 75014 Paris

Ⓜ Line 4, Porte d'Orléans

🚋 Line T3, Porte d'Orléans

🚌 Lines 28 & 38

🖼 48.823559 N, 2.324737 E

🌐 www.autopassioncafe.fr

📞 +33 1 45 43 20 20

BMW George V, Paris

The lifestyle boutique. (Courtesy BMW Paris) / The spectacular glass façade of the BMW George V building. (Courtesy BMW Paris)

BMW France already had a directly owned dealership in the 15th arrondissement of Paris, but in May 2012 it opened the first of a new generation of retail stores worldwide. Located just off the Champs-Élysées, it covers more than 1100m² (nearly 12,000ft²). The main windows alone measure more than 35m² (370ft²), so you s houldn't miss it!

Inside, there is a strong high-tech theme, with huge touch screens, an LED Media Wall, and a special kidney sculpture inspired by the distinctive radiator grilles of all BMW's cars. Most of the display area around the central plaza is devoted to the latest production cars, including models from the M performance line and its latest electric models. The focus on technology continues with presentations of its connected infotainment and safety features. BMW supports historic events including the Tour Auto, and classics such as an original 328, 502 or M1 Procar are often shown too, as well as historic prototypes like a 1602 Electric from 1972.

At the other end of the store, with an additional entrance from the rue François 1er, you'll find a BMW Lifestyle boutique, selling all the latest branded merchandise.

Practical information

🕐 Open Monday to Saturday, 10am-8pm

🏠 38, avenue George V, 75008 Paris

Ⓜ Line 1, George V

🚌 Line 73

🖼 48.869535 N, 2.301224 E

🌐 brandstore.bmw.fr

📞 +33 1 40 69 43 00

The central plaza, here displaying a BMW M3 Convertible. (Courtesy BMW Paris)

Museums Shows & Tours **Market Place** Motorsport Circuits

Bonhams auctions, Paris

Pre-sale viewing in the main hall of the Grand Palais. (Courtesy Bonhams) / A cool 2 million euros to get behind this wheel! (Courtesy Bonhams)

Bonhams will already be well known to many European collectors, holding regular sales in the UK and on the Continent. The rules governing auctions in France are quite strict, which helps explain why the company was a late arrival in Paris, in 2011. But Bonhams has more than made up for this delayed start with the quality of the cars on offer and the sheer style of its presentation. Its sale is now one of several major auctions scheduled during Rétromobile (page 20), making it a fantastic time of year to visit Paris.

As with the start of the Tour Auto a couple of months later, Bonhams' annual sale, 'Les Grandes Marques du Monde,' is held in the magnificent surroundings of the Grand Palais. Under its huge glass and metal canopy, potential buyers can view as many as 150 cars, motorbikes and maybe even a plane. Some of the cars are exceptional and command high prices: a 1929 Bugatti Type 35B and a 1966 Ferrari 275 GTB, for instance, both sold for well over 1.5 million euros.

Delightful Alfa Romeo Giulietta SZ 'Coda Tronca.' (Courtesy Bonhams)

At this end of the market, most buyers are from outside France, whether from the US or other European countries.

Practical information

🕐 February every year

🏠 Grand Palais, avenue Winston Churchill, 75008 Paris

Ⓜ Lines 1 & 13, Champs-Élysées-Clémenceau

🚌 Lines 42, 73, 83 & 93

🗺 48.866063 N, 2.313826 E

🌐 www.bonhams.com

📞 +33 1 42 61 10 11

✉ eurocars@bonhams.com

Citroën C42 & DS World, Paris

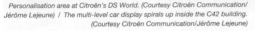

Personalisation area at Citroën's DS World. (Courtesy Citroën Communication/ Jérôme Lejeune) / The multi-level car display spirals up inside the C42 building. (Courtesy Citroën Communication/Jérôme Lejeune)

Citroën has owned this site on the Champs-Élysées since 1927, and for a long time it was a main dealership. After a sombre period as a steak restaurant, Citroën completely transformed the building with a bold glass and steel facade by the architect Manuelle Gautrand. Re-opened in 2007, it's now an international showcase for the marque.

The dramatic design of the building takes visitors up a spiral staircase, to see a car displayed on each level. Imaginative thematic exhibitions have included many of Citroën's concept cars, but its heritage is not forgotten, and displays have featured French presidential cars, the story of the 2CV, and Citroën's WRC-winning rally cars. A small shop sells a limited range of merchandise.

A short walk away, at 33, rue François 1er, you'll find the DS World Paris. The second store of its kind (the first was in Shanghai), this elegant showroom focuses on luxury and style 'à la française.' Current DS models are shown, together with unique DS accessories, and a special personalisation area where customers can configure their car. The top floor is dedicated to the original 'Déesse' and visitors can even book a tour through Paris in a DS.

The stunning glass front of Citroën's C42 showroom. (Courtesy Citroën Communication/Jérôme Lejeune)

Practical information

🕐 Open every day, 10am-8pm or later

🏠 42, avenue des Champs-Élysées, 75008 Paris

Ⓜ Lines 1 & 9, Franklin D Roosevelt

🚌 Lines 32, 42, 73 & 80

🖥 48.869939 N, 2.307327 E

🌐 www.citroen.fr/univers-citroen/vitrines-citroen/citroen-c-42.html

📞 +33 1 56 43 36 70

Museums

Shows & Tours

Market Place

Motorsport

Circuits

Doc'Auto, Paris

Chantal Pougeux, the welcoming owner of the bookshop, with a rare Bugatti title. / This modest shop front hides a wealth of treasures.

Situated on a quiet side-street in the 17th arrondissement of Paris, the unassuming shop front of Doc'Auto hides a wealth of treasures. Since opening the shop in 1986, Chantal Pougeux has acquired an unrivalled knowledge – and stock – of historic motoring literature.

Her original specialisation was in brochures and catalogues, especially for cars between the two world wars, and the shop is still the best place in France to try and find these. As these documents have grown increasingly rare, so the shop has built up its book business. The stock includes secondhand books and new titles which have gone out-of-print; if you missed out on a limited-edition work when it appeared, you may still find it here. There are many French books, of course, but also plenty of titles in English, German and Italian. Marque histories and motorsport titles are well represented, and you'll often find bound sets of old motoring magazines like *Sport Auto*. Madame Pougeux

is happy to let customers browse for as long as they like, so allow plenty of time for your visit!

If you can't make it to Paris, Doc'Auto is also developing its website for online sales.

Just some of the well-stocked shelves.

Practical information

🕐 Open Monday to Friday, 2.30-7pm; closed in July & August

🏠 70, rue Laugier, 75017 Paris

Ⓜ Line 3, Pereire or Porte de Champerret

🚌 Lines 92 & 93

🖥 48.884184 N, 2.292435 E

🌐 www.librairie-docauto.com

📞 +33 1 43 80 84 99

✉ docauto@wanadoo.fr

Galerie Vitesse, Paris

Géo Ham's famous Casque bleu. (Courtesy Galerie Vitesse)

Although shows like Rétromobile (page 20) display the work of many artists for a few days, there's only one gallery in Paris where you can view a wide range of motoring art all year round. Founded in 1987 by Isabelle Nicolosi, the Galerie Vitesse is a unique venue at which to enjoy drawings, paintings and sculptures.

The gallery alternates temporary exhibitions devoted to a single artist with permanent displays of the 20 or more artists it represents. Cars – and especially sports and racing models – predominate, but you'll also find the works of artists like Lucio Perinotto, who specialises in painting historic planes.

There is too little space to list all the artists here, but personal favourites include the paintings of Hideki Yoshida, originally from Japan; the striking triptychs of the Polish artist Kapica, and the finely-hewn sculptures of Emmanuel Zurini.

The gallery also regularly sells the works of famous artists from the last century, like Géo Ham and Paul Bouvot, as well as original illustrations for books and magazines such as *L'Action Automobile*. If the originals are out of your reach, the gallery offers reprints and posters of many of the artists which it represents.

Drawing of a Bugatti Atlantic by Paul Bouvot. (Courtesy Galerie Vitesse)

Practical information

🕐 Open Tuesday to Saturday, 2-7pm

🏠 48, rue de Berri, 75008 Paris

Ⓜ Line 9, Saint-Philippe-du-Roule

🚌 Lines 22, 43, 52, 83 & 93

🖥 48.874702 N, 2.308212 E

🌐 www.galerievitesse.com

📞 +33 1 42 25 48 13

✉ contact@galerievitesse.com or galerievitesse@gmail.com

Librairie Passion Automobile, Paris

The extensive stock of new motoring books. / The friendly manager, Raphaël Galdos, with one of his favourite titles.

The perfect counterpart to Doc'Auto (page 40), the Librairie Passion Automobile sells only new books. There has been a bookshop specialising in motoring books on this site since the late 1940s, and originally it concentrated on technical manuals. Part of the leading automotive publishing group ETAI, the shop was completely refitted in the 2000s. If you're travelling with friends or family who aren't so interested in cars, there are plenty of other shops nearby which they can visit while you're browsing.

French technical manuals are now only a small part of the shop's extensive inventory, although it still focuses on motoring books, together with a smaller selection for enthusiasts of motorbikes, aviation and toys. As you'd expect for a shop in the French capital, owners of French cars are especially well served, and the helpful manager, Raphaël Galdos, runs his own classic Panhard. The shop also holds a good range of titles

for other marques, including English, German and Italian. Motorsport is another of its strengths, with videos as well as books on the races, circuits and drivers all on offer.

If you can't visit the shop in person, it offers an efficient mail-order service, by phone or through its website.

The shop front on the busy rue de Rennes.

Practical information

🕐 Open Monday to Saturday (exact hours on website)

🏠 83, rue de Rennes, 75006 Paris

Ⓜ Line 4, Saint-Sulpice or line 12, Rennes

🚌 Lines 95 & 96

🗺 48.850082 N, 2.329937 E

🌐 www.librairie-passionautomobile.com

📞 +33 1 45 48 15 14

✉ passionautomobile@etai.fr

Mercedes-Benz Center, Rueil-Malmaison

Mercedes McLaren SLR line-up, outside the Center. (Courtesy Mercedes-Benz France) / Temporary exhibition of Studio Harcourt photographs held in the Center.

Mercedes was one of the first car manufacturers to invest in a new generation of customer centres, at Brooklands in the UK or here in 2005 at Rueil-Malmaison, just off the A86 autoroute and close to Versailles and Saint-Germain-en-Laye.

The focus is mainly on its newest cars, but for the Mercedes enthusiast there's plenty to see in this large and airy building. At any one time, some 60 cars are displayed, and there are dedicated viewing areas on the upper floor for the high-end AMG versions and premium models of the day, like the Mercedes-Maybach S-Class. Test drives can be arranged for almost any model in the range.

Mercedes-Benz France has built up a collection of classic Mercedes – including a 300 SLR and a 450 SEL 6.9 – and these are regularly shown in the Center. The central atrium is sometimes used for temporary exhibitions of art and photography, and there is a small restaurant, 'La Bulle,' revamped at the end of 2013, where you can enjoy lunch or a coffee among the cars.

Practical information

🕐 Open Monday to Saturday, 9am-7pm

🏠 344 avenue Napoléon Bonaparte, 92500 Rueil-Malmaison

🖼 48.870021 N, 2.156417 E

🌐 paris.mercedes.fr/passion/mercedes-benz%20center/accueil

📞 +33 1 56 84 51 00

✉ paris.mercedes@daimler.com

Replica of 1886 Benz Patentwagen tricycle.

43

Mercedes-Benz Gallery, Paris

At the start of the 20th century, Mercedes' importer in France created the grandly named 'Mercedes Palace,' at 70, avenue des Champs-Élysées. Today, the company has moved up the avenue to this bold and modern display space, which offers a regularly changing programme of special exhibitions. Often, these highlight Mercedes' involvement in racing, with cars from its Formula 1 and DTM programmes, or limited edition sports cars from AMG.

Other displays focus more on style and luxury, such as the extensive 'designo' programme. As long ago as 2004, the company created a sensation by showing a CLK personalised by Giorgio Armani, which

The launch of the Mercedes-Benz CLS Shooting Brake. (Courtesy Mercedes-Benz France) / The Mercedes AMG Petronas Formula 1 car. (Courtesy Mercedes-Benz France)

was one of the first cars to use matt paintwork. The Gallery includes a large boutique, which sells the usual range of branded merchandise, but is particularly noteworthy for its wide range of scale models, including many historic cars.

Take the chance to visit this showroom while you can: faced with ever higher rents, Mercedes will leave its historic home by the end of 2017, giving way to a famous brand of confectionery! After that, or if you have a bit more time in Paris, you can see more of Mercedes' current range by visiting the Mercedes-Benz Center at Rueil-Malmaison (previous page).

Red-themed store front for an AMG promotion. (Courtesy Mercedes-Benz France)

Practical information

🕐 Open 7 days a week, 10.30am-10pm (8pm on Sundays)

🏠 118, avenue des Champs-Élysées, 75008 Paris

Ⓜ Line 1, George V

🚌 Line 73

🖼 48.872434 N, 2.300619 E

🌐 www.paris.mercedes.fr/ passion/mercedes-benz-champs-elysees/accueil

📞 +33 1 53 83 00 53

✉ accueil-ce@daimler.com

MotorVillage, Paris

MotorVillage illuminated at night. (Courtesy MotorVillage – Fiat France) / Alfa Romeo 1900 Sprint. (Courtesy MotorVillage – Fiat France)

Museums   Shows & Tours   **Market Place**   Motorsport   Circuits

Feeling in need of some refreshment? Why not stop at the Fiat group's MotorVillage, where you can enjoy an Italian-strength ristretto at the street-level Fiat Caffè!

Opened in 2010, this is one of the newest sites for the car enthusiast on the Champs-Élysées. Built to an imaginative plan by the French architect Jean-Michel Wilmotte, MotorVillage is a showcase for the best in Italian automotive history and design. The building's key feature is a central glass tube, 14m (46ft) high, and a single car is displayed on each of five levels. You'll also find dedicated boutiques for each marque, selling clothing and other goodies.

A regular programme of special exhibitions shows off the history and sporting traditions of each marque: Fiat, Abarth, Alfa Romeo, Lancia, Maserati and Jeep. Recent shows have included a look back at the group's history since 1900, the parts taken by its cars in the cinema, and a celebration of their race and rally victories. Many of the models displayed are brought in especially from Italy, giving visitors the chance to see cars like the first ever production Fiat 500 or a record-breaking Abarth 750 Bertone.

MotorVillage also features an outstanding Italian restaurant, NoLita, established by a Michelin-starred chef.

NoLita restaurant. (Courtesy MotorVillage – Fiat France)

Practical information

🕐 Open every day, 11am-8pm (Fridays and Saturdays 9pm; Sundays 7pm)

🏠 2, rond-point des Champs-Élysées, 75008 Paris

Ⓜ Lines 1 & 9, Franklin D Roosevelt

🚌 Lines 28, 32, 80, 83 & 92

🗺 48.869717 N, 2.310766 E

🌐 www.motorvillage.fr

📞 +33 1 53 75 78 84 (Boutique)

Osenat auctions, Fontainebleau

1968 Maserati Mistral 4000, with period yellow headlamps. (Courtesy Osenat) / 1929 Chenard et Walcker 1500 Grand Sport Ç Torpille. (Courtesy Osenat)

In 2016, the town of Fontainebleau, an hour's drive south of Paris, celebrated the 200th anniversary of its auction house. Now run by Jean-Pierre Osenat, it's the largest firm of auctioneers outside the capital and specialises in 19th century paintings, Empire furniture and classic cars.

A notch down from Artcurial (page 34), Osenat's auctions offer a broad range of historic cars, from vintage models through to the 1990s. There will usually be at least one 'star lot' at each sale, such as the Chapron-bodied Delahaye 135MS sold in late 2016 for €200,000, but most of the cars go for much less. Osenat often sells complete collections, such as that of Roger Brioult, the founder of the *Revue Technique Automobile*, or when museums have closed down. Osenat's auctions are also an outstanding opportunity to buy automobilia, with a huge selection of metal signs, books and magazines at the start of each sale.

Osenat's motoring auctions are held in the company's salerooms opposite the famous château in Fontainebleau. To view the cars during the week before each sale, however, you'll need to visit their premises at Moret-sur-Loing, a few miles further south.

1951 Talbot T26 Lago Record. (Courtesy Osenat)

Practical information

🕐 Regular sales throughout the year, on Sundays at 2pm

🏠 9-11, rue Royale, 77300 Fontainebleau

🖼 48.402662 N, 2.695421 E

🌐 www.osenat.fr

📞 +33 1 64 22 27 62

✉ contact@osenat.com

Peugeot Avenue, Paris

Just launched second-generation Peugeot 3008 SUV. (Courtesy Peugeot)

Peugeot's showroom at the top of the Champs-Élysées is a small one, with space for just three or four cars, but that doesn't stop 2.5 million visitors squeezing in each year. Exhibits frequently include new or forthcoming models, often highlighting Peugeot's investment in new technologies: that might mean its latest sporting variant, such as the 308 R Hybrid, or an ambitious prototype like the fuel cell-powered H2O Concept.

But Peugeot also remembers its heritage, with classic models loaned from its museum in Sochaux frequently displayed alongside new cars: a record-breaking 404 Diesel from 1965 or an Eclipse from the 1930s, for instance, next to the latest 3008. At the back of the showroom, re-designed for 2015, is a retail counter where you can buy scale models, and even household items like the pepper mills still manufactured by the company.

For the moment, PSA's corporate headquarters remains nearby at 75, avenue de la Grande Armée, giving fans of the marque another chance to see find the complete range of cars on show, but in 2017 Peugeot will leave this head office as it continues its restructuring.

Practical information

🕐 Open every day, 10.30am-8pm (11pm Thurs-Sat)

🏠 136, avenue des Champs-Élysées, 75008 Paris

Ⓜ Line 1, George V

🚌 Line 73

🗺 48.872419 N, 2.29946 E

🌐 www.peugeot.com/fr/marque-peugeot#peugeot-avenue

📞 +33 1 42 89 30 20

Modern concept cars like this Peugeot Quartz are also regularly exhibited. (Courtesy Peugeot)

Le Rendez-Vous Toyota, Paris

Looking to the future: the FT-HS concept. (Toyota Motor Europe/Olivier Sochard) / Toyota's most famous sports car, the 2000 GT. (Courtesy Toyota Motor Europe/Olivier Sochard)

Alongside the big French manufacturers and German prestige brands, it may at first seem surprising to find Toyota on the Champs-Élysées, especially as Japanese cars have a smaller market share in France. But Toyota is a significant contributor to the French economy, employing nearly 4000 people at its plant in Valenciennes, where the Yaris is built, and it enjoys a strong positive image thanks to its association with hybrid technology.

Toyota's showroom is one of the newest to open, and typically devotes much of its space to the company's hybrid production models and concept cars, like the FT-HS. For the enthusiast, though, there are sometimes displays of new sporting models, like the FT86 Coupé or the TS040 hybrid race car. Toyota regularly brings in cars from Japan or other European collections - such as the Louwman Museum in the Netherlands – to showcase its heritage. Whilst the 2000 GT remains the company's best known sports car, the showroom has also given visitors the chance to see cars like the 1965 Sport 800, or a Celica GT Coupé from the following decade. For the moment at least, however, Lexus cars are not shown and you can't buy any Toyota-branded goodies.

Practical information

🕐 Open every day, 11am-8pm (11pm Thurs-Sat)

🏠 79, avenue des Champs-Élysées, 75008 Paris

Ⓜ Line 1, George V

🚌 Line 73

🖥 48.871216 N, 2.302668 E

🌐 www.toyota.fr/world-of-toyota/about-toyota/rendez-vous/index-new-fr.json

📞 +33 800 86 96 82 (Toyota France)

Celebrating Toyota's 75th anniversary: the Sport 800. (Courtesy Toyota Motor Europe/Olivier Sochard)

Museums

Shows & Tours

Market Place

Motorsport

Circuits

RM Sotheby's auction, Paris

Display of the Porsche 550 Spyder recreated the 1955 Frankfurt Motor Show, where it was first presented. / Mussolini's gift to his mistress, an Alfa Romeo 6C 2500 Sport Berlinetta by Touring.

RM Sotheby's claims to be the world's largest auction house for 'investment-quality automobiles'. That will inevitably mean that many of the cars it sells are out of reach, but its auctions do give everyone the chance to see some of the world's most prestigious cars, often with a story to tell.

RM's own history goes back 35 years and it arrived in Europe in 2007. After organising sales in London, Maranello, Monaco and on Lake Como, it held its first sale in Paris in 2014. It proved an immediate success, with sales totalling nearly €18M. The auction now takes place each year during Rétromobile (page 16), in a marquee at the Invalides which it shares with the Exposition Concept Cars (page 28).

RM Sotheby's catalogue covers cars from the earliest years of motoring through to the latest 21st century supercars, but many of its star lots have been prewar coachbuilt coupés and convertibles or post-war GTs. In 2016, for example, a 1962 Ferrari 400 Superamerica LWB Coupé Aerodinamico by Pininfarina vied for honours with a Wendler-bodied Porsche 550 Spyder. The previous year, the 1939 Alfa Romeo 6C 2500 Sport Berlinetta by Touring had allegedly been given by Mussolini to his lover, Claretta Petacci.

One of the oldest cars for sale, a 1900 Bardon Type A Tonneau.

Practical information

🕐 February every year

🏠 In front of the Invalides dome, place Vauban, 75007 Paris

Ⓜ Line 13, Varenne

🚌 Lines 82 & 92

📷 48.853881 N, 2.31237 E

🌐 www.rmsothebys.com/auctions/

📞 +44 20 7851 7070

✉ information@rmsothebys.com

49

Coupes de Printemps, Montlhéry

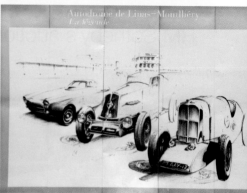

Porsche 910. (Courtesy Paris Auto Events) / Mural depicting the history of the track.

When the Autodrome at Montlhéry (page 53) revived its programme of sporting events in 2008, the Coupes de Printemps was one of the first to take its place on the calendar. Now well established and open to the public, it provides one of the first opportunities each year for enthusiastic drivers to give their cars a shakedown, ahead of the major historic events like the Tour Auto (page 22) later in the season.

Up to 100 pre-1972 cars take part, split into different series. Many of them have an impressive sporting pedigree, cars like the ex-Trintignant Bugatti type 51, a Gordini type 15 driven by Fangio, or a Porsche 910 which raced at the Nürburgring in 1968. Others – such as a DB Panhard HBR5 in 1958/9 or a Ford GT40 from the following decade – saw their moment of glory at Le Mans. The organisers also do a great job attracting some unusual racers, such as the improbable-looking Morgan Monotrace or stylish Porsche 356 Carrera Abarth.

If you're not lucky enough to be driving one of these yourself, you can get up close to all the cars in the paddock or enjoy the great view over the start line from the terrace.

Paul Belmondo behind the wheel of an Alpine A441.

Practical information

🕐 March every year

🏠 Autodrome de Linas-Montlhéry, avenue Georges Boillot, 91310 Linas

🖥 48.621999 N, 2.247294 E

🌐 www.coupesdeprintemps.com

📞 +33 1 69 80 17 00

✉ pae@utaceram.com

Les Grandes Heures Automobiles, Montlhéry

Group B Peugeot 205 T16 in the paddock. / Beautiful – and rare – Triumph Italia parked beside the track.

After a diffident start in 2015, Franz Hummel and his team really hit their stride for the second edition of this event. It has already established itself as the top event at Montlhéry and the most impressive historic motorsport gathering in the Ile-de-France. Its formula for success? A constantly changing programme of demonstrations on track – including some spectacular sessions after nightfall – and a friendly, informal atmosphere with easy access to the cars in the paddock. Affordable prices helped attract 15,000 spectators, despite the rain.

For 2016, the outstanding selection of cars on track ranged from prewar Bugattis and others which had raced at Montlhéry in period to spectacular Group B rally cars. The latter included an original Audi Quattro, a Lancia 037 and a first-generation Mazda RX-7, but Bruno Saby, driving a Peugeot 205 T16, was in a class of his own. Among the older cars, Peter Mullin from California and Philippe Moch brought along some remarkable Voisins, including the 1927 Speed Record car.

Away from the track, many clubs put on a good show of their members' cars, with a good turn-out last year by MG and Porsche, as well as official support from L'Aventure Peugeot (page 206).

Practical information

🕐 September every year

🏠 Autodrome de Linas-Montlhéry, avenue Georges Boillot, 91310 Linas

🖼 48.621999 N, 2.247294 E

🌐 www.lesgrandesheures automobiles.com

📞 + 33 4 50 91 98 19

✉ contact@lesgrandes heuresautomobiles.com

Bugatti pressing on through the chicane.

Vintage Revival, Montlhéry

1926 Bugatti Type 36 single-seater at speed on the banking / Dutch-registered Lagonda 3-Litre Tourer from 1933 leading the grid.

There are many ways to enjoy the old racetrack at Montlhéry (page 53), but few can match the special atmosphere of the Vintage Revival. First held in 2011, this biannual meeting is for cars, three-wheelers ('cyclecars') and motorbikes built before 1940, the very ones which raced here when new.

This event is all about the action on track, with 240 cars taking part and another hundred to admire in the paddock. After a series of grouped runs, the weekend finishes with a final parade lap on Sunday afternoon. At each event one make is honoured: Voisin in 2013, and Salmson in 2015, for example. Marques such as Amilcar or Bugatti are almost commonplace; here you can see rarities from long gone manufacturers like Guyot or SCAT, and curiosities such as the Bédélia cyclecar, in which the passenger sits in front of the driver. Some of the cars taking part – like the Amilcar C6 – are the actual vehicles which set speed records here in the 1920s and '30s.

The Revival is well supported by owners' clubs, for whom special rates to take part are offered. 70% of participants are from outside France, and commentary is given in English and French, adding to the international atmosphere of the meeting.

1923 Rolland-Pilain A22 GP in the paddock.

Practical information

🕐 Held biennially in April or May (odd years)

🏠 Autodrome de Linas-Montlhéry, avenue Georges Boillot, 91310 Linas

🗺 48.621999 N, 2.247294 E

🌐 www.vintage-revival.fr

📞 +33 3 86 57 10 67

✉ vintage-revival-montlhery@outlook.com

Autodrome de Linas-Montlhéry

Built in a record-breaking six months in 1924, the Autodrome at Montlhéry is a place which every enthusiast should visit at least once. From the 1920s to the '50s, its legendary banked track was the setting for countless races and speed records, and later for some of France's first historic races. At the start of the 21st century, however, it seemed that its closure was inevitable and that the Grand Prix de l'Âge d'Or in 2004 would be the last event held there.

Happily, the owners of the track, UTAC, decided just four years later to invest heavily in a new programme of events and facilities for visitors. Today the circuit at Montlhéry – the last in the world to retain its original layout – hosts nearly 30 events a year for clubs and the public alike. At the top of its 51-degree slope, drivers can once again run hands-off at 180km/h (112mph). In 2014 Montlhéry celebrated its 90th anniversary in style, when a new pavilion opened at the centre of the track to welcome visitors.

Celebrating 90 years of the Montlhéry circuit in 2014. (Courtesy Paris Auto Events) / Alfas speed off the banking. (Courtesy Paris Auto Events)

The circuit also offers a range of driving courses, including special programmes for the police and road testers.

Lotus and Caterham owners gather on a summer evening. (Courtesy Paris Auto Events)

Practical information

🕐 Events throughout the year

🏠 Autodrome de Linas-Montlhéry, avenue Georges Boillot, 91310 Linas

🖳 48.621999 N, 2.247294 E

🌐 www.parisautoevents.com

📞 +33 1 69 80 17 00

✉ pae@utaceram.com

Circuit length: 3405m

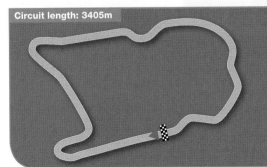

Circuits Automobiles LFG, La Ferté-Gaucher

Located about 70km (43 miles) east of Paris, la Ferté-Gaucher is the biggest circuit in this area. Laid out by the Austrian F1 designer Franz Schreiner, the purpose-built track opened in 2009.

The circuit is actually made up of three different tracks: a fast circuit, 2km (1.2 miles) long, a short technical circuit with 9 corners, and the main circuit of 3.6km (2.2 miles). This features a 500m (550yd) straight and 14 corners of different degrees of difficulty. It has been homologated by the FFSA for speeds in excess of 200km/h (125mph) and is well rated by the specialist press for its mix of speed and technical difficulty. It's no surprise that it is regularly used by the motoring press to test high-performance cars.

La Ferté-Gaucher offers a broad array of driving courses through its on-site partners. Options range from road safety to drifting and performance driving in cars including a Dodge Viper and the X-Bow two-seaters in the newly created KTM Academy. You can also experience the track in your own car on one of many open days, or book it for the exclusive use of a club. The French Corvette Club, for example, celebrated the 60th anniversary of the Corvette here.

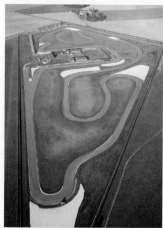

Aerial view of the circuit. (Courtesy Circuits Automobiles LFG) / Indoor driving simulator. (Courtesy Circuits Automobiles LFG)

Chevrolet Corvette Pace Car. (Courtesy Circuits Automobiles LFG)

Circuit length: 3600m

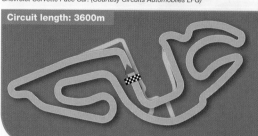

Practical information

🕐 Open year-round: book in advance

🏠 Route de Choisy, 77320 La Ferté-Gaucher

🖥 48.757289 N, 3.278287 E

🌐 www.circuitslfg.fr

📞 +33 1 64 65 92 12

✉ info@circuitslfg.fr

Circuit JP Beltoise, Trappes

The circuit at Trappes is small – just 1.6km (1 mile) in length – but has the advantage of being only 25km (16 miles) away from Paris. Originally designed as a speed ring for the testing of heavy goods vehicles, it was taken over in 1986 by the late Jean-Pierre Beltoise, the former French motorcycle champion and Formula 1 driver for Matra and BRM. He developed an original approach to driver safety training called 'Conduire Juste,' and this is the mainstay of the courses offered at Trappes, which include a track driving option using high-performance models from VW.

Ferrari F430 used for driving courses. (Courtesy Circuit JP Beltoise) / Aerial view of the circuit. (Courtesy Circuit JP Beltoise) / Jean-Pierre Beltoise, seen here at a book signing session in 2013.

For sports car enthusiasts, however, the circuit is also used by companies such as Pilotage Passion and Pole Position for its own driving courses in the latest models from Porsche, Ferrari, Lamborghini and Audi. These are popular choices for the quick familiarisation experiences often offered as gifts, but many provide limited time behind the wheel. For a longer drive, the circuit is available for exclusive club hire, and there is a karting track on site as well. In all these activities, the emphasis now is on training and leisure rather than competition.

Practical information

🕐 Open all year

🏠 Avenue des Frères Lumière, ZA Trappes-Elancourt, 78190 Trappes

🖼 48.757521 N, 1.987779 E

🌐 www.conduirejuste.com

📞 +33 1 30 51 23 23

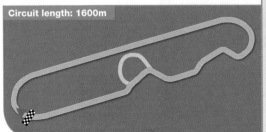

Circuit length: 1600m

Circuits de l'Ouest Parisien, Dreux

Pro'Pulsion supercar driving course. (Courtesy Circuits de l'Ouest Parisien) / MCC Rallye du Cœur. (Courtesy Circuits de l'Ouest Parisien)

This circuit, an hour's drive west of Paris, was opened in 1959 by the French tyre manufacturer Kléber-Colombes, which used it as test track. It went on to gain a reputation as a rallycross venue, but today the rallycross circuit is only part of an extensive set of facilities, which include tracks for 4-wheel drives, karting and quads.

The main asphalt track has been re-surfaced and extended over the past few years, and is now 2100m (1.3 miles) in length. The addition of sand traps and run-off areas has improved safety and ensured its continued homologation by the FFSA. Although flat, the circuit has a good variety of corners (five right and two left); a car like a Porsche Cayman Cup can lap it in under a minute.

There is a wide range of driving courses available, provided by Pro'Pulsion, whose cars have included the Aston Martin V8 Vantage and Peugeot RCZ R, as well as models from Lamborghini, Ferrari and Porsche. Drifting courses in a BMW M3 are also offered, and there are regular track days throughout the year when you can bring your own car. The clubhouse and reception facilities make it a good venue for club events.

Practical information

🕐 Open all year

🏠 Address: Chemin Notre-Dame de la Ronde, ZI Nord, 28103 Dreux

🖥 48.751848 N, 1.362829 E

🌐 www.circuitouestparisien.com

📞 +33 2 37 62 50 00

✉ contact@circuitouestparisien.com

Circuit length: 2100m

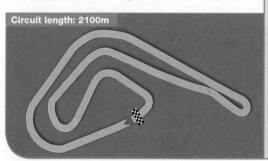

Western France

From Normandy and Brittany, to the vineyards of Bordeaux ... not forgetting Le Mans!

This region covers Normandy, Brittany, the Pays de la Loire and much of la Nouvelle-Aquitaine; it stretches from the western Channel ports in the North, down the Atlantic coast to the vineyards of Bordeaux.

A t its centre – in automotive, if not strictly geographical terms – is Le Mans, home to the world's most famous endurance race for over 90 years. Le Mans is a place every enthusiast should visit at least once, whether for the 24 Hours race or one of the classic events held there.

Historic motorsport fans are also in for a treat at Angoulême, where the Circuit

The concours d'élégance in Deauville.

Racing through the night at Le Mans. (Courtesy Toyota Motorsport GmbH)

des Remparts is one of the few races still run on an original street circuit. Until the 1950s, many more French towns held their own Grand Prix races – there were four in Normandy alone – and today several of these hold revival events, featuring demonstrations on specially recreated circuits.

The coastal resorts of Normandy and Brittany host many of France's finest concours d'élégance, like those at Deauville and La Baule. Further inland you can visit the museums at Le Mans, Châtellerault or Lohéac – which also hosts France's biggest autojumble – or drive on one of the many fine circuits in the region.

The Circuit des Remparts in Angoulême.

Contents

Museums

Shows & Tours

Market Place

Motorsport

Circuits

Manoir de l'Automobile, Lohéac

Lohéac is renowned for its collection of Alpine berlinettes.

With more than 400 cars on show, the Manoir de l'Automobile is one of France's top car museums. Half-an-hour's drive south of Rennes, the beautiful village of Lohéac is a haven for enthusiasts. As well as its museum, which opened in 1988, they can enjoy its circuit and frequent events. The village owes its revival to one man, Michel Hommell, who moved here in 1973 and has built up a thriving magazine business; for several years, the Hommell sports cars were built here, and the former factory still maintains them.

The museum has a strong focus on sports and racing cars, and features exceptional displays of Hommell's own cars, from the very first prototype, and the largest permanent collection of

Once a farm building, the Manoir is built in the traditional stone of the region. / Stained-glass window in the 'Chapelle des moteurs.'

The famous Formula 1 hall.

Alpine sports cars. Cars on show include early A106 and A108 models, as well as the famous A110 berlinettes and the later A310. There are less common French sports cars from the 1950s and '60s, too, from manufacturers such as Rispal, René Bonnet and UMAP, and more recent Le Mans contenders such as a Jaguar XJR-11 and Pescarolo's Courage C36.

Rally cars are a major strength of the Manoir, which has an exceptional set of Group B cars, including the Lancia 037 that won the World Rally Championship in 1984, a Delta S4, and Peugeot 205 Turbo 16. But even these are just an appetizer before the Formula 1 hall, with its breathtaking line-up of 18 F1 cars from the 1980s and '90s, from constructors including Ligier, Jordan and McLaren.

Other highlights of the museum include the display of engines in the 'Chapelle des moteurs' and the collection of 3000 model cars, complete with 30 beautiful dioramas by Francis Costanzo. On the upper floor, a series of displays recreate village life and add to the museum's appeal for all the family.

Practical information

🕐 Open all year, closed Mondays except in July & August

🏠 Rue du Manoir, 35550 Lohéac

🗺 47.861251 N, -1.894743 W

🌐 www.manoir-automobile.fr

📞 +33 2 99 34 02 32

✉ musee@sfep.fr

Citroën's 'Petite Rosalie' leads this display of prewar models.

Château de Vernon

Two Maseratis: a 1963 3500 GT Sebring and 1973 Merak. / Simca 5 and 8 in the 'Nursery.'

At a time when many car museums in France have closed, it's encouraging to see a new collection open to the public. Not far from the Val de Vienne circuit (page 102), the château is a beautiful 17th century listed building, which has been meticulously restored over the past decade.

Its owner, Jean-Pierre Nylin, began his collection of nearly 50 vehicles with a 1953 MG TD, and sports cars from the 1950s onwards continue to be a focus of the displays. English makes are well represented by a rare Jaguar SS 3.5 Cabriolet from 1940, and an original LHD Bentley Type R from 1953. Other marques include a 1959 Facel Vega HK500, a personal favourite of the owner, and an unusual Dinalpin, an A110 berlinette built under licence from Alpine in Mexico. More recent high-performance models include a couple of fine Maseratis, one of only three Lotus Esprit Sport 300s in France, and a Dodge Viper GTS prepared to Le Mans racing spec by Oreca. The charmingly named 'Nursery' section of the collection houses some small cars, including a couple of prewar Simcas, a Fiat 500 and a Mini Countryman. All the cars are in running order, and generally in good condition.

Practical information

🕐 Open every day (26pm) except Monday in July & August, on Sundays (2-6pm) in June & September; by arrangement for groups at other times

🏠 1, rue du Château, 86340 Vernon

🗺 46.440824 N, 0.476596 E

🌐 www.tourisme-vienne. com/fr/activite/728/ musee-automobile-de-vernon

📞 +33 5 49 45 28 72

✉ jpnylinvernon@orange.fr

The beautifully restored exterior of the Château de Vernon.

Museums

Le Monde de Jacques, Saint-Laurent du Mottay

In front of the Château de la Houssaye. / The entrance to the collection. (Courtesy Le Monde de Jacques)

This delightful site not far from Angers really deserves a section of its own, as there is no other place in this guide quite like it. Imagine stepping back in time to join a car-loving family at a country house party and you are ready to enter the world of Jacques Bru and his partner, Aline Luneteau.

In a château re-built in the 19th century, they have assembled an eclectic mix of old cars and automobilia. One building houses a selection of prewar cars, including a rare 1922 Zédel and an immaculate 1939 Renault Primaquatre cabriolet, often used for family trips. Next door there are more recent classics, from an Austin-Healey Sprite and Triumph TR3, to the legendary Citroën DS and 2CV. Throughout the château you'll find old motoring books, catalogues and posters to browse through, as well as film and slot car racing rooms to enjoy.

But the motoring décor is only part of what makes this site so special. Jacques and Aline encourage you to stay and enjoy walks in the park, fishing, and horse rides from the stables nearby. Whether for a family or a club, they'll be happy to arrange picnics, wine-tastings and even hot air ballooning.

Practical information

🕐 Open all year, but book in advance

🏠 Château de la Houssaye, 49410 Saint-Laurent du Mottay

📠 47.351315 N, -0.963589 W

🌐 www.lemondedejacques.fr

📞 +33 (2) 41 68 14 96

✉ collections@lemondedejacques.fr

Starting a vintage Peugeot Lion, one of the earliest cars in the collection. (Courtesy Le Monde de Jacques)

Museums

Shows & Tours

Market Place

Motorsport

Circuits

Musée Auto Moto Vélo de Châtellerault

This museum must be one of the best-kept secrets for visitors from outside the region, but is well worth a stop if you're following the old Nationale 10 or heading to the Futuroscope. You won't miss the distinctive twin chimneys of the building, a former arms factory.

Re-opened as a museum by the town authorities in 1998, its impressive and well-presented collection of nearly 200 vehicles covers cars, motorbikes and cycles. Indeed, it's one of the biggest motorcycle museums in France, displaying models from long-gone manufacturers such as Aiglon, Moto-Rêve or René Gillet, as well as a huge collection of scooters from the 1950s.

Welcome to the museum!
(Courtesy Musées de Châtellerault)

The cars on show, many of them French, are informatively presented in chronological order, beginning with a pre-1900 Panhard & Levassor. They include popular models such as the Citroën Traction Avant, but also rarities such as a unique replica of a 1906 Brouhot, or a Longchamp de Courcy prototype from 1953. Some of the finest cars, however, must be the 1929 Voisin C14 Coach, the beautifully restored Georges Irat MDU from 1937, or the 1949 Delahaye 135M with its elegant bodywork by Guilloré. Looking ahead, the museum is building up a collection of electric cars.

Practical information

🕐 Open February-December, but days vary by season (see website for full details)

🏠 5, rue Clément Krebs, 86100 Châtellerault

🖳 46.813163 N, 0.535428 E

🌐 www.ville-chatellerault.fr/animations/musees

📞 +33 5 49 20 30 99

✉ musees.chatellerault@alienor.org

La Manufacture, home to the museum. (Courtesy Musées de Châtellerault) / 1961 Dodge Lancer and Simca 1000 in this re-created garage.

Museums

Shows & Tours

Market Place

Motorsport

Circuits

Musée Automobile de Vendée, Talmont-Saint-Hilaire

Racing cars in the foreground, with vintage models along the back wall. / 1913 Mors RX outside the museum entrance.

Talmont-Saint Hilaire is just 10km (6 miles) from the beaches of les Sables-d'Olonne. Gaston Giron, the father of the museum's current owner, was a local garage proprietor and there is a reconstruction of the Mathis dealership he ran inside the museum. He began collecting long before the classic car movement existed, and the museum will celebrate its 50th anniversary in 2017. Now there are nearly 140 cars on show, with more waiting their turn to be restored in the workshop, and the third generation of the family is already involved in running the museum.

Veteran and vintage cars are a great strength of this collection, which includes an 1885 De Dion Bouton steamer, an 1898 Aster (one of only two survivors) and a curious Morgan Monotrace from 1926, fitted with two small stabilizer wheels to use when parking. Some of the cars on display were built in the region: there is a 1912 Barre from Niort and two cars designed or assembled by Brissonneau & Lotz, which was founded in Nantes. There are racers too, from a 1923 Bugatti Brescia to a 1968 Costin Nathan, whilst a fine display of period advertising posters lines the walls.

Practical information

🕐 Open from April 1 to October 1 (see website for exact details), and by appointment for groups in February-March and October-December

🏠 Route des Sables d'Olonne, 85440 Talmont-Saint-Hilaire

🖼 46.477167 N, -1.667507 W

🌐 www.musee-auto-vendee.com

📞 +33 2 51 22 05 81

✉ musee.auto@wanadoo.fr

1912 Renault AG1 (the famous 'taxi de la Marne'), seen here beside the sea. (Courtesy Musée Automobile de Vendée)

Musée de Mécanique Naturelle, Giverny

The entrance to the museum. / All the engines are in working order.

The village of Giverny is famous the world over for the beautiful house and gardens of Claude Monet, and there is now a modern museum of Impressionist art to enjoy as well. But if you feel like you've seen one water lily too many, just a few minutes' walk away from Monet's home you'll find this unique museum devoted to stationary engines of all kinds. Established in 1955 by Adolphe Guillemard, an agricultural mechanic, it's now run by his sons.

The family has built up a huge collection of engines from the 19th and 20th centuries: agricultural machinery, power generators, sawing machines and more. Some of the earliest engines are steam-driven, followed by petrol and diesel machines, like the huge Carel diesel engine from Belgium. The exhibits come from all over Europe and even the US. Many of the machines – like the 1824 veneer saw – have been beautifully restored and most are in working order. The owners will be happy to explain their workings to visitors, and maybe even start them up.

The museum is open throughout the year and hosts a special meeting for collectors from across Europe in September, 'Le moteur est dans le pré.'

This three-cylinder Carel diesel engine weighs 17 tons!

Practical information

🕐 Open all year, but times vary, so call in advance to check

🏠 2, rue Blanche Hoschedé Monet, 27620 Giverny

🖥 49.0770818 N, 1.5293493 E

🌐 www.vernon-visite.org/rf2/giverny4.shtml

📞 +33 2 32 21 26 33

✉ meseum@aol.com

Musée du Moteur, Saumur

This enormous Sulzer diesel engine weighs in at 23 tons. / The museum is housed in this Baltard-style building: a former factory.
(Courtesy Musée du Moteur)

This museum is the only one in France devoted to combustion engines of all kinds, from 1898 to the present day, and its modest setting in a suburb of Saumur belies the richness of its exhibits. The museum owes its creation in 1986 to a local technical college, and its former students continue to donate engines so that its collections remain up-to-date. Try to take a guided tour if you can, as these are especially informative.

The visit begins in an educational area which explains how internal combustion engines for cars (both petrol and diesel) work, with a special display on Wankel engines. The route through the museum then moves on to planes and trains, and even an Ariane IV rocket engine. There are industrial power units, too, like the huge 1907 Winterthur engine from the mill at Gennes, and a fascinating model of the Stirling external combustion engine.

Car engines on show range from a rare Majola Type A from 1911, to the motor which powered Peugeot's Le Mans-winning 905 in 1993. As well as production engines, there are prototypes like the Perkins diesel, developed from the 3.5-litre V8 petrol engine in the Range Rover.

Majola Type A from 1911.

Practical information

🕐 Open mid-April to early October, Tuesday to Saturday 2-6pm, and at other times for groups (check website for latest details)

🏠 Rue Alphonse Caillaud, 49400 Saumur

📧 47.25056 N, -0.08778 W

🌐 www.museedumoteur.fr

📞 +33 2 41 50 26 10

✉ contact@museedumoteur.fr

Museums

Shows & Tours

Market Place

Motorsport

Circuits

Musée Populaire chez Manuel, Migné-Auxances

1909 Renault AX 'doctor's coupé.' / A well-stocked bar!

This museum is surely one of the most extraordinary places in this guide. Located between Poitiers and the Futuroscope, it's a collection of curiosities more than a car museum. Nothing can really prepare you for the surprise as you move from room to room: everywhere you look there are thousands of objects – furniture, toys and clothes among them – which pay tribute to a way of life which has now disappeared.

Among the exhibits are many vehicles, most of them well worn: vintage motorbikes from Alcyon, Ravat and Monet-Goyon; cars such as the 1923 Amilcar near the entrance, or the prewar Renault AX and Monasix in the next room. The collections of microcars from the postwar years and 60 pedal cars are particularly noteworthy. Outside, there's more to see, like the school bus or charming Poulain chocolate van from the 1950s, and even a Sikorsky helicopter behind the museum!

The current owner's father, Manuel Ribeiro, began collecting as he travelled around France, and opened this museum in 1977. His son Jean-Claude is now well past retirement age himself, but his daughter is already starting to help maintain this unique site.

Small postwar models from Renault, Fiat, Panhard, and more.

Practical information

🕐 Open all year, but call in advance to check

🏠 37, avenue de Châtellerault, 86440 Migné-Auxances

🗺 46.6273 N, 0.354945 E

🌐 www.musee-chez-manuel.com

📞 +33 6 05 39 01 11

✉ contact@musee-chez-manuel.com

Musée de Sanxet, Pomport

The one-off Casimir Ragot Spéciale racer from 1930. / The Château de Sanxet's current buildings date back to the 16ᵗʰ century.

If you like your museums smart and shiny, this won't be the place for you. To call the cars on display 'well patinated' would be an understatement! But don't let this put you off: Bertrand de Passemar, a retired winegrower and former amateur racer, has built a fascinating collection of 35 cars, many of them rare or with interesting histories.

The star of the show is the one-off Casimir Ragot Spéciale from Bordeaux, which runs on a heady mix of petrol and alcohol. Take your pick nearby from a 1923 Citroën 'tank' racer, a superb 1929 Rally ABC roadster or a post-war Jowett Javelin which competed in the Monte Carlo Rally. The 1949 Triumph Roadster undergoing restoration was originally owned by the film director Visconti, whose family had property in the area. And don't miss the extraordinary flight simulator used by the French army in 1939!

The history of Sanxet goes back to 700, and the château was later the starting point for the Hundred Years War. Set in the heart of Monbazillac, its vineyards produce one of the oldest sweet white wines in the world, so you can finish your visit with a wine tasting.

Practical information

🕐 Open all year, but call in advance to check

🏠 Château de Sanxet, 24240 Pomport

📧 44.805638 N, 0.436007 E

🌐 www.sanxet.com

📞 +33 6 27 19 19 39

✉ sanxet@sanxet.com

Two unique models: a 1923 Citroën 'tank' racer next to a Jowett Javelin with Ghia bodywork.

Museums

Musée des 24 Heures-Circuit de la Sarthe, Le Mans

Le Mans-winning cars through the years. (Courtesy Dominique Breugnot/teamdbc-pictures.com)

At the start of 2017 the museum was taken over by the ACO (Automobile Club de l'Ouest) and will ultimately become part of a new 'Le Mans Resort' experience, so expect to see big changes in the coming years. But even now, it is well worth joining the nearly 70,000 fans who visit it every year. It is really three museums in one, telling the story of car manufacturing in Le Mans and of motoring in the 20th century, as well as celebrating the world's most famous endurance race. Both Bollée and Renault built cars in the area around Le Mans, and their models are included in the display of 150 cars. The many other French cars on show include fascinating prototypes, such as the turbine-powered Socéma Grégoire from 1952, and rotary-engined Citroën C35.

But, of course, the racing cars steal the show, whether it's the Bentley 3 Litre which won in 1924, or the 166 MM that heralded Ferrari's first entry (and victory) in 1949, Matra's MS670B from 1974, or the recent Audi R8. Other areas of the museum go behind the scenes, or present the drivers who won at Le Mans, complete with archive videos and period posters.

Practical information

🕐 Open year-round, Jan: Fri-Mon 11am-6pm, Feb-Mar and Oct-Dec: daily except Tues, 11am-6pm, Apr-Sep: daily 10am-7pm

🏠 9, place Luigi Chinetti, 72100 Le Mans

🖼 47.956227 N, 0.207749 E

🌐 musee24h.sarthe.com/

📞 +33 2 43 72 72 24

✉ See website

Replica of the rotary-engined Mazda 787B, the first Japanese car to win at Le Mans. (Courtesy Dominique Breugnot/teamdbc-pictures.com)

Les Anciennes en Vallée de l'Eure Classic, Saint Aubin-sur-Gaillon

Museums

Shows & Tours

Market Place

Motorsport

Circuits

Rarely seen TVRs from the final years of production.

You may be excused for not recognising the name of this village of 1800 inhabitants, about 90km (56 miles) west of Paris. In just a few years, however, the energetic local club, Volants et Vallée, has built this late summer show into a lively gathering, which attracts up to 2,000 cars and 12,000 visitors. It has now outgrown its original location at nearby Breuilpont and moved in 2015 to a new site just off the A13 autoroute. Now there is almost too much space for the cars of all ages, parts stands and live entertainment.

Ever-popular Renault Dauphines.

There's a good variety of cars on show, from 2CVs and beach buggies to the majestic Mercedes 600s of a local garage which specialises in the model. Local owners bring along rare models such as a police specification Matra Djet 5S or a Tornado sports car. The event regularly marks key model anniversaries, such as the 60th birthdays of the Chevrolet Corvette and Triumph TR2, and is well supported by owners' clubs including DeLorean and TVR, whose cars are much less common in France than in the UK.

Practical information

🕐 Early September every year

🏠 Ritchie Bros. Auctioneers, off junction 17 of A13 autoroute, 27600 Saint Aubin-sur-Gaillon.

📧 49.135730 N, 1.316419 E

🌐 www.lva-auto.fr/minisite/volants-et-vallee

📞 +33 6 61 39 46 06

✉️ volants.vallee@orange.fr

Massive Berliet desert truck.

Concours d'élégance, La Baule

Prize-winning 1913 Hudson. / Fashion models part of the show.

Enthusiasts in France are spoiled for choice among its many concours d'élégance each summer, but the show in La Baule is exceptional for a couple of reasons. First, it's the oldest such event still held – the 2017 edition will be the 87th. Secondly, it takes place at night, culminating in a grand firework display. The whole show is a very lavish production, playing to a packed house of 4000 spectators at La Baule's prestigious racecourse. With live music, professional dancers and fashion models, the whole family can enjoy the evening. You can buy tickets in advance from the Comité des Fêtes in La Baule.

As you would expect, the 60 or more cars shown are just as classy, and participants come from all over Europe. The cars are presented in chronological order and winners in 2016 included a magnificent Delaunay-Belleville 'Torpédo' from 1930 and a superbly restored BMW 327. There are plenty of rarities too, like the unique Frua-bodied Citroën SM.

The concours d'élégance is the highlight of a week of motoring events in La Baule, which include a children's car show, a day-long sale of automobilia, and a road trip to the salt pans at Guérande.

Scale model Delahaye in the children's concours.

Practical information

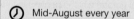

🕐 Mid-August every year

🏠 Stade François André, avenue de Joyeuse, 44500 La Baule-Escoublac

🖼 47.28356 N, -2.412303 W

🌐 www. comitedesfeteslabaule.com

📞 +33 2 40 60 66 98

✉ comfeteslabaule@ wanadoo.fr

Museums

Shows & Tours

Market Place

Motorsport

Circuits

Coupe Florio Saint-Brieuc

*This British-registered Lancia Fulvia HF is a regular entrant in historic events. / Vauxhall 30/98, one of the oldest cars competing.
(Both courtesy Anthony Ménard)*

The very first Coupe Florio in Saint-Brieuc was held in 1927, thanks to the efforts of Lucien Rosengart. The following year, the race returned to Italy and more than 80 years would pass before it was revived in France. The new event was an immediate success, attracting 400 cars and 70,000 spectators to its fifth edition in 2015, many of them from the UK.

The weekend starts with a stylish concours d'élégance on Friday evening in the city centre. Winners last time included a remarkable 1899 Lacroix. On the following day, participants can join a road trip in the attractive countryside nearby. Saturday is also the day for scrutineering, giving the public the chance to get up close to the cars in the Parc des Promenades.

The highlight of the weekend comes on Sunday, when qualifying tests take place in the morning and the main demonstration sessions (run on regularity principles) are held in the afternoon. Starting from the port, the 2.7km (1.7 mile) circuit climbs up to the town centre. Although there are plenty of sporting models from the '60s and '70s, the route also resounds regularly to monsters like David Biggins' 1913 Mercedes Grand Prix replica.

Practical information

🕐 End of August/early September, biennially (odd years)

🏠 Parc des Promenades, 22000 Saint-Brieuc

🖥 48.513494 N, -2.755761 W

🌐 www.lacoupeflorio.fr

✉ saintbrieucentreprises@gmail.com

Ford Escort RS2000 on the street circuit. (Courtesy wild-club.com/GLD)

Museums

Shows & Tours

Market Place

Motorsport

Circuits

Dieppe Rétro

The cliffs of Dieppe provide a backdrop for these English and French open-top tourers. / One of several Bentleys taking part.

Thanks to its direct ferry sailing from Newhaven, Dieppe is one of the easiest destinations in this guide for British visitors to reach. Little wonder then that many British enthusiasts come over for this event. Its contribution to French motor racing history, however, is sometimes forgotten. The first Paris-Dieppe motor race took place in 1897, and, ten years later, the Automobile Club de France organised its second Grand Prix here, devising a 77km (48 miles) circuit which drivers lapped 10 times. The same circuit was used the following year and again in 1912, this time extended to 20 laps.

For nearly 30 years, the association Dieppe Rétro has celebrated the city's motoring past and organised a series of events for classic car enthusiasts. The format varies, so it's worth checking their website for the latest details. The association commemorated the centenary of each of the Grand Prix races in Dieppe, but in other years they've run trips through the countryside or along the coast, with a stop for lunch in the beautiful seaside village nearby of Veules-les-Roses. Distances tend to be short, so it's a popular outing for vintage and even some veteran models.

Practical information

🕐 Early September every year

🏠 Grande Rue, 76200 Dieppe (may vary)

🖼️ 49.926689 N, 1.077755 E

🌐 www.diepperetro.org

📞 +33 2 35 82 49 29

✉️ caillot.jacqueline@wanadoo.fr

Delightful mascot on a Citroën Traction Avant cabriolet.

Elégance Rétrospective Automobile, Sarlat

Original publicity vehicle from the 1958 Tour de France cycle race. / Exceptional Figoni & Falaschi-bodied Delahaye cabriolet in the concours d'élégance.

Sarlat-la-Canéda lies at the heart of the Dordogne and is as popular with British and Dutch tourists as it is with the French. Every two years, Sarlat has a special appeal for lovers of classic cars, when it hosts this stylish show in the shade of the Parc du Plantier, just a few minutes' walk from the beautiful old town.

More than 100 cars are displayed, with a strong prewar presence, often including the great French makes of Delage, Delahaye and Panhard, as well as rarer models such as the Delaugère et Clayette from 1910 at the last show. British makes are also well represented by cars – often in exceptional condition – from the likes of AC, Lagonda and Rolls-Royce. In the past, the organisers have even set up an impromptu paddock, complete with straw bales, for racers such as the unique Jean Gali from 1948 with its engine from a Citroën Traction Avant.

The highlight of the event is the concours d'élégance on Sunday afternoon. Although this often features some prestigious cars, the emphasis is on having fun, with many of the participants putting on a lively show to the sound of period music.

Practical information

🕐 July, biennially (odd years)

🏠 Parc du Plantier, 24200 Sarlat-la-Canéda

🖼 44.888001 N, 1.219476 E

🌐 www.retroautosarlat.fr

📞 +33 6 88 59 31 54

✉ contactretroautosarlat@gmail.com

Unique 1948 Jean Gali single-seat racer based on Citroën Traction Avant.

Rallye Cadillac Côtes de Bordeaux

Rally participants line up beside the vines during lunch at the Château de Broustaret.

Long before Cadillac became famous as an American make of car, it was the name of a village in the Gironde, whose vineyards produce some of Bordeaux's sweet white wines. The area around it now makes a wonderful setting for an annual tour for classic cars, part of a weekend of events organised by the local winegrowers. As well as trying the local wines (there are red and dry white wines from the Côtes de Bordeaux too), these include tasting classes, exhibitions and competitions the whole family can take part in.

One of the biggest events of its kind in the area, the rally takes nearly 100 cars on a beautiful route through the vineyards and past many well-known châteaux. Participants are broken up into small groups of 6-10 cars, each visiting three châteaux and answering a series of questions along the way. The itinerary is not too challenging though, so even pre-war cars can easily keep up. Popular French models or British sports cars from the post-war years add to the diverse range of cars taking part. If you want to join them, you'll need to book at the start of the year.

Looking out across the vineyards of Bordeaux. (Courtesy Olivier Goudeau)

Practical information

🕐 May/June every year, usually at Whitsun

🏠 33410 Cadillac (check website for more details)

🖳 44.637639 N, -0.319108 W

🌐 www. cadillaccotesdebordeaux. com/accueil

📞 +33 5 57 98 19 20

Rallye Paris-Deauville

The grand start from Paris' Place Vendôme. (Courtesy Alain Besnard/Club de l'Auto) / Rare 1960 Alvis TD21 with Graber coachwork at the concours d'élégance.

Deauville is well known as one of France's swankiest resorts, famed for its boardwalk and film festival, but it also has a long association with the car. Keen to hold a motor race of its own, it launched the Grand Prix de Deauville in 1936. Sadly, two drivers were killed on the ill-suited track and the event was never repeated.

Since 1967, however, Deauville has also hosted a prestigious concours d'élégance, which is the culmination of the Rallye Paris-Deauville. Starting – security permitting – from the Place Vendôme in Paris, where they are seen off by the Garde républicaine, no less, participants enjoy a day driving through Normandy, and a gala dinner in Deauville. On Sunday, they take part in a stringent concours d'état (to judge the car in best condition) and the concours d'élégance, held at the racecourse on the edge of the town. For more than 30 years there's even been a competition for the best hat!

Admission to view the cars is free and it's a great chance to enjoy some stylish cars presented by their immaculately attired owners. Entries range from prewar classics to 1960s Ferraris, with one 'marque d'honneur' each year; these have included Packard, Delahaye, Bentley and Rolls-Royce.

Practical information

🕐 End September/early October every year (may become biennial)

🏠 Hippodrome de la Touques, 45 avenue Hocquart de Turtot, 14800 Deauville

🖼 49.355288 N, 0.078047 E

🌐 www.clubdelauto.org

✉ Contact form on website

1937 Delage D8-120 Cabriolet at the concours d'état.

Museums

Shows & Tours

Market Place

Motorsport

Circuits

Rallye Dior Paris-Granville

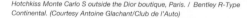

Hotchkiss Monte Carlo S outside the Dior boutique, Paris. / Bentley R-Type Continental. (Courtesy Antoine Glachant/Club de l'Auto)

Like the autumn event in Deauville (page 77), the Rallye Dior Paris-Granville is organised by the Club de l'Auto, one of the most elegant clubs in France, open to owners of all makes of car built before 1970. With support from the Dior fashion house, the tour takes participants from various starting points (in Paris or to the west) to finish in Granville. It was there that Christian Dior was born, and the famous designer is still remembered at the museum in the family's former home, the Villa Les Rhumbs.

This well-organised tour takes place over three days, with a leisurely run through the countryside on Saturday, before participants arrive in Granville for dinner. The following morning, the cars line up on in the centre of Granville, in the bay of Mont Saint-Michel, before taking part in a concours d'élégance on Sunday afternoon, which everyone can enjoy. Style and luxury are the watchwords for this event, whether you're a lucky participant or just a spectator eyeing up a coachbuilt Bentley, a spotless Hotchkiss Monte Carlo S, or a more recent Lancia Flavia Sport Zagato. For the participants, the weekend concludes with a gala dinner that evening, and another scenic drive on Monday.

Practical information

🕐 May every other year (odd years)

🏠 Cours Jonville, 50400 Granville

🗺 48.838067 N, -1.596337 W

🌐 www.clubdelauto.org

✉ Contact form on website

This 1940 Packard convertible won the Grand Prix in the 2015 concours d'élégance.

Rallye International du Pays de Fougères

Triumph Roadster from Jersey in Dol-de-Bretagne.
/ Delage and other participants in front of the Mairie at Sées.
(Both courtesy G Nédélec-APPF)

This pretty area of Brittany is only 80km (50 miles) or so from the port of Saint-Malo. That makes it an easy drive for visitors from Southern England and helps explain the enduring success of this event among British enthusiasts. During its 20-year history other entrants have come from ten different countries in Europe, and even the USA and Australia. The tour follows a different route each year, taking crews through the countryside from old towns such as Sées and Dol-de-Bretagne to seaside resorts like Dinard or the bay of Saint-Brieuc. There are visits to châteaux like those at Fougères or Hurlières and cathedrals along the way, and entrants can choose to take part for the whole weekend or just one day. This helps keep costs down, and the event offers excellent value. Spaces soon fill up, so book early if you want to take part.

The rally is open to 150 cars from before 1967, with an increasing number of prewar models to be seen. One or two marques are honoured each year and British manufacturers like Alvis, Aston Martin or Rover are usually well represented, alongside coachbuilt models from the great French marques such as Bugatti, Delage or Delahaye.

Prewar Lagonda in the beautiful Brittany countryside.
(Courtesy G Nédélec-APPF)

Practical information

🕐 May every year

🏠 Different route each year (see website for details)

🌐 www.rallye-fougeres.org

✉️ appf@rallye-fougeres.org

Rétro Festival Caen

Proud participants in the concours d'élégance. / 2016 Festival celebrated taxis from around the world. (Courtesy Rétro Festival Caen)

Caen is a great base from which to tour Normandy, so why not plan your trip to coincide with its annual classic car event? The Festival offers a varied range of activities over a busy weekend. For 2017, the event returns to its original site at the city's racecourse: rather dusty, but a more pleasant setting than the modern exhibition centre. The programme includes a small auction of classic cars as well as the usual display of historic cars and traders' stands.

Sunday afternoon is given over to a lavish concours d'élégance, in which each car is presented to the accompaniment of music of its time. Points are awarded not just for the cars, but also for their owners' matching attire.

The highlight of the weekend, however, is the recreation of the old Circuit de la Prairie, on the city streets near the racecourse. Back in the 1950s, Caen hosted its own Grand Prix, won in 1958 by a young Stirling Moss. Today, groups of cars and motorcycles – from 1920s cyclecars to high-performance sports cars of the '70s – can lap the makeshift track, providing a wonderful free show for everyone.

Alpine A310 V6 on the street circuit.

Practical information

🕐 Late June/early July every year

🏠 Hippodrome de Caen, boulevard Yves Guillou, 14000 Caen

🖥 49.17694 N, -0.36694 W

🌐 www.retrofestival.fr

📞 + 33 9 67 12 50 34

✉ retrofestivalcaen@gmail.com

Salon Auto Moto Rétro, Rouen

Museums

Shows & Tours

Market Place

Motorsport

Circuits

The Blues Brothers help present this 1958 Cadillac. / Alpine always has a strong presence in Rouen.

Sadly, there's nothing left to see of the old circuit at Rouen-les-Essarts, which closed in 1993, but Rouen remains a beautiful city to visit, its cathedral immortalised in the paintings of Monet. Each autumn it holds a popular classic car show, which attracts nearly 20,000 enthusiasts. The organisers have done a great job developing it, enlarging the exhibition space over the years and adding a dedicated car park for classic cars. There's a big central display, too, usually devoted to a single make such as Alfa Romeo in 2015, for example. But this isn't a snobbish event; the show has a friendly, down-to-earth atmosphere, and plenty of traders' stands, both inside the halls and outdoors, selling books and parts at affordable prices.

Rouen is close to Dieppe, the historic home of Alpine; its supporters always put on a good show for the local marque, with an exceptional display for the factory's 60th anniversary in 2016. The landing beaches of Normandy are also nearby, and one of the halls usually features a display of military vehicles from World War II. As well as Jeeps, the local clubs often set up good displays of American cars of all periods.

Practical information

🕐 September every year

🏠 Parc des Expositions, Rue Marcel Cavelier, 76550 Petit-Couronne

🖼 49.389536 N, 1.052932 E

🌐 www.salonautomotoretro.com

📞 +33 2 35 18 28 28

✉ Contact form on website

Display of WWII military vehicles, inspired by the landing beaches in Normandy.

Western France

Sport et Collection, Le Vigeant

Ferrari 360 Challenge Stradale. / Maserati club stand.

I f ever a pastime seemed like the preserve of a selfish and wealthy few, a racetrack meeting of 500 Ferraris would surely be the one! In the case of Sport et Collection, however, nothing could be further from the truth; over 20 years this fantastic event has raised no less than €3.5M for cancer treatment at the regional hospital in Poitiers.

If you're fortunate enough to own a Ferrari or another top-class GT, this weekend is a great opportunity to drive your car on a fine circuit. But for the 40,000 spectators it's a special occasion too, from the moment you enter the paddock; one side – a sea of red – is reserved for Ferraris, the other for everything from Aston Martin to Rondeau. Modern-day F458s seem almost ordinary; you can see erstwhile F1 cars or racers like the 166 MM which won at Le Mans in 1949 in action here. There's a growing historic presence, with some cars – such as a Ghia-bodied 195S from 1951 – loaned by the factory museum. There are great views of the circuit from the control tower on the main straight, and – a special treat – from the restaurant during the night time session.

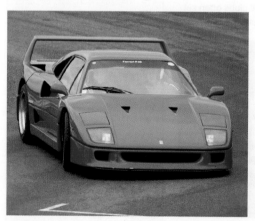

Ferrari F40 on track.

Practical information

🕐 June every year

🏠 Circuit du Val de Vienne, 86150 Le Vigeant

🖥 46.195921 N, 0.632242 E

🌐 www.sportetcollection.info

📞 +33 5 49 39 34 25

✉ sport.et.collection@free.fr

Tour de Bretagne

I f you had to guess which event in this region attracted the most spectators, you'd probably think of the 24 Hours race at Le Mans (page 90). If the organisers' estimates are to be believed, however, first place on the podium goes to the Tour de Bretagne, which brings 300,000 people out on the streets to wave on the cars!

For more than 35 years, the Tour has been a moveable feast of motoring history. It takes a different route each year, but the principle remains the same: a leisurely trip over three days on the most picturesque roads of the region. The distances are deliberately kept short, allowing cars like a Renault AX from the start of the last century to take part. Each day's itinerary fans out from the same town or village, which changes each year: Bains-sur-Oust in 2015, Fouesnant in 2016. Nearly 700 participants, many of them in period clothing, join in, driving a mix of cars, buses, lorries and motorbikes; you might see a Vélosolex tucked in between a Salmson saloon and a Berliet truck. And if any of them should run into difficulty, a historic breakdown truck won't be far away!

The medieval 'Ville Close' in Concarneau.

Practical information

🕐 May every year

🏠 Different route each year (see website for details)

🌐 www.abva.net

📞 +33 6 67 95 23 97

✉ jacquelinenovack@orange.fr

The village in Lohéac, a regular staging post for the Tour de Bretagne.

Traversée de Bordeaux

Dawn start from the place des Quinconces, Bordeaux. / Splendid Jaguar XK120 in the courtyard of the Château Latresne.

After the success of the Traversée de Paris (page 31), several other French cities (Bordeaux, Lyon and Rennes among them) have created their own drives through the city as a celebration of the story of motoring. In Bordeaux, local enthusiasts soon gave this initiative their support, and it's grown into a much bigger event. The drive itself, limited to cars at least 30 years old, is now the highlight of a weekend of activities, including club stands and a parts fair. The popularity of the winter event has encouraged the organisers to create a second drive in September, the 'Traversée estivale.'

The event is based around the Place des Quinconces, right where the Bordeaux Grand Prix ran from 1951 to 1955. Special displays mark major anniversaries, whether for particular cars – like the 50th anniversary of the Ford Mustang – or key moments in the city's history.

Unlike the event in Paris, the Traversée itself, held on Sunday morning, takes the 200 participants out of the city for a 100km (60 miles) drive through the surrounding countryside. The route changes each year; it might, for instance, have an aviation theme, stopping off at the aerodrome at Saucats-Léognan or the aeronautical centre at Latresne.

Practical information

🕐 February and September every year

🏠 Place des Quinconces, 33000 Bordeaux

🖼 44.845395 N, -0.574696 W

🌐 www.atlanticoldtimer.com

📞 + 33 6 41 32 07 77

✉ atlanticold@gmail.com

Morning stop at the aerodrome at Saucats-Léognan.

Autobrocante, Lohéac

The Manoir de l'Automobile, setting for the event. / Demonstrations of Renault's F1 cars a big draw this weekend. (Courtesy Le Manoir de l'Automobile)

If you want an excuse to visit – or revisit – Brittany, the annual autojumble at Lohéac could be just what you need! First held nearly 25 years ago, it's become the biggest event of its kind in France, attracting 450 traders from France and abroad, 70% of whom come back year-on-year. Some 13,000 visitors come to look through the extensive range of parts, models, books and other automobilia; it's an especially good event for owners of French cars looking for hard-to-find items. The Autobrocante is much more than just a parts fair though. Like the famous autojumbles at Beaulieu in England, the Autobrocante takes full advantage of its location at Le Manoir de l'Automobile (page 60). The museum is very crowded this weekend, but is a must if you haven't been before. Thanks to generous support from Renault Classic, there are spectacular demonstrations of historic Renault Formula 1 cars on the circuit beside the museum, driven by former champions like Michel Leclère or Alain Serpaggi. Rally cars are regularly celebrated too, with the much-loved Jean Ragnotti a frequent visitor. National and regional clubs often host meetings during the weekend of the Autobrocante, with 50th anniversary celebrations of the Renault 8 Gordini a notable success.

Practical information

🕐 Early October every year

🏠 Le Manoir de l'Automobile, rue du Manoir, 35550 Lohéac

🖥 47.861251 N, -1.894743 W

🌐 www.manoir-automobile.fr

📞 +33 2 99 34 02 32

✉ musee@sfep.fr

There's no mistaking that Lohéac is the village of the car!

Circuit des Remparts, Angoulême

In the paddocks. / The owners of this Panhard PL17 get into the spirit of the Swinging Sixties at the concours d'élégance.

The Circuit des Remparts is one of the great historic motorsport events in France, right up there next to Le Mans, Monaco and Pau. If you haven't been before, it's hard to imagine the atmosphere in the city, as cars of the period race around the same track they lapped more than 60 years ago. The first Grand Prix was held here in 1939, and, altogether, seven Grands Prix were staged in Angoulême between then and 1955. The race was revived in 1978, when Fangio returned as its patron to storm around the track in his Mercedes W196. Since then, the organisers have done a fantastic job to keep the event alive, despite increasingly stringent safety requirements and financial pressures.

The circuit around the ramparts of the old town is just 1.279km (0.8 miles) long and has hardly changed since 1939. It is a small, technical track with many tight corners, demanding maximum

Lunch stop for rally participants at the Château de la Rochefoucauld.

Bugatti Type 30 heading up to the cathedral.

concentration from the drivers. The races are split into several categories, including prewar sports, Touring and GT classes, many named after a famous driver from the circuit's past. Practice takes place on Sunday morning, followed by the races in the afternoon. The highlight of the weekend – and the contest for which Angoulême is most famous – comes when the prewar Bugattis battle for honours. Giant screens around the track make it easy to follow the whole race.

Sunday's race day is just part of a full programme, which begins on Friday evening with a lively concours d'élégance at the Champ de Mars. On Saturday, up to 300 participants meet at the Chai Magélis for a day-long rally, stopping at châteaux along the way and returning to the shopping centre in the city where visitors can admire them once again.

Practical information

🕐 September every year

🏠 Place de l'Hôtel de Ville, 16000 Angoulême

🖥 45.648618 N, 0.156212 E

🌐 www.circuit-des-remparts. com

📞 +33 5 45 94 95 67

✉ circuit-des-remparts@ orange.fr

Citroën MEP racers are waved off.

Le Mans Classic

1932 MG Midget on track. (Courtesy Colin Murrell)

For lovers of historic motorsport, this is one of the greatest events in Europe, which deservedly attracts well over 120,000 fans. Since its creation in 2002, Peter Auto and the Automobile Club de l'Ouest have made it into a very special occasion which really captures the spirit of the 24 Hours races of the past. The main roads around Arnage are closed for the weekend, giving participants a unique opportunity to lap the main circuit of 13.6km (8.5 miles). Altogether, 450 cars are selected from those eligible to take part, separated into categories covering the years from 1923 to 1979. Whether you're following a prewar Blower Bentley, a Ford GT40 from the Sixties, or a humble MG Midget, it's an extraordinary sight. Many winners of the past, like Derek Bell or Henri Pescarolo, and current champions such as Romain Dumas take part, and the standard of racing is impressively high.

As well as watching the races themselves, there's much more to enjoy during the weekend. At the heart of the Village is the elite Le Mans Heritage Club, reserved for some of the finest cars which raced at Le Mans in period, starring models from manufacturers such as Bentley,

Group C grid – a successful addition to the weekend's racing programme in 2016.

Museums

Shows & Tours

Market Place

Motorsport

Circuits

Remarkable display of 1960s racing transporters – a big hit with the public.

Delage or Ferrari. Other recent centrepiece exhibits have included the racing transporters of the 1960s or Jaguar's remarkable XJ13. Artcurial stages a major auction of sports and racing cars, while 'Little Big Mans' is a special competition for miniature cars piloted by children aged 6-12, drawing as many as 80 entrants each year.

Perhaps best of all though is the huge area taken over by clubs from all over the world, where over 150 groups present 8000 pre-1966 cars from more than 50 makes. From impromptu picnics to parades on the track, there's always something happening.

Jaguar brought the unique XJ13 back to Le Mans 50 years after its planned début at the track.

Practical information

🕐 July every two years (even years)

🏠 Circuit des 24 Heures, 72100 Le Mans

📷 47.956245 N, 0.20744 E

🌐 www.lemansclassic.com

📞 +33 1 42 59 73 40

✉ Contact form on website

Museums

Shows & Tours

Market Place

Motorsport

Circuits

Le Mans 24 Hours

Porsche drivers Tandy, Bamber, and Hulkenberg celebrate victory with Porsche in 2015. (Courtesy Porsche)

More than just a motorsport event, the Le Mans 24 Hours race, first held in 1923, has become part of French popular culture, on a par with the Tour de France cycle race and the Roland-Garros tennis championship. A quarter-of-a-million fans flock to the circuit, enjoying the funfairs and partying through

Night-time pit stop for the Toyota TS030 Hybrid. (Courtesy Toyota Motorsport GmbH)

the night. But at heart it is still the world's greatest endurance race, especially in the flagship LMP1 category, where the fearless drivers reach over 340km/h (210mph) on the famous Hunaudières straight. Each race brings its own surprises, as Porsche's breathtaking final lap win over Toyota in 2016 proved once again.

The event remains a constantly changing showcase for the latest technology, whether the cars are powered by petrol, diesel or now hybrid electric engines. The old adage, "Win on Sunday, sell on Monday", has never been truer than at Le Mans, with huge stakes for the manufacturers taking part. Audi may have pulled out of endurance racing after 2016, but the return of companies such as Porsche and Ford ensures that there are always new cars to watch alongside old favourites, and fresh battles being fought. Especially if you are travelling a long way to Le Mans, it's well worth coming early, as there's a lot to see before the race weekend, beginning with scrutineering on Sunday, testing on Wednesday and Thursday, and then the pitwalk, and parade by all the drivers through the city on Friday. Many car clubs and specialist tour operators organise trips to the race. One of the event's traditions, ever since it began in the 1920s, is to camp overnight, and there are dedicated camping areas in the heart of the circuit. However you come, though, book well in advance!

Aston Martin brings its cars back to the Hôtel de France in La Chartre-sur-le-Loir. (Courtesy Drew Gibson/Aston Martin)

Lotus T128 in the pit lane. (Courtesy Alexis Toureau/ACO)

Practical information

🕐 June every year

🏠 Circuit des 24 Heures, 72100 Le Mans

🗺 47.956245 N, 0.20744 E

🌐 www.lemans.org

✉ Contact form on website

Museums

Shows & Tours

Market Place

Motorsport

Circuits

Classic British Welcome, Saint-Saturnin

The Le Mans 24 Hours race (previous page) has become so popular with British enthusiasts, that since 2001 it has laid on its own pre-race event especially for them. And now this sideshow for the British has become so successful that each year more and more French fans come to it!

For most of the year, Saint-Saturnin is a quiet little village, close to the junction of the A11 and A28 autoroutes just north of Le Mans. But on the Friday before the race, it's taken over by 5000 motorsport fans, who gather in the local community centre to enjoy food, films, live music and an exhibition of cars from previous races. Outside there's an eclectic mix of nearly 1000 sports cars on show; Aston Martin, Porsche and TVR are all well represented, but you might

Classic Le Mans racers are displayed inside the exhibition hall. / Audi drivers on parade before the race. (Courtesy Arnaud Cornilleau/ACO)

also spot a road-going Ultima GTR or an intriguing Marcos Mantis. One marque is honoured each year, but everyone is welcome to come along. There are often VIP guests too, such as Bernard Ollivier from Alpine or former champions like Jürgen Barth. The day concludes with the departure of the Saint-Saturnin Cavalcade to join the drivers' parade that evening in the centre of Le Mans.

The crowded parking area at the Val de Vray. (Courtesy Stéphane Auvrignon/Classic British Welcome)

Practical information

🕐 June every year

🏠 Centre culturel du Val de Vray, rue de l'Église, 72650 Saint-Saturnin

📷 48.06169 N, 0.15532 E

🌐 www.classicbw.org

✉ Contact form on website

Museums | Shows & Tours | Market Place | Motorsport | Circuits

Course de côte (hill climb), Étretat

One minute is all it takes for the fastest competitors to scurry up the 1620m (1770yd) hill to the hamlet of Bénouville. This friendly event has been run by an enthusiastic group of volunteers for nearly 20 years; the road is now well surfaced with modern crash barriers, but it still makes for a good test of car and driver. The climb is popular with British competitors and enjoys strong support from the Frazer-Nash club. This climb is one of many such VHC events in France, but few can match the beauty of the cliffs of Étretat.

The weekend begins with scrutineering on Saturday morning – held until now in front of the town hall in Étretat –- before entrants move up to the farmyard in Bénouville which is the base for the event. There's time for free practice and qualifying sessions on Saturday afternoon, before the actual race sessions on Sunday. Nearly 50 historic cars take part, split into classes by age – from pre-1947 cars (stretching back to the 1920s, in fact), as well as many newer sports prototypes and GTi's. Although cars as big as a Ford Galaxie have taken part, the climb is best suited to smaller models.

Well-travelled Wolseley Hornet Special. / Getting it sideways in this Alfa Romeo GT.

Practical information

🕐 Late August every year

🏠 Rue de l'Aiguille de Belval, 76790 Bénouville

🖼 49.715632 N, 0.243806 E

🌐 www.asacotedalbatre.com

✉ asacotedalbatre@hotmail.fr

1929 Morgan Super Aero pressing on.

Museums   Shows & Tours   Market Place   **Motorsport**   Circuits

Grand Prix Historique, Bressuire

Traditional Le Mans-style start. / Step back in time inside this Lotus. (Both courtesy Rachel Jabot Ferreiro)

Halfway between Angers and Niort, Bressuire is a place whose connections with the history of motorsport could easily have been forgotten, were it not for the commitment of a local enthusiast, Jean-Claude Fillon. In 2004, he published a book, *Les années circuit*, re-telling the story of the Grand Prix races held there from 1951-54. The wave of interest this inspired encouraged Fillon to revive the event and, in 2006, the Grand Prix Historique de Bressuire was born.

The 750m (820yd) route through the town, the Circuit Alain Métayer, follows part of the original layout, and drivers sprint across the track in a popular Le Mans-style racing start. Modern-day safety requirements mean that the event is no longer run as a race, but participants and spectators alike can enjoy several demonstration sessions for each group of cars, with a night-time session on Saturday a popular addition to the programme. Access for spectators is free, and there are many good vantage points around the circuit.

The cars taking part include cyclecars, single-seaters, sports cars and touring cars from manufacturers like Panhard, Peugeot and Renault. After Ferrari and Gordini, it will be the turn of Porsche to take the honours in 2017.

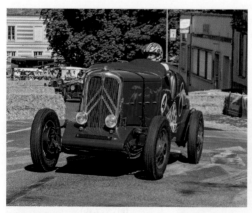

Citroën's 'Petite Rosalie' leads the pack up the hill.
(Courtesy Rachel Jabot Ferreiro)

Practical information

🕐 June every year

🏠 Place Saint-Jacques,
79300 Bressuire

🖼 46.837229 N, -0.494374 W

🌐 auto-retro-bressuirais.
wifeo.com

✉ clfillon@wanadoo.fr

Western France 🏁

Grand Prix Rétro, Le Puy-Notre-Dame

Some of the many Darmont and Morgan three-wheelers taking part. / Riley and MG lead this group past the vineyards.

Unlike many of the revival events presented in this region, nothing in Le Puy-Notre-Dame's past destined it to host a historic Grand Prix. Not far from Doué-la-Fontaine, the village was better known for its 13th century church and palatable white wine. But that was to reckon without the passion of a local winegrower and Bugatti owner, who decided with his friends that Le Puy should have an event of its own!

Now, 20 years later, the Grand Prix Rétro of Le Puy-Notre-Dame attracts 150 cars – many over from the UK – and more than 8000 spectators. After participants tour the countryside on Saturday, Sunday is race day, with demonstrations on the ad hoc, 1.5km (0.9 miles) circuit, between the vineyards and old stone walls of the village. Entry is limited to vehicles pre-1940 or 1950 (depending on the category), and there are classes for cars, motorbikes and sidecar combinations. Cyclecars are a great favourite here, and dozens of models from Morgan, Darmont, and Sandford fill the makeshift paddock beside the village hall. If you come in an even year you can also enjoy the night-time run through the village on Saturday.

All the way over!

Practical information

🕐 Late July every year

🏠 Rue de la Mairie, 49260 Le Puy-Notre-Dame

🖼 47.124918 N, -0.229968 W

🌐 www.grandprixretro-puynotredame.com

✉ contact@grandprixretro-puynotredame.com

95

Circuit Automobile EIA, Pont-l'Évêque

The circuit at Pont-l'Évêque is situated just a few miles inland from the coastal resorts of Deauville and Trouville, and its club house looks out over the beautiful countryside of the Vallée d'Auge. If you want to add a track day session to a holiday in Normandy, it's a great location to choose. The main track, laid out in a large natural park, is 2000m (1.25 miles) in length and

Aerial view of the circuit. (Courtesy Circuit Automobile EIA)

has several tight corners, making it a relatively slow and technical circuit. There's also a karting circuit 800m (875yd) long, which is fully homologated by the FFSA, the French motorsports federation, and space to try out quads.

The main circuit is available for clubs to hire, but EIA also has its own fleet of cars with plenty of choice for the driving courses it runs. Current options include FWD Renault Clio 4 RS cars, and RWD Caterham 7, Lotus Elise, Opel Speedster and Toyota GT86 models. If you'd like a bit more power, the centre has a Lotus Exige 240 and Porsche 997 Carrera S, or you could join one of the special driving safety courses run by EIA in association with BMW France.

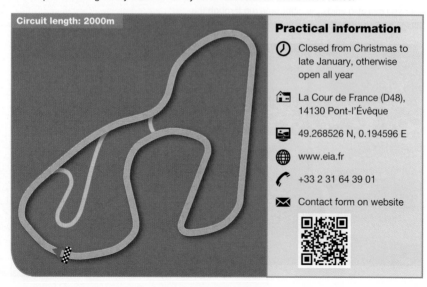

Circuit length: 2000m

Practical information

🕐 Closed from Christmas to late January, otherwise open all year

🏠 La Cour de France (D48), 14130 Pont-l'Évêque

📇 49.268526 N, 0.194596 E

🌐 www.eia.fr

📞 +33 2 31 64 39 01

✉ Contact form on website

Circuit de Bordeaux-Mérignac

Just five minutes' drive from the airport at Mérignac, this circuit is home to a wide variety of activities, which share a strong sporting emphasis. Relatively short (1760m/1920yd), it features two 400m (440yd) straights and a rapid chicane. Several manufacturers, including Porsche, Ferrari, Honda and Mazda, have used it for testing, and the whole track can be hired by clubs

Originally presented at the Paris Motor Show in 2014, the Lamborghini Huracan can now be driven on track at Bordeaux.

at rates which compare well with many other circuits. There are plenty of open days too, and inexpensive, one-hour starter sessions are available. If you would prefer to take one of the courses run by GTRS Racing Event, choices include an Audi R8, Ferrari F430, Lamborghini Huracan and Porsche 911 Turbo. Alternatively, why not try a nimble Renault Mégane RS or a recent American muscle car such as a Chevrolet Corvette? If all that seems too much, children from 10 can do their first lap in a Smart!

Above all, the circuit at Mérignac has made a name for itself with lovers of drifting, and has hosted rounds of the European Drift Championship. The layout of the track, which can be partially flooded, lends itself well to drifting, and you can take lessons in a specially-prepared BMW M3.

Practical information

🕐 Open all year

🏠 Rue Marcel Issartier, 33700 Mérignac

🖥 44.84653 N, -0.719343 W

🌐 www.circuit-bordeaux-merignac.com

📞 +33 5 56 34 21 63

✉ contact@gtrsopendays.com

Circuit length: 1760m

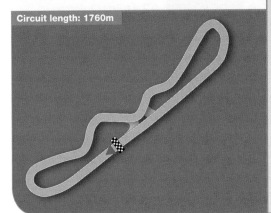

Circuit de Haute-Saintonge, La Genétouze

This circuit, halfway between Bordeaux and Angoulême, is one of the newest in France and was built according to principles of sustainable development. Since it opened in 2009, the motoring press has acclaimed the pleasure of driving on the 2200m (1.4 miles) track. Quick and naturally undulating, it features seven corners and two

Aerial view of the circuit. (Courtesy Circuit de Haute-Saintonge)

straights, each of 650m (710yd). Safety is paramount: the circuit has generous run-off areas and a sophisticated monitoring system which uses multiple surveillance cameras and warning lights.

The circuit does not run its own driving school, but works with training partners who offer a good range of high-performance models, whether you prefer your thrills German, Italian or even Japanese style. Drivers can bring their own cars to regular open days and the whole track – together with the reception facilities in the old farmhouse beside it – can be hired by clubs.

Next to the main circuit, there's an 1100m (1200yd) karting track, which is also used for economy and safe driving courses. The facilities at Haute-Saintonge are managed by Julien Beltoise, from the famous racing family, and the safe driving courses here follow the same approach known as 'Conduire Juste,' which his father developed at Trappes (page 55), outside Paris.

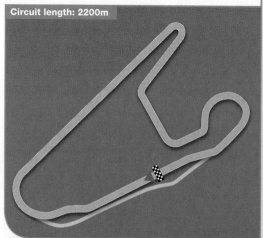

Circuit length: 2200m

Practical information

🕐 Closed Christmas to mid-January; otherwise open all year

🏠 Le Petit Châtaignier, 17360 La Genétouze

🖳 45.24189 N, -0.097884 W

🌐 www. circuitdehautesaintonge. com

📞 +33 5 46 04 08 10

✉ Contact form on website

Circuit de Lohéac

Subaru Impreza WRX outside the entrance to the circuit. / Record-breaking Hommell barquette, on display in Le Manoir de l'Automobile.

The first ever rallycross event in France was held at Lohéac, back in 1976, and rallycross remains a key part of Lohéac's programme of activities today. The round of the European Rallycross Championship held here each August/September attracts 40,000 spectators, and it's the best place in France to take a rallycross driving course. Training cars include a Peugeot 206 RC and Subaru Impreza, and there are half- and full-day courses, as well as inexpensive discovery laps with one of the instructors.

Lohéac also has a traditional asphalt track, 2.5km (1.6 miles) long, which offers a good balance of speed and technical difficulty. There are regular open days (often on Sundays) for individual enthusiasts and a wide range of driving courses using GTs – including the latest 4WD Ford Focus RS – as well as a Formula Renault single-seater or Funyo sports prototype. If you're planning a visit to the circuit, it's well worth allowing some extra time in Lohéac, where the Hommell sports cars were built. The museum in Le Manoir de L'Automobile (page 60), next to the circuit, is one of the best in France, and there are plenty of places to eat and stay in the charming old village.

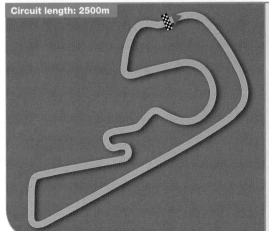

Circuit length: 2500m

Practical information

🕐 Open all year

🏠 Rue du Manoir, 35550 Lohéac

📷 47.861251 N, -1.894743 W

🌐 www.conduirealoheac.fr

📞 +33 2 99 34 16 77

✉ contact@conduirealoheac.fr

Circuits

Museums   Shows & Tours   Market Place   Motorsport   Circuits

Circuit de Loire-Atlantique, Fay-de-Bretagne

The city of Nantes had only a fleeting connection with motorsport, when its one-and-only Grand Prix took place in 1946. The nearby circuit at Fay-de-Bretagne was never homologated for competition either, but was built in 1992 as a test track for Venturi, whose sports cars were assembled nearby in Couëron. Although it's now owned and managed by the 'département' of the Loire-Atlantique, it maintains a strong allegiance to the marque,

A pair of Venturi 400GTs, seen here at Magny-Cours.

with a workshop on site which specialises in Venturi cars and prepares LMP2 prototypes for endurance races.

The local authorities are keen to develop safety and economy driving courses, but there are plenty more options for track day enthusiasts. Patrice Roussel, a former F3 and Le Mans driver, now heads the 'Extrême Limite' driving school at the track. You can bring your own car for open practice or individual coaching sessions, or join a course in the school's own cars. These include Formula 4 and Formula Renault 2.0 single-seaters and a Tatuus PY012 sports prototype, which offers a healthy power-to-weight ratio of 1000bhp per ton. At 3.2km (2 miles), the track is a decent length and there is a main straight of 950m (1040yd).

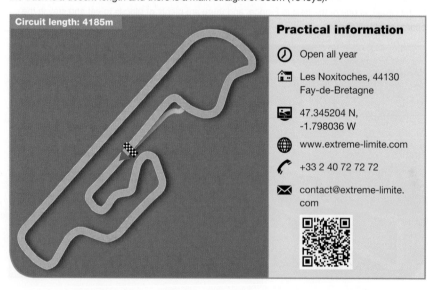

Circuit length: 4185m

Practical information

🕐 Open all year

🏠 Les Noxitoches, 44130 Fay-de-Bretagne

🗺 47.345204 N, -1.798036 W

🌐 www.extreme-limite.com

📞 +33 2 40 72 72 72

✉ contact@extreme-limite.com

Circuit Renault, Saint-Just

Aerial view of the circuit. (Courtesy Circuit Renault)

Originally known as the Circuit de l'Eure, after the area west of Paris where it's located, this is an unusual circuit. In its layout, the 2.5km (1.6 miles) circuit is typical of many. Where it differs, however, is in its focus on driver safety. Many tracks have diversified into road safety and economy driving courses to boost their income, but the Circuit Renault, which opened in 2010, now concentrates solely on these. Exclusively using recent Renault cars, such as the Mégane or Zoë, with petrol, diesel and electric power, the circuit has developed a series of courses called 'Renault Spirit,' comprising modules on driving skills, using electronic aids like ABS and ESP to best effect, and eco-driving. Many courses cater to business car users, but there are also sessions for members of the public, from newly qualified drivers to those over 75.

The stone-built club house has classrooms for theory sessions and a gallery displaying Renault's contributions to safety technology. Renault likens the whole site to a university-style campus dedicated to improving road safety, and has partnered with the University of Aix-Marseille to create a special diploma in the management of driving safety.

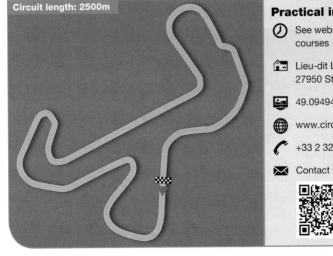

Circuit length: 2500m

Practical information

🕐 See website for current courses

🏠 Lieu-dit La Corne Haute, 27950 St Just

🖼️ 49.09494 N, 1.42778 E

🌐 www.circuit-renault.fr

📞 +33 2 32 64 68 68

✉️ Contact form on website

Circuit du Val de Vienne, Le Vigeant

An hour's drive south of Poitiers, the Val de Vienne circuit opened in 1990, but was completely modernised at the start of 2012. The pits and control tower were updated and improved, as were the restaurants and facilities for spectators. It now rates as one of the best circuits in the region, and is deservedly popular with car and motorbike fans alike, for whom it hosts a wide range of events from April to October. One of the most famous is the annual Sport et Collection weekend (page 82), but there are also FFSA championship races, and frequent club events for makes including Peugeot, Porsche and VW.

The main track is 3.729km (2.3 miles) and largely flat. It's known for its sharp turns, and especially for its double bends, where the second corner is tighter than the first, which can force drivers into a delicate mid-corner braking manoeuvre. Training choices include Caterhams and Ligier JS Sport prototypes, as well as specially-equipped Renault Clios for skid control classes. Open practice sessions are held from March to November, but many of these are reserved for holders of racing licences.

A trio of Ferraris in front of the new control tower. / Ford Mustang club members line up at the start.

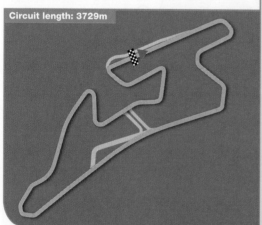

Circuit length: 3729m

Practical information

🕐 Open all year, but most events April-October

🏠 Circuit du Val de Vienne, 86150 Le Vigeant

📷 46.195921 N, 0.632242 E

🌐 www.circuitvaldevienne.com

📞 +33 5 49 91 79 17

✉ info@lesdeuxarbres.com

Circuit des 24 Heures du Mans

Pescarolo prototype, used by the Le Mans Driver School. (Courtesy Jean-René Roger/ACO)

U nless you're a top-class professional or entrant in Le Mans Classic (page 88), you won't get the chance to drive the full 24 Hour circuit at Le Mans. Outside race weeks you can drive part of the circuit along the regular 'Routes Nationales' or try either of the permanent race tracks here.

The better known of the two is the Circuit Bugatti, which incorporates 1500m (1640yd) of the full circuit. It's a major motorsport venue in its own right, hosting 24 Hour truck and motorbike races, as well as DTM car races and major European car club meets. 4.2km (2.6 miles) long, the track is fully equipped with extensive safety and pit facilities and has been extensively renovated for 2017.

Somewhat shorter, at 2.8km (1.7 miles), the Circuit Maison Blanche was updated in 2007, and gives enthusiasts an alternative circuit to try. The ACO offers a great range of track experiences on both circuits, from individual lessons in your own car to driving courses in a Pescarolo prototype. Since 2015 Porsche owners have been able to enjoy a brand-new Porsche Experience Centre, with luxurious viewing and hospitality areas and displays of Porsche's historic cars.

Practical information

🕐 Open all year

🏠 Circuit des 24 Heures, 72100 Le Mans

🖥 47.956245 N, 0.20744 E

🌐 www.lemansdriver.fr

📞 +33 2 43 40 24 30

✉ Contact form on website

Circuit length: 4185m (Circuit Bugatti)

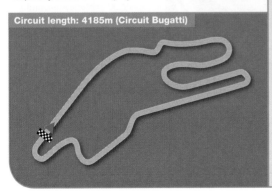

Piste Fontenay Pôle 85, Fontenay-le-Comte

Aerial view of the circuit. (Courtesy Piste Fontenay Pôle 85)

Less than an hour's drive from the historic port of La Rochelle, this circuit is part of a new business park funded by local authorities, and dedicated to technological innovation in the automotive sector. The track was conceived with equipment manufacturers in mind, as a modern venue where they can test tyres, brakes and suspension components. Altogether, it's 2.4km (1.5 miles) in length, and can be split into two separate loops. The main straight is nearly 800m (860yd), allowing for speeds of up to 280km/h (174mph). The website gives an interesting explanation of how each aspect of the circuit's design helps test particular conditions.

However, from its 2010 opening the site was also designed for enthusiasts. There are currently no open track days, but the circuit can be booked by clubs for their exclusive use. Several recent events held at Fontenay-le-Conte have showcased innovation in electric cars, including the Formula E Venturi show car, a prototype from the Trophée Andros (page 184) and the Renault Twizy F1. The circuit also hosted the 70 cars competing in the latest Vendée Electrique Tour.

Practical information

🕐 Closed mid-December to mid-January, otherwise open all year

🏠 60, rue de Chambouin, 85200 Fontenay-le-Comte

🖼 46.43756 N, -0.789946 W

🌐 www.innovation-automobile.com

📞 +33 2 51 69 00 78

✉ Contact form on website

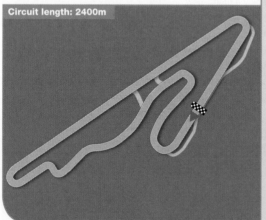

Circuit length: 2400m

Southern France

If ever a region in France is sure to appeal to lovers of motorsport, this must be it.

In the south-east, the tiny principality of Monaco is home to two of Europe's most famous motorsport events: the Grand Prix de Monaco in Formula 1 and the Rallye de Monte Carlo. Both modern events have their historic counterparts, too, as the cars – and sometimes the drivers – that raced in period relive their battles of old. Historic motorsport fans can enjoy more on-street action in the old city of Pau, at the foot of the Pyrenees.

In this chapter, you'll find information on no fewer than twelve racetracks in the region, from one of the most modern and sophisticated facilities in Europe, the Circuit Paul Ricard at Le Castellet, to two ice-driving circuits which operate at ski resorts in the winter.

Southern France is renowned for its great weather and beautiful countryside. Whether you're visiting a museum in the Gorges du Verdon, attending a classic car show beside the sea in Bandol or Monte Carlo, or taking part in a rally around Corsica, there are dozens of things for the enthusiast to enjoy against the stunning backdrop of the Mediterranean.

The Grand Prix de Monaco F1. (Courtesy J M Folleté/ACM)

Contents

Yssingeaux
Le Puy-en-Velay
A7
Romans-sur-Isère
Le Pont-de-Claix
Valence
Regional
Natural Park
Briançon
26
Italy
E15
Ecrins
National Park
Privas
Gap
36
Aubenas
Montélimar
Pierrelatte
Nyons
24 **40**
Bollène
Digne-les-Bains
23
Orange
23
30
Alès
Carpentras
PROVENCE-ALPES-CÔTE D'AZUR
E714
Avignon
2
11
32
L'Isle-sur-la-Sorgue
13
Manosque
1
8
15
Nîmes
5
Apt
Nice
Menton
10
Beaucaire
3
Grasse
Monaco
Montpellier
Arles
39
Salon de Provence
Pertuis
n-Provence
Draguignan
25
Antibes
16
Miramas
31
A8
Vitrolles
Gardanne
9
Fréjus
19
Istres
22
6
Brignoles
18
Martigues
37
Sainte-Maxime
Marseille
35
La Ciotat
La Crau
Hyères
4
Toulon

Bastia **12**
Calvi
28 Corte
Cervione
CORSICA
Ghisonaccia
Ajaccio **21**
Sartène
Porto-Vecchio
27
Bonifacio
Sardinia

The Grand Prix de Pau Historique (top). / The Ronde Hivernale at Serre Chevalier.
(Courtesy Circuit de Serre Chevalier)

Southern France

Museums
Shows & Tours
Market Place
Motorsport
Circuits

Citromuseum, Castellane

Fire service Méhari heads this line-up of 2CV family members. / CX Safari, originally from Berkshire in southern England, next to rotary-engined GS Birotor and M35.

For Citroën enthusiasts, this museum, located amid the breathtaking scenery of the Gorges du Verdon, is an absolute must. Opened in 2004, it houses 90 Citroën cars from the late 1940s to 1990. One hall is devoted to the air-cooled cars, from the first 2CVs to the last GSA models, another to the water-cooled models, from the Traction Avant to the CX. The museum's owner, Henri Fradet, visited more than 4000 Citroën agents across France as he built up this unique collection.

What makes the museum so special, however – and well worth a visit by all enthusiasts, not just Citroën fans – is the history of each car, which is presented in English and French. All the cars are in outstanding unrestored condition and many have incredibly low mileages, with the record currently held by a 1983 GSA Spécial showing just 41km (25 miles) on the clock! Others are a tribute to the care their owners took, like the 1954 2CV with its door cards still protected by the original brown paper. There are rare model variants and prototypes, too, such as the sole surviving CX 2500 GTi 'Régamo,' built to test the new suspension for the forthcoming XM.

The Gorges du Verdon on the road to Castellane.

Practical information

🕐 Open every day (2-6pm) from mid-April to mid-October; all day (10am-6pm) in July & August

🏠 Route de la Palud, 04120 Castellane (opposite the Camping International camp site)

🖥 43.857459 N, 6.499149 E

🌐 www.citromuseum.com

📞 +33 4 92 83 76 09

✉ citromuseum@orange.fr

The collection of historic cars of the Prince of Monaco

A passionate car enthusiast, Prince Rainier III built up his collection over 40 years before opening this museum in 1993. It's very much a personal collection, with the 100 cars chosen because of their interest to the Prince or connections with the history of Monaco. There are some prestigious models used for grand occasions, like the 1956 Chrysler Imperial limousine, but many popular cars too, such as the 1959 Fiat Jolly with its wicker seats. Many of the cars were used by members of the royal family, like the 1971 Lotus Super Seven, Prince Albert's first car. The 1954 Sunbeam-Talbot recalls the film *To Catch a Thief*, starring Grace Kelly and shot in Monaco.

1959 Renault Floride given by the manufacturer to Princess Grace.
(Courtesy Collection de SAS le Prince de Monaco)

The vehicles on show stretch back from a 2004 Venturi Fetish electric sports car to 19th century horse-drawn carriages and early cars and motorbikes. There's a 1911 Renault which Prince Rainier drove for the opening of the Monaco Grand Prix in 1962, and a Humber 350 motorbike which his grandfather used to ride from Monaco to his estate in northern France.

The details here show the current location of the collection, but there are plans to move to a new, purpose-built site in 2018/19.

Practical information

🕐 Open every day (10am-6pm) except Christmas Day

🏠 Les Terrasses de Fontvieille, 98000 Monaco

🚌 Lines 5 & 6, Centre Commercial de Fontvieille

📧 43.730904 N, 7.417123 E

🌐 www.palais.mc

📞 + 377 92 05 28 56

✉ mtcc@mtcc.mc

1989 Ferrari F1 raced by Nigel Mansell.
(Courtesy Collection de SAS le Prince de Monaco)

Museums

Musée Automobile de Provence, Orgon

The museum entrance, just off the Nationale 7. / Rare Voisin Biscooter from 1947 squeezed in next to Bugatti bicycle.

Don't be put off by the unprepossessing building and the cars outside which have seen better days; this is a friendly and interesting museum to visit. Set on the old Nationale 7 between Avignon and Aix-en-Provence, the museum is run by Pierre Dellière and was established by his father in 1967. He led an adventurous life, even riding the Vespa 125 on display from Saigon to Paris in 1953, a trip of 16,000km (10,000 miles).

The main hall has about 20 vehicles on show, including an unusual Voisin Biscooter from 1947, and several Bugattis, one a Le Mans-winning Type 57 'tank'. The 1962 Cooper T61, which Pierre Dellière now competes in, was originally raced by José Rosinski. The sporting theme continues in the second room, which features another 20 more recent cars, some of them for sale by local club members. Temporary exhibitions – for Simca last summer, for example – add to the interest of the displays.

The museum makes an excellent place for clubs to meet, with a comfortable café next to the exhibition area and regular live music sessions on weekend evenings. For 40 years it has hosted an annual autojumble in June.

Practical information

🕐 Open all year, Tuesday to Saturday (2-6pm) or by appointment; closed on public holidays

🏠 D7n, 13660 Orgon

🖥 43.7928 N, 5.025703 E

🌐 www.musee-auto-provence.com

📞 +33 4 90 73 36 53

✉ museeauto@orange.fr

Citroën models of all ages on show.

Les Anglaises ont la Côte, Bandol

Magnificent setting beside the Mediterranean. / Welcome to the show! (Both courtesy Les Anglaises Ont la Côte)

I t would be tempting fate to say that the sun always shines in Bandol, but the sun is nearly always out for this event! Inspired by the long running Swiss Classic British Car Meeting in Morges, this is one of two big shows in France for owners of British cars. Each year the local car club takes over the seafront for a display of nearly 350 cars.

British cars of all makes are welcome: there's no need to register, just come along on the day. There's usually a good showing of sports cars from the 1960s and '70s, including Jaguar, MG and Triumph, and some models rarely seen in France. Space is reserved near the entrance for some special cars, such as a replica of a 1910 Sherborn Grand Prix car or an Aston Martin DB2/4 from 1954.

The show makes for a great day out; as well as looking at the cars, you can enjoy an aperitif on the seafront, dance to Sixties pop music, or even take a boat trip to one of the nearby islands. Bandol has plenty of excellent restaurants, too, offering fine sea views.

Practical information

🕐 May/June every year, on a Sunday (10am-5pm)

🏠 Allée Alfred Vivien, 83150 Bandol

🖼 43.135244 N, 5.753996 E

🌐 www. lesanglaisesontlacote.org

📞 +33 6 17 80 14 78

✉ contact@ lesanglaisesontlacote.org

Triumph and Jaguar convertibles line up on the quayside.

Museums

Shows & Tours

Market Place

Motorsport

Circuits

Avignon Motor Festival

Prestigious Horch 853A Sport from Saulius Karosas' collection. / Concours entrants with their 1948 Alvis TA14.

The first time you visit this show, you're sure to be surprised by its size, with nearly 400 exhibitors spread across a dozen exhibition halls. Relatively unknown outside France, it has quickly become one of the three biggest classic car shows in the country, attracting nearly 50,000 visitors. There's a huge variety of things to see in the halls dedicated to motorcycles, trucks and buses, tractors, modern sports cars and motorsport.

In 2016, the highlights were a celebration of BMW's centenary and a display of historic Abarth racers from Michel Pont's collection at Savigny-lès-Beaune (page 165). The previous year, there was a stunning array of cars from the 1930s with bodywork by Erdmann & Rossi, brought to Avignon by the Lithuanian collector Saulius Karosas. Other recent exhibits have ranged from Vespa scooters to Renault F1 cars. The car clubs taking part really help make the show too, while there is a vast selection of parts and automobilia to choose from.

Apart from the displays, there is a concours d'élégance and a fashion show to enjoy. There are demonstration runs on-site for everything from tractors to dragsters and maybe even a flypast by a historic plane.

Practical information

🕐 March every year

🏠 Parc des Expositions, Chemin des Félons, 84140 Avignon

🚆 Avignon mainline & TGV stations, then bus or taxi

🚌 Lines 3, 4 & 17 (Friday & Saturday only)

📷 43.905716 N, 4.894452 E

🌐 www.avignon-motor-festival.com

📞 +33 4 90 83 27 29

✉ trajectoiresconcept@orange.fr

Lancia Delta Integrale and Peugeot 205 T16 in the display of competition cars.

Bouchon de Tourves

Citroëns jam the streets. / This Ford Thunderbird squeezes through. (Both courtesy Thierry Dubois, www.nationale7.com)

I f you spend most of the year stuck in traffic jams getting to work, you could be excused for not wanting to spend your holidays in one! But the Bouchon de Tourves – which takes place in August every two years – is a traffic jam with a difference, with all the vehicles trapped in it dating back to the 1960s or before. Until 1968, when it was finally bypassed, the village of Tourves, situated between Aix-en-Provence and Fréjus, was one of the most notorious bottlenecks on the famous Nationale 7. In its centre the Grande Rue (a misnomer if ever there was one) narrows to just 4m (13ft); on a record-breaking day in August 1965, 28,000 cars became stuck there and the queues stretched back 6km (3.7 miles).

Since 2011 the Bouchon de Tourves has been a light-hearted celebration of summers past, its participants in period dress re-enacting roadside breakdowns or arguments between holidaymakers from Paris and Marseille. Starting from the recently-opened Musée des Gueules Rouges (named after the red dust that covered the faces of the local bauxite miners), entrants try and drive through the village as many times as they can, before retiring for a well-earned pastis or picnic lunch.

Practical information

🕐 August 15 biennially (odd years)

🏠 Musée des Gueules Rouges, off Avenue Gambetta, 83170 Tourves

🖼 43.41103 N, 5.919898 E

🌐 routenationale7. blogspot.fr/search/label/ Bouchon%20de%20 Tourves

✉ nationale7historique provence@gmail.com

Beautifully-restored Berliet truck from the Var. (Courtesy Thierry Dubois, www.nationale7.com)

Classic Festival, Nogaro

Historic airplanes take off from the airstrip next to the circuit. / More than 400 cars in the parade lap for charity.

Take the successful formula of Classic Days at Magny-Cours (page 172), add the legendary good food and hospitality of the Gers, sprinkle liberally with some autumn sunshine, and you get the winning recipe for this hugely enjoyable event. Since its first edition in 2014, this weekend meeting based around the Circuit Paul Armagnac (page 146) has quickly established itself as one of the leading events in the south-west.

Some of France's best-known drivers – Henri Pescarolo in 2015, Jean Ragnotti in 2016 – put on impressive demonstration drives. All participants can enjoy plenty of time behind the wheel or simply join the parade lap to raise money for charity. Between sessions on track, visitors can look at more than 1000 cars taking part in the paddocks, visit the traders' stands or walk over to the airstrip nearby to admire 35 historic airplanes, some of which fly over the circuit.

It is the involvement of the whole town that really makes the Classic Festival special. On Saturday evening, the classic cars parade through the town centre, while live music, a giant aperitif, games of *pétanque* and even bull-running sessions ('courses landaises') in the arena all add to the spectacle.

Pescarolo delighted the crowds in this 1976 Inaltera.

Practical information

🕐 October every year

🏠 Circuit Paul Armagnac, 32110 Nogaro

🖥 43.765907 N, -0.038014 W

🌐 www.classicfestival.fr

📞 + 33 5 55 25 27 26

✉ contact@classicfestival.fr

French Riviera Classic & Sport, Nice

Lancia Flaminia Sport Zagato, shown here at Essen, the perfect embodiment of 'la dolce vita.' / Something to please everyone! (Courtesy French Riviera Classic & Sport)

Given the number of well-heeled enthusiasts who live along the Mediterranean coast, it's surprising there are so few classic car shows in the area. It has taken a while for the Côte d'Azur to find the winning formula for a major classic car show, but this event – under the patronage of rally driver Jean-Claude Andruet – seems to be well on its way. A football stadium may seem an unlikely setting for a car show, but its circular layout ensures that everyone gets to walk all the way round and so see all the cars on display. For 2017, when the event will be held for the third time, there will also be an area outside the stadium for demonstrations of Formula 1 cars, Group B rally cars and Grand Prix motorbikes.

The last edition took cars and the cinema as its theme, with a special focus on films shot on the Riviera. In 2017 visitors will be able to enjoy 'la dolce vita,' with cars on loan from the collections of HSH the Prince of Monaco (page 109) and Adrien Maeght. The weekend's programme also features plenty of club exhibits, a parts fair and an auction of classic cars.

Practical information

🕐 Check website for dates; 2017 edition in June

🏠 Stade de Nice - Allianz Riviera, Boulevard des Jardiniers, 06200 Nice

📧 43.704 N, 7.191 E

🌐 www.fr-cms.com

📞 + 33 4 93 21 95 01

✉️ info@fr-cms.com

Seen on track at Montlhéry, ex-Michèle Mouton Group B Audi quattro.

Southern France

Rétro Auto Forum du Var, Fréjus

Celebrating 50 years of the Porsche 911. / 'Barn find' 2CV on the award-winning stand of the 2CV Club Varois.

Less popular than some of the resorts along the Mediterranean coast, Fréjus is about halfway between Cannes and Sainte-Maxime. This show started in 2008 to fill a gap in an area with many car enthusiasts but no major regional event. Like many provincial shows, it has grown quickly and now attracts 140 exhibitors and over 15,000 visitors. It's well supported by local clubs, many of whom have a lot of fun decorating their stands; last year, there were even reconstructions of a complete Shell service station and a Citroën sales office.

Above all, the organisers have been successful in staging an interesting series of special exhibitions, bringing in cars from well outside the region. These have often marked key anniversaries through the years, whether for Porsche's 911, Citroën's Traction Avant or DS. Former French race and rally drivers, such as Jean-Pierre Jaussaud and Jean Ragnotti, regularly visit the show and are happy to sign autographs for their fans.

The show takes place in a nature park close to the sea: if you're visiting with your family, they can enjoy the sandy beach two minutes away, or the cycle paths and sports facilities in the park.

One of two rare Vermorel models taking part in the road run.

Practical information

🕐 May/June every year

🏠 Base Nature François Léotard (car access: rue des Batteries), 83600 Fréjus

🖥 43.424209 N, 6.737793 E

🌐 https://frejus.fr

📞 +33 4 94 51 83 83

✉ tourisme@frejus.fr

Museums
Shows & Tours
Market Place
Motorsport
Circuits

Salon Auto Moto Prestige et Collection, Nîmes

Reconstruction of an old garage on a club stand. / Pre-1980 sports cars the theme in 2017. (Courtesy Retro Organisation)

The city of Nîmes can trace its history back to Roman times and is a popular tourist destination. If you're planning to visit its famous arena next winter, this classic car show is one of the first events of the season. One of the smaller shows in this guide, it is well supported by local and national clubs, and less common marques such as NSU or the Renault Rambler Club often take part. Under new management since 2015, the organisers have worked hard to attract a wider range of traders, and the show is now a good place to find parts, books and brochures or scale models. For enthusiasts who bring their own classic, there is a large dedicated parking area.

The major exhibits each year often have a sporting focus: in 2017, Jean-Pierre Coppola and Françoise Conconi will show their Alpine A110, fresh from the Rallye Monte Carlo Historique (page 130). In previous years MG and Abarth have both been honoured, while special displays have marked the 50th anniversary of the Ford Mustang and recalled the cars of the James Bond films.

Cars from the James Bond films.

Practical information

🕐 February every year

🏠 Parc des Expositions, avenue du Languedoc, 30000 Nîmes

🗺 43.816973 N, 4.363038 E

🌐 www.retro-organisation. com

✉ Contact form on website

Museums · Shows & Tours · Market Place · Motorsport · Circuits

Top Marques, Monaco

Pagani Huayra makes its Monaco début. / *Carbon fibre and alcantara details in this Gumpert Apollo S.*

In Monaco, the exotic soon seems ordinary; the exceptional mundane. In the street leading to the Grimaldi Forum, the waterfront venue for this show, the car showrooms welcome buyers of McLaren, Ferrari and Bentley rather than Citroën or Renault. But, for some, a standard Lamborghini is not enough; for these customers, Top Marques is the show. As you walk past the powerboats and helicopter parked outside the exhibition centre, you enter another world; the premium whiskies and exclusive watches on display are just small change before you reach the cars.

Although the mainstream supercar manufacturers all show their latest models, Top Marques is, above all, the place to compare limited production hypercars such as the 2000bhp Berus or Donkervoort's D8-GTO RS, the fastest and lightest model ever built by the Dutch manufacturer. Specialists in up-market personalisation such as Mansory, TechArt or Hamann offer massive power increases, mirror finish bodywork, or one-off interiors: everything is possible ... although the results are often of questionable taste. For cars which are ready for the road, you can take a test drive along part of the Monaco F1 Grand Prix circuit, which has to beat trying the latest SUV on the local ring road!

Practical information

🕐 April every year

🏠 Grimaldi Forum, 10, avenue Princesse Grace, 98000 Monaco

🚌 Line 6, Grimaldi Forum/ Musée Sauber

📷 43.744007 N, 7.431408 E

🌐 www.topmarquesmonaco. com

📞 + 377 97 70 12 77

✉ Contact form on website

Personalised Porsche Cayenne by Hamann.

Trophée en Corse

Porsche 356 against a backdrop of the Mediterranean. / Lotuses old and new enjoying the trip.
(Both courtesy Rallystory)

Where the Tour de Corse Historique (page 139) has a strongly sporting bent, the emphasis for Rallystory's annual tour of Corsica is on leisure and enjoyment. Taking their inspiration from the 1921 Corsican Grand Prix, the organisers prepare a different route each year, divided into six stages and covering about 1000km (620 miles) around the island. Entrants meet in Marseille for the ferry crossing to Bastia, or another of the island's ports, and then spend three days on the island's winding backroads, staying in 4-star hotels and enjoying meals on the beach or quayside. There are no average speed requirements or special stages on closed roads, simply a beautiful route to follow and prizes for everyone who stays on course.

Clearly, the formula appeals; the Trophée en Corse will soon celebrate its 25th anniversary and attracts over 100 participants. Entry is open to all classic cars, primarily covering the period from 1945-80. It's understandably popular among owners of sports cars from manufacturers such as Alpine, Lotus and Porsche, who come to enjoy the so-called 'island of 10,000 corners.' There's also a smaller GT category, open to more recent GT and rally cars.

The distinctive logo for the event.
(Courtesy Rallystory)

Practical information

🕐 October every year

🏠 Different route around Corsica each year

🌐 www.rallystory.com

📞 +33 1 42 12 07 08

✉ contact@rallystory.com

Bourse-expo de Cavaillon

A varied lineup of sports models on the organisers' stand. (Courtesy Écurie les Trapadelles) / The historic Écurie les Trapadelles logo.

If you are heading down to Provence in December, Cavaillon is an easy stop off the A7 autoroute between Avignon and Aix-en-Provence, and only a few kilometres from the Musée Automobile de Provence in Orgon (page 110). A mix of autojumble and classic car show, it's one of the last meetings of the year. With more than 15 editions already behind it, the long-established local club, the Écurie des Trapadelles, has made this a successful event, attracting over 4000 visitors. There is a waiting list for new exhibitors. Prices are reasonable, especially compared with some of the bigger shows, and there's a good range of parts for pre- and post-war French cars.

The central displays are very varied. French makes often take the honours, as with the exhibition of 26 Peugeot cars, from a 1916 Bébé Peugeot to a 205 Turbo 16 from the 1980s. A couple of years later, Renault – showing one car from each decade from 1925 to 1990 – shared top billing with a splendid array of Italian sports cars, including a rare Alfa Romeo Giulietta Sprint Veloce *allegerita* and a well-patinated Ferrari 250 GT convertible which once belonged to Yves Montand.

Practical information

🕐 December every year

🏠 Marché d'Intérêt National, 15, avenue Pierre Grand, 84300 Cavaillon

🖥 43.824638 N, 5.04176 E

🌐 www.trapadelles.fr

📞 See Contacts section of website

✉ contact@trapadelles.fr

Plenty of parts to look over. (Courtesy Écurie les Trapadelles)

Motors Mania, Pau

The sign says it all! / A good stock of books, models and artwork.

At a time when many specialist booksellers are now only to be found online, it's a pleasure to be able to browse the shelves of this charming shop in Pau. Opened by Christophe Lavielle in 2003, it's located in the beautiful old area of the city near the château. During the Grand Prix Historique (page 126), Motors Mania sometimes also takes a stand in the paddock.

Altogether it carries some 3500 titles, mainly in French but with some in English and German, too. As you would expect in this location, it is especially strong on motorsport books, but the range is extensive, featuring books on motorbikes and even tractors. Motors Mania stocks both new titles and selected secondhand books, as well as magazines and technical manuals. There's a selection of scale models and motoring art as well, including affordable posters and reproductions. If you're looking for an old programme from one of Pau's original races, or a print by photographers of the day like Lartigue or Dieuzaide, this is a good place to try. If you can't make it to Pau, the shop operates a mail-order service through its website and will ship worldwide.

The shop front in the historic quarter near the Château.

Practical information

🕐 Open Tuesday-Saturday, 11am-1pm and 3-7pm

🏠 28, rue Henri IV, 64007 Pau

🖼 43.294562 N, -0.374294 W

🌐 www.motors-mania.com

📞 +33 9 60 11 75 84

✉ motorsmania@wanadoo.fr or contact form on website

Museums

Shows & Tours

Market Place

Motorsport

Circuits

Grand Prix Historique de Monaco

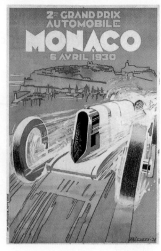

O f all the motor races in the world, the Grand Prix de Monaco is surely the best known and most prestigious. Held on the 'archetypal street circuit,' in the words of the British motoring writer Richard Meaden, its history stretches back to 1929. The original idea for the race came from Anthony Noghès, a member of a wealthy local family who also inspired the Rallye de Monte Carlo, and to this day the last corner on the 3.3km (2.1 miles) circuit is named after him. The narrow, hilly track has undergone a few changes to improve its safety, but the layout remains essentially the same.

As interest in historic racing has grown over the past 25 years, it was a natural step for the Automobile Club de Monaco (ACM) to launch a new event to re-create

Poster from the second ever Grand Prix, 1930. (Courtesy Musée Automobile de Vendée)

the atmosphere of the Grands Prix of the past. Given the opportunity to drive on this legendary circuit, the event was an immediate success and celebrated its 10th edition in 2016. Held every two years, it gives enthusiasts the chance to relive the great races from the 1930s to the 1970s. The period feel is ensured by grouping the cars into categories by age, starting with prewar Grand Prix cars and running through to Formula 1 cars of 1973-78, like the McLaren M26. In between, there are hard fought battles between 1950s sports cars, like the Jaguar C-Type, and the first rear-engined Grand Prix cars from manufacturers such as Brabham. Two days of

McLaren M23 leads Lotus 77 around the harbour.

Maserati 150S/200S and 300S charging up the hill towards the Casino. / Jaguar C-Type refilling in the pits.

testing lead up to the races themselves on Sunday, and the cars run for 10-18 laps, depending on their age. Spectators can also enjoy demonstration laps of outstanding race cars, or join the bidding at one of the prestigious auctions of historic cars often held during the race weekend.

Demonstration lap by the 'Silver Arrows' Auto Union, here passing in front of the Casino.

Practical information

🕐 May, biennially (even years)

🏠 ACM, 23, boulevard Albert 1er, 98000 Monaco

🗺 43.735825 N, 7.421032 E

🌐 www.acm.mc

📞 + 377 93 15 26 00

✉ info@acm.mc

Museums

Shows & Tours

Market Place

Motorsport

Circuits

123

Museums   Shows & Tours   Market Place   **Motorsport**   Circuits

Grand Prix de Monaco F1

Ferrari F2012 in Monte Carlo. (Courtesy J M Folleté/ACM)

Whenever you choose to visit Monaco, it's a special experience. From the glamour of the casino in Monte Carlo, to the millionaires' yachts moored in the harbour, it has a unique appeal. Even Bernie Ecclestone, the supremo of Formula 1 racing, conceded, "This place gives us more than we give it." Modern safety requirements have seen the end of many races on city streets, but Monaco continues with its unrivalled setting by the sea and famous tunnel, from which the drivers emerge blind at speeds of up to 270km/h (nearly 170mph). Over the years, it's seen its share of famous accidents, and some drivers – such as Alberto Ascari in 1955 – have even ended up in the harbour! But it has also witnessed some epic victories, like the string of five consecutive wins by Ayrton Senna from 1989-93. More than any other, it's the race every driver wants to win.

The modern Formula 1 Grand Prix – usually the sixth race in the F1 World Championship season – is the culmination of four different races. There are other contests for GP2 and Renault Series 2.0 single-seaters, as well as Porsches competing in the Mobil 1 Super Cup. Practice

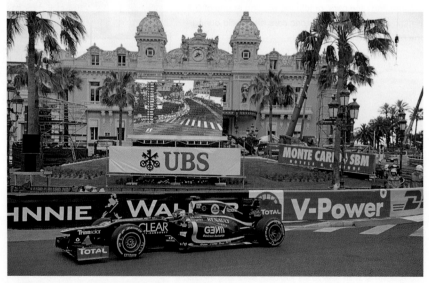

Lotus-Renault passing in front of the Casino. (Courtesy J M Folleté/ACM)

Red Bull Racing RB8 on the waterfront. (Courtesy J M Folleté/ACM)

begins on Thursday and the excitement builds until the Formula 1 race on Sunday afternoon, which lasts for 78 laps or two hours.

With the world's highest GDP and some of its most valuable real estate, everything in Monaco is expensive. Unfortunately, that goes for the Grand Prix too, and hotel rooms overlooking the track reach astronomical prices. But the Automobile Club de Monaco (ACM) does its best to offer a range of packages, from the most expensive grandstand seats to standing room in front of giant screens. And if you visit Monaco outside race week, you can drive the circuit for free!

The Monaco coastline, seen from the sea. (Courtesy Top Marques, Monaco)

Practical information

🕐 May every year

🏠 ACM, 23, boulevard Albert 1er, 98000 Monaco

🖼 43.735825 N, 7.421032 E

🌐 www.acm.mc

📞 + 377 93 15 26 00

✉ info@acm.mc

Grand Prix de Pau Historique

Minis line up at the start.

Set against the dramatic backdrop of the Pyrenees, Pau is one of a handful of places where motor races are still held on the streets of the city. Popular with the English since the 19th century, Pau has a motorsport history even longer than that of Monaco: the first Grand Prix here was held in 1900. The current circuit remains virtually unchanged since 1935 and the great prewar races dominated by Nuvolari, Wimille and Lang. The historic event was revived at the start of the 21st century and is part of ten days of racing, with the modern Grand Prix for Formula 3, Formula 4 and GT4 cars. The modern event has continued to be a great training ground for future stars of Formula 1; Lewis Hamilton won here in 2005, and Romain Grosjean the next year.

There are many ways to enjoy a visit to Pau; as a competitor, as a visitor with your own classic car, or simply as a spectator. Since HVM Racing took over the organisation of the races from Peter Auto, the atmosphere has been less elitist and some of the grids less prestigious. Most of the races now feature Formula Junior, Formula Ford, and Formula 3 single-seaters,

Formula Ford single-seaters press on up the hill away from the station.

British enthusiasts' cars in the Parc Beaumont. / Below: Sometimes things get out of shape ...

as well as pre-76 GT & Touring cars and Maxi 1000 Trophée contenders like the Mini Cooper.

The 2.8km (1.7 miles) circuit is a challenging track for the competitors, with the tight Virage de la Gare and Épingle du Lycée catching out the unwary. For spectators, there are good views from the different stands, but be ready to walk a fair way around the paddocks and circuit. On Sunday, the Parc Beaumont hosts a display of up to 800 classic cars, and club members can drive around the circuit at lunchtime.

Porsche 356 Carrera 2 approaches the tight corner by the station.

Practical information

🕐 May every year

🏠 1, boulevard Aragon, 64000 Pau

🖼 43.294002 N, -0.368336 W

🌐 www.hvmracing.fr

📞 +33 1 41 22 20 10

✉ contact@hvmracing.fr

Motorsport

Museums   Shows & Tours   Market Place   **Motorsport**   Circuits

Rallye Monte Carlo

A new entrant in 2017, Toyota's Yaris WRC car was previewed at the Paris Motor Show.

It is hard to imagine now that the wealthy principality of Monaco should need to find ways to attract more visitors, but a hundred years ago, it faced tough competition from neighbouring resorts such as Nice. The Rallye Monte Carlo began less as the motorsport event we know today, and more as a grand occasion for members of high society. The first rally in 1911 was run as a regularity event, and some cars were even driven by the owner's chauffeur. Gradually, the rally took on a more overtly sporting character, and gave manufacturers the chance to test the performance and durability of their cars. When the World Rally Championship was created in 1973, the 'Monte' took its place as the opening event of the season. Over the years, it became synonymous with the often arduous winter conditions and demanding concentration drives, from starting points in cities as far away as Athens or Tallinn.

Since the end of the 1990s, the event has been centred around Monte Carlo, but as Citroën, Ford, Toyota and Hyundai fight for honours today, the rally retains an unrivalled appeal for competitors and fans alike. The exact route changes every year, but the website of the Automobile Club de Monaco gives plenty of information on the 15 special stages which make up the rally: check out where you can see the competitors in action or return with your own car later in the year. The most famous stage of all is run at night on the Col de Turini, which tops out at 1607m (5272ft), and where thousands of fans ensure a unique atmosphere. Alternatively, head to the Casino in Monte Carlo for the traditional departure ceremony, or cheer winners like Sébastien Ogier as Prince Albert presents the awards in front of the Palace, back in Monaco.

Ford Fiesta RS WRC from the Qatar M-Sport World Rally Team. (Courtesy Frédéric Chambert)

Loeb and Elena on their last outing in the Rallye de Monte Carlo.
(Courtesy Frédéric Chambert)

2016 winners from the Volkswagen and Hyundai teams.
(Courtesy Volkswagen Motorsport GmbH)

Practical information

🕐 January every year

🏠 ACM, 23, boulevard Albert 1er, 98000 Monaco

🖼 43.735825 N, 7.421032 E

🌐 www.acm.mc

📞 + 377 93 15 26 00

✉ info@acm.mc

Rallye Monte Carlo Historique

Alpine A110 takes to the departure ramp, to be flagged off by Prince Albert.

After the FIA changed the regulations for international rallying in the 1990s, the Automobile Club de Monaco (ACM) decided to introduce a new historic event, to recapture the spirit of the great rallies of the past. Like the Grand Prix Historique de Monaco (page 122), which the Club also organises, it quickly became one of the highlights of the historic motorsport calendar.

Open to models of cars which competed in the original Monte Carlo rallies from 1955-1980, the rally attracts over 300 crews from 30 different countries. The organisers have revived the popular concentration runs, with entrants starting from cities including Barcelona, Lisbon, Copenhagen and Glasgow, before joining up for the series of regularity stages. These include many of the most famous routes in the history of the rally, such as the Col de Turini or the Col de Braus in the mountains behind Monaco. The rally programme and website give lots of information on where to see the cars in action. You can also get up close to the cars and drivers as they prepare to leave the waterfront in Monaco, where Prince Albert and former champions wave them off.

The participants gather at dusk on the Quai Albert 1er, Monaco.

Paddy Hopkirk pressing on to victory in 1964. (Courtesy BMW Group)

Many of the cars competing – like the Porsche 911, Lancia Fulvia and Opel Ascona – were winners in their day. Increasingly, however, the rally attracts cars less commonly seen in competition, such as an Australian Holden or Polski-Fiats and Zastavas from Eastern Europe. In 2016, one Belgian competitor even took part in an Austin FX3 London taxi, just as Tony Brooks had done in 1961. The participants include former rallymen such as Jean Ragnotti, driving a Renault 5 Turbo as he did 35 years before, modern champions like Daniel Elena (this time behind the wheel), and amateur enthusiasts, for whom it may be a once in a lifetime opportunity.

Practical information

🕐 January every year

🏠 ACM, 23, boulevard Albert 1er, 98000 Monaco

📧 43.735825 N, 7.421032 E

🌐 www.acm.mc

📞 + 377 93 15 26 00

✉ info@acm.mc

Jean Ragnotti's Renault 5 Turbo. (Courtesy Renault UK Limited)

Les 100 Tours, Nogaro

Victorious Citroën GS. (Courtesy Philippe Hortail, les 100 Tours)

Oysters for lunch!
(Courtesy Philippe Hortail, les 100 Tours)

In the Circuits sections of this guide you'll find plenty of information on track days, driving courses and hiring tracks for club events. For owners of historic cars there are races and demonstration events too. The organisers of the 100 Tours take a different approach, extending the concept of 'regularity' from road rallies to the track. After a practice session, each crew (driving cars at least 15 years old) sets a lap time which they have to stick to as closely as possible for the following hundred laps. Novice drivers can take it easy, whilst more ambitious competitors can set themselves a tougher target. And if the weather takes a turn for the worse during the day, that just adds to the challenge! As the Citroën GS which won in 2016 shows, outright speed isn't everything.

During the year, the 100 Tours organisation visits several different tracks, but the circuit at Nogaro in the Gers (page 146) is a longstanding favourite. Participants in the series of races compete for the Trophée Alain Fabre, which celebrates its 20th anniversary in 2017. Good food contributes to a pleasurable day out and the organisers help to raise money for research into eye diseases.

Magnificent Porsche 906 Carrera 6 waiting in the stands.
(Courtesy Philippe Hortail, les 100 Tours)

Practical information

🕐 September/October every year

🏠 Circuit Paul Armagnac, 32110 Nogaro

🖥 43.765907 N, -0.038014 W

🌐 www.les100tours.fr

📞 +33 6 09 90 60 85

✉ pdamaz@orange.fr

Corse Sud Classic Rallye

The calanques at Bonifacio. / AC Cobra on the road. (Courtesy Gérard Sacco)

I f the Tour de Corse Historique (page 139) seems too demanding, and the Trophée en Corse (page 119) is beyond your budget, this well-established rally might be just the way to enjoy the wonderful scenery of the 'Ile de Beauté.' The organisers offer a complete package including the ferry crossing from Marseille, accommodation, meals and breakdown assistance. After a short run on the first day, participants cover about 700km (430 miles) over the next three days, based out of a resort such as Porticcio. The rally is conducted on regularity principles, with an average speed of no more than 50km/h (31mph) on the open road.

There is room for a maximum of 40 cars, split into different classes covering the period 1950-90, and a special category for all-women crews. The rally attracts a good mix of cars; entries might range from a pocket-sized Honda S800 up to a Ferrari 348, while the last event was won by an Audi quattro. Participants from outside France are welcomed, and – to add to the competitive spirit – entrants are encouraged to form teams of three to five crews. Places usually fill quickly, so plan on booking by the end of the previous year.

Practical information

🕐 May every year

🏠 Different route each year around Corsica

🌐 http://corseclassicrallye.fr/

📞 +33 6 84 35 89 82

✉ new.racing.team@ wanadoo.fr or contact form on website

CG Coupé in the parc fermé. (Courtesy Thomas Sorel)

Les Dix Mille Tours, Circuit du Castellet

Heading down the main straight. / Saloon cars join the fray.

The final event of the season organised by Peter Auto, the Dix Mille Tours sees out the year in style. One of the finest circuits in Europe, the usually mild weather of Provence and an exceptional grid of historic racers ... what's not to like? It's no surprise therefore to see the paddock filled with expensive transporters from across Europe, and up to 300 cars take part in three days of practice and racing. Highlights of the weekend include the races for Group C prototypes, like the Porsche 962, and the Trofeo Nastro Rosso, an exceptional grid of pre-'66 Italian sports and GT cars from Ferrari 250 Berlinettas to the Alfa Romeo TZ. Meanwhile, the Sixties Endurance races let lightweight Jaguar E-Types and AC Cobras fight for position, whilst prototypes and GT cars from 1966-79 battle in the Classic Endurance class.

For spectators, the Circuit Paul Ricard (page 147) offers excellent viewing facilities. Visitors can enjoy demonstrations of exceptional cars like the McLaren F1 GTR or Venturi 600 LM, or browse the traders' village. For owners of classic cars, there's room in the paddock for several hundred cars and the chance to enjoy time on track each day.

McLaren F1 GTR returns to the pits.

Practical information

🕐 October every year

🏠 Circuit Paul Ricard, 2760 route des Hauts du Camp, 83330 Le Castellet

🖥 43.248619 N, 5.788899 E

🌐 www.dixmilletours.com

📞 +33 1 42 59 73 40

✉ Contact form on website

Mont Ventoux

The shadow of the observation tower in the early evening light. / The summit is at over 1900m (6000ft).

Like the Klausen pass in Switzerland or Pikes Peak in Colorado, Mont Ventoux is one of the world's most famous hill climbs. Although best known today as a stage on the Tour de France cycle race, it was renowned as a motorsport event from 1902-73. In the 1930s it was the scene of epic victories by drivers like Hans Stuck, who charged up the mountain in his V16-engined Auto Union. In 2013, Sébastien Loeb used it for the final testing of his Peugeot 208 T16 before shattering the record at Pikes Peak.

The classic way to the mountain's 1912m (6272ft) summit is to take the D974 from the village of Bédoin. The 21.6km (13.4 miles) southern route rises from the vineyards and through woods before reaching the bleak, moon-like landscape beyond Le Chalet Reynard. As the road climbs, the gradient steepens and the temperature plummets. Even on a mild evening in late May, it may be -1°C (30°F) at the summit. In winter, 3m (10ft) high snow poles mark the edge of the road. Exact dates depend on the weather, but the road from Bédoin is usually closed from mid-November until mid-April, and the northern route down through Malaucène until mid-May.

The Peugeot 208 T16 which Loeb took to victory at Pikes Peak.
(Courtesy Peugeot)

Practical information

🕐 Opening period: see main text

🏠 Le Mont Ventoux, 84340 Beaumont-du-Ventoux

📧 44.1735 N, 5.27829 E

🌐 www.bedoin.org

📞 +33 4 90 65 63 95

✉ Contact form on website

Passion et partage, Alès

Do you sometimes feel a bit selfish enjoying a day out on track? If you do, 'Passion et partage' could be a good way to ease your conscience and let others share the fun! Organised by the local Rotary Club, this event raises as much as €25,000 each year in aid of handicapped children. Most of the money collected comes from track rides for the public, so you can give others lots of pleasure as you help raise funds, or perhaps experience a ride yourself in an unfamiliar car.

Time on track is split into a series of 20-minute sessions, culminating in a final parade lap at the end of the day. The event attracts the usual track day suspects, such as the Lotus Elise, Caterham or Porsche 911, but also a surprising variety of upcoming classics, such as the Renault 5GT Turbo, VW Golf GTi and Honda Integra. The organisers also stage a modest outdoor show of classic cars, and sometimes put on special demonstration drives on the track, as when Luc Costermans, the former holder of the land speed record for blind drivers, drove around the circuit in a Renault Mégane RS, following rally-style pace notes from his sighted co-pilot.

Top: Eye-catching logo for the event. / The locally-built PGO Cévennes, seen here at the Avignon Motor Festival.

Practical information

🕐 September-November every year (depending on track availability)

🏠 Pôle mécanique d'Alès-Cévennes, Vallon Fontanes, 30520 St Martin de Valgalgues

📧 44.15502 N, 4.071045 E

🌐 www.passion-partage.com

📞 +33 6 74 09 78 82

✉ passionetpartage@gmail.com

Lotus owners enjoying time on track.

Rallye Hivernal Classic, Vallauris

Opel Kadett GT/E on the road. (Courtesy Thierry Mouchet/Studio Christine)

If ever proof were needed that you can have great fun taking your classic out in any season, this rally is surely it! The association Event Classic Car, which organises this winter regularity event, has a decidedly sporting outlook and organises several competitive rallies throughout the year. The Rallye Hivernal Classic has taken place for more than a dozen years. Participants cover about 400km (250 miles) over a two-day weekend, starting from the Golfe Juan on the Mediterranean coast, between Antibes and Cannes, and climbing up through the beautiful mountain roads behind the coast to the ski resort of Le Val d'Allos.

Some of the regularity stages are held on closed roads and there are sessions – which the public can watch – on the temporary ice circuit at Le Val d'Allos, as well as a gymkhana when the competitors return to Golfe Juan. It's the only winter rally on the Côte d'Azur, and the conditions in January can be tough, making this an often challenging event. That doesn't deter 50-60 crews each year, increasingly driving 'Youngtimers' - recent classics from the 1980s and 1990s, such as the Lancia Delta Integrale, Datsun 280Z, Opel Manta or BMW 325i.

Practical information

🕐 January every year

🏠 Quai Napoléon, 06220 Vallauris (Golfe Juan)

🗺 43.566689 N, 7.078011 E

🌐 www.eventclassiccar.fr

📞 +33 4 93 69 90 40

✉ eventclassiccar@sfr.fr

Alfa Romeo Giulia in the snow at Le Val d'Allos. (Courtesy Thierry Mouchet/Studio Christine)

Ronde Hivernale Historique, Serre Chevalier

There's a Renault 11 in there somewhere! (Courtesy Circuit de Serre Chevalier)

Volvo PV544 leading an Opel Ascona in the Ronde Hivernale. (Courtesy Circuit de Serre Chevalier)

Of all the events that take place on the ice circuit at Serre Chevalier (page 148), the Ronde Hivernale is the most famous, and certainly the best way to re-capture the atmosphere of the first races held here in the 1970s. Cars taking part must be at least 25 years old, and you can expect to see a good range of mainly rear-wheel drive sporting machinery from the 1960s to 1980s. For the circuit's 40th anniversary in 2011, more than 100 drivers took part, some of them the sons of fathers who competed when the circuit opened.

The Ronde begins with an evening session on Friday, and continues through Saturday and Sunday. All the drivers get the chance to take part in several series of laps, comprising both regularity and longer endurance sessions. To add more variety, the laps are split into different sets going both ways around the 810m (885yd) circuit. The walls of ice surrounding the track can be unforgiving, but if you feel uncertain about taking part, the circuit organises special courses in driving on ice. Or simply come as a spectator and enjoy watching the regularity sessions and final parade lap.

Alpine A110 berlinettes racing in 1973. (Courtesy Circuit de Serre Chevalier)

Practical information

🕐 January every year

🏠 Circuit de Serre Chevalier, 22, route de Grenoble, 05240 La Salle des Alpes

🖼 44.953207 N, 6.551355 E

🌐 www.circuitserrechevalier.com

📞 +33 4 92 24 78 44

✉ contact@circuitserrechevalier.com

Tour de Corse Historique

The Mediterranean provides a stunning setting for this Alpine A110. / Lancia 037 on the road. (Both courtesy Frédéric Chambert)

Sometimes known as the rally of 10,000 corners, the Tour de Corse was first held in 1956, and quickly established a reputation as Europe's ultimate tarmac rally. Since the turn of the century Corsica has played host to this revival event, one of the most demanding historic rallies in this guide.

Over five days, participants cover up to 1200km (750 miles), including nearly 350km (220 miles) on 18 special stages against the clock. Some of these are run at night, others on the original tarmac of the 1960s rally. The event has become ever more popular, thanks to the beautiful scenery of the island, the exciting if sometimes dangerous roads, and the professionalism of the organisers. There is room for only 250 or so cars, and as many as 200 would-be entrants are turned away, so book early if you want to take part. You'll join an impressive line-up of competitors, like Erik Comas, Jean-Charles Rédélé or Romain Dumas, piloting cars such as the Lancia Stratos, Alpine A110 or Porsche 911 3.0 RS. If you can't follow the rally, why not return and drive the famous special stages in your own car?

Villagers enjoying watching one of the night stages. (Courtesy Frédéric Chambert)

Practical information

🕐 October every year

🏠 Different route around Corsica each year

🌐 www.tourdecorse-historique.fr

📞 +33 4 95 70 67 33

✉ tourdecorsehistorique2a@gmail.com

Museums

Shows & Tours

Market Place

Motorsport

Circuits

Tour de Corse WRC

Citroen's DS3 WRC competing in Corsica in 2015. (Courtesy Citroën Communication) / Hyundai's brand-new i20 WRC car. (Courtesy Hyundai Motorsport)

After five years in Alsace, the French round of the World Rally Championship (WRC) returned to Corsica in 2015. Its history is the stuff of rallying legend, perhaps never more so than in 1970 when Bernard Darniche won every special stage on the rally, an exploit Sébastien Loeb would repeat in 2005.

The modern rally is made up of ten special stages, taking competitors from the coastal roads to the mountains inland and back to the sea. The FFSA's website (see link below) provides a fascinating insight into what it is like to drive each stage, even indicating when drivers will need to do a handbrake turn! You'll also find plenty of practical information there (in English and French) on where and when to see the cars.

For 2017 a new chapter opens in the WRC's history, with Volkswagen's withdrawal from rallying and four-time world champion Sébastien Ogier's move to the M-Sport Ford team. Citroën and Hyundai will return to fight for honours, while Toyota will enter its new Yaris WRC for the first time.

Just a few of Corsica's famous 10,000 corners. (Courtesy Tour de Corse/S Presse)

Practical information

🕐 April (from 2017); previously October

🏠 Different route around Corsica each year

🌐 www.tourdecorse.com

📞 +33 4 95 29 01 00

✉ tourdecorse@ffsa.org

Circuit d'Albi

There has been a motor racing circuit in Albi since 1932, but the current track, sometimes known as the Circuit du Séquestre, dates from 1962. It's been regularly updated ever since, with improvements to its safety equipment and regular changes to its layout. 3.565km (2.2 miles) long, it's a fast track, with several straights and good opportunities for overtaking, but can be hard

The final of the French Drift Championship was held here. (Courtesy Circuit d'Albi)

on your brakes. The weather can be very hot, making it trying for drivers as well.

The most famous event here is the Grand Prix Automobile d'Albi, which has been held more or less continuously since 1933. Albi's calendar is certainly pretty diverse; in recent years, it has also staged the finals of the French superbike championship and the French drift championship.

If you'd prefer to get on the track yourself, there are regular, relatively inexpensive open days, and courses including high-end GT cars like the Audi R8 or Lamborghini Gallardo and drifting sessions in a BMW M3 or Nissan Skyline R33.

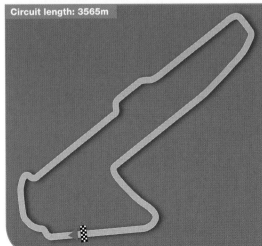

Circuit length: 3565m

Practical information

🕐 Open all year; for details, see calendar on circuit website

🏠 81990 Le Séquestre (next to Aerodrome)

🖥 43.915787 N, 2.118679 E

🌐 www.circuit-albi.fr

📞 +33 5 63 43 04 04

✉ contact@circuit-albi.fr

Circuit AT2000, Isola 2000

Just 90km (56 miles) from Nice, Isola 2000 owes its name to its altitude; an average 2000m (6500ft) above sea level. Since its construction in the early '70s, it's become one of the most important ski resorts in the French Alps, boasting 120km (75 miles) of pistes. If you enjoy cars as much as skiing, it's a great place for a winter holiday, with one of the top ice driving circuits in France. Established in 1993, the Circuit AT2000 has become famous for one of the key stages in the Trophée Andros ice driving championship (page 184), which is keenly followed in France.

The circuit is 800m (875yd) long, with two straights, five right- and two left-hand corners – or vice versa, as the direction of the track can be reversed. The whole circuit can be hired by clubs for private use, or you can take ice driving classes in the school run by Arnaud Trévisol, a former professional racer. As if to prove that you don't need lots of power to have fun, the school uses Nissan Micras! If you're feeling more competitive, the circuit also organises racing days featuring specially designed snow karts.

The circuit at Isola 2000. (Courtesy AT2000) / The Trophée Andros at Isola 2000. (Courtesy Trophée Andros/B. Bade)

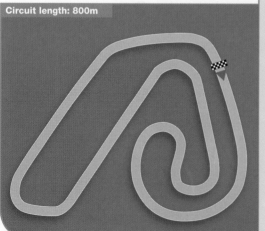

Circuit length: 800m

Practical information

🕐 Open during winter season (exact dates depend on weather)

🏠 06420 Isola 2000

🚌 Line 750 from Nice airport and railway station

🖥 44.191 N, 7.148 E

🌐 www.sportsloisirs.net

📞 +33 4 93 23 91 32

✉ contact@circuitdeglace.com

Circuit du Grand Sambuc, Vauvenargues

Tucked away in the hills of Provence at an altitude of 500m (1640ft), the Circuit du Grand Sambuc can be tricky to find. But persevere and you'll discover a beautiful track in a gently undulating setting, from which you can enjoy great views across Provence. Manufacturers such as Renault sometimes use the track for their new model launches.

Track-focused Lotus Elise Cup R. (Courtesy Lotus Cars)

Built in 1985, the circuit is relatively short, at 2km (1.2 miles) in its longest configuration, which includes a main straight of 800m (875yd) ending in a chicane. What it lacks in length, it makes up for in the technical challenges of its corners, some of them cambered, and alternating rapid changes of direction. The quickest cars – such as a French-built Norma M20 sports prototype – can lap it in comfortably less than a minute.

Lotus has chosen Le Grand Sambuc as the base for its official Lotus Academy, offering individual coaching in its Elise Cup and Exige V6 Cup models. If you'd prefer to try a Porsche Cayman or 997 GT3, or maybe a nimble Renault Clio, the circuit's training partner, Spark Motorsport, also provides training sessions and passenger rides in these.

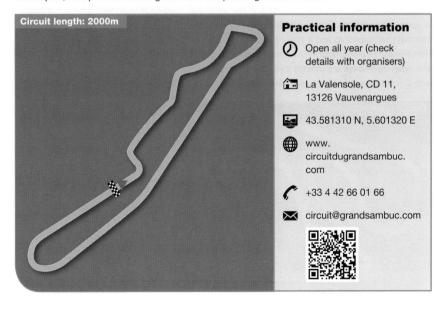

Circuit length: 2000m

Practical information

🕐 Open all year (check details with organisers)

🏠 La Valensole, CD 11, 13126 Vauvenargues

🖥 43.581310 N, 5.601320 E

🌐 www. circuitdugrandsambuc. com

📞 +33 4 42 66 01 66

✉ circuit@grandsambuc.com

Circuit de Nîmes-Lédenon

The story of the circuit at Lédenon, just north of Nîmes, is that of one family's determination; with his wife, Sylvie, Jean-Claude Bondurand built this circuit from nothing, even driving the bulldozer to clear the ground himself! Still privately managed by the family, the track has been steadily improved over the past 40 years, and since 2010 has been

Mazda RX-7 drift car on the circuit's stand at the Avignon Motor Festival.

homologated by the FIA to hold all races except Formula 1. Only the sometimes difficult access to the circuit is a reminder of its modest beginnings.

For drivers, the main track is best known for the fact that it runs anticlockwise. 3.15km (1.96 miles), it's a varied and hilly circuit, comprising several blind corners and a famous triple left. The location is exposed to the Mistral wind, which can sometimes unsettle motorbikes and even cars.

Lédenon is deservedly popular and is in use up to 300 days each year, with a full programme of competitive events. These include races in the FFSA national championship and a major historic meeting, the HistoRacing Festival, held in October. Driving courses and open track days are offered throughout the year, with a smaller second track used for karting.

Practical information

🕐 Open all year; for details, see calendar on circuit website

🏠 30210 Lédenon

🖼 43.92299 N, 4.503733 E

🌐 www.ledenon.com

📞 +33 4 66 37 11 37

✉ info@ledenon.com

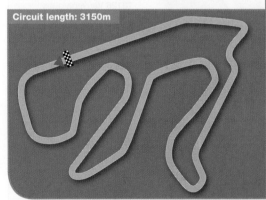

Circuit length: 3150m

Museums Shows & Tours Market Place Motorsport Circuits

Circuit de Pau-Arnos

Pau is a long way from northern France or the UK, but if you are planning to attend the Grand Prix Historique in Pau (page 126) or tour the Pyrenees, this circuit is well worth seeking out. Its undulating, parkland setting is reminiscent of tracks in the UK, like Brands Hatch or Cadwell Park; the French magazine *Sport Auto* described it as one of the most beautiful circuits in the country. Designed by the

Looking over the circuit from the stands.

French champion Jean-Pierre Beltoise with the safety of drivers paramount, the track opened in 1986. At 3.03km (1.9 miles) long, it's a highly technical circuit; car drivers and motorbike riders alike enjoy its rich variety of corners. Spectators too appreciate the good views from the stands.

Spaces for events at Arnos fill up quickly, but GTRO, its training partner, offers a range of courses with choices including the latest GTs such as the Porsche 991, Ferrari 458 Spéciale and Lamborghini Huracan, American hot rod-inspired 'Legends Cars' or a Martini MK75E Formula 3 single-seater. When the track is not in use for training sessions, it can be booked by clubs for their exclusive use or enjoyed by individual enthusiasts in their own cars.

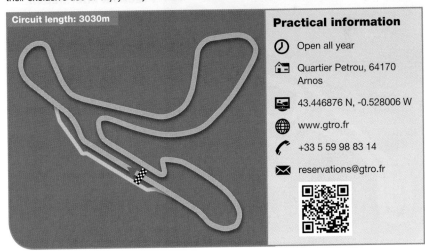

Circuit length: 3030m

Practical information

🕐 Open all year

🏠 Quartier Petrou, 64170 Arnos

📷 43.446876 N, -0.528006 W

🌐 www.gtro.fr

📞 +33 5 59 98 83 14

✉ reservations@gtro.fr

Circuit Paul Armagnac, Nogaro

FFSA GT3 racers line up by Nogaro's distinctive control tower. / Single-seaters on track during the Classic Festival.

In the rural heart of France, Nogaro is about 70km (43 miles) north of Pau. It's one of France's most famous motorsport venues, renowned for its friendly atmosphere and good food as much as for the action on track. After a somewhat turbulent history in the 1960s, the circuit has been progressively extended and improved. New stands were built in 2007 and there are plans in hand to resurface the track. It is now 3.636km (2.26 miles) long and offers a good balance of speed and technical difficulty.

Nogaro is best known for the Coupes de Pâques, marking the start of the GT season, but this is only one of many events held there, which cater to followers of modern and historic motorsport alike. The autumn is an especially rich time of year, giving fans the chance to watch the long running Grand Prix de Nogaro for modern GT cars and Historic' Tour for classic racers. In 2014 a new event, the Classic Festival (page 114), was launched, inspired by the similar event at Magny-Cours. Monthly track days are run for cars and motorbikes, and driving courses are offered in Renault Mégane and Clio 4 RS cars, as well as Formula Renault single-seaters.

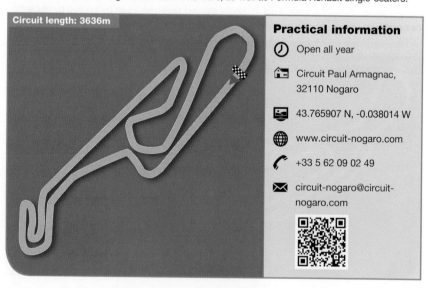

Circuit length: 3636m

Practical information

🕐 Open all year

🏠 Circuit Paul Armagnac, 32110 Nogaro

📇 43.765907 N, -0.038014 W

🌐 www.circuit-nogaro.com

📞 +33 5 62 09 02 49

✉ circuit-nogaro@circuit-nogaro.com

Circuit Paul Ricard, Le Castellet

The pit lane at the circuit / The unmistakable blue lines of the circuit. (Both courtesy Circuit Paul Ricard)

From the blue skies of Provence to the legendary blue lines at the edge of the track, this could only be the Circuit Paul Ricard. The abrasive surfaces of the coloured lines progressively slow cars and contribute to the circuit's outstanding safety record. They are just part of the technological arsenal of this advanced track, with its elaborate signalling systems and automated sprinklers. Completely re-designed in 2002, and welcoming competitors and the public alike with excellent facilities like the Grand Prix Hall, luxury hotels and even an airstrip next to the track, it's one of the most sophisticated circuits in Europe. No wonder that when Formula 1 returns to France in 2018, the Grand Prix de France will be held here at Le Castellet.

The 5.8km (3.6 miles) track can be configured in no fewer than 180 different ways. Cars reach exceptionally high speeds along the 1.8km (1.1 miles) of the Mistral straight and the track is often used by race teams and manufacturers for testing. Hiring the main circuit is prohibitively expensive for most clubs, but you can experience the smaller Driving Center track in an extensive range of GT cars and Mitjet racers.

Practical information

🕐 Open all year

🏠 Circuit Paul Ricard, 2760 route des Hauts du Camp, 83330 Le Castellet

🖥 43.248619 N, 5.788899 E

🌐 www.circuitpaulricard.com

📞 +33 4 94 98 36 66

✉ circuit@circuitpaulricard.com

Circuit length: 5800m

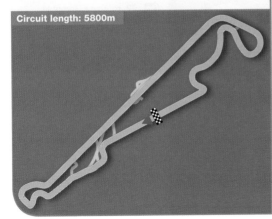

Circuit de Serre Chevalier

Home to ice racing for more than 40 years. / Competitors in the Coupe Glacée DAF. (Both courtesy Circuit de Serre Chevalier)

A few kilometres north of Briançon, Serre Chevalier is one of the biggest ski resorts in the Hautes Alpes, and the ice driving circuit created by the former rally driver Claude Laurent just adds to its appeal. The 810m (885yd) long circuit is built of artificial snow on an asphalt base, which is watered daily: this ensures a constant depth of ice and consistent driving conditions. Naturally sunny during the day, the circuit is fully lit at night.

Together with Chamonix, Serre Chevalier was the first place in France to hold races on ice, and it continues to stage a busy programme of events, especially in January when the weather conditions are usually best. These include the Ronde Hivernale (page 138), the newer Sprint Hivernal, and the Coupe Glacée DAF. All these events attract good crowds; you can watch from the outdoor stands or from the warmth of the restaurant.

Serre Chevalier is also known for its excellent range of ice driving courses, using powerful 4WD cars from Subaru; these vary in length from 20-minute 'taster' sessions to intensive full-day courses, and you can focus on driving safely or for competition.

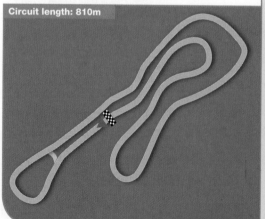

Circuit length: 810m

Practical information

🕐 Mid-December to mid-March (depending on weather)

🏠 22, route de Grenoble, 05240 La Salle des Alpes

🖥 44.953207 N, 6.551355 E

🌐 www.circuitserrechevalier.com

📞 +33 4 92 24 78 44

✉ contact@circuitserrechevalier.com

Circuit du Var, Le Luc

Comparisons are often unfair, and it certainly wouldn't be right to match this circuit against its prestigious neighbour at Le Castellet (page 147). But the circuit at Le Luc lets you enjoy the sunny climate of Provence for a wider range of budgets. Operated by the local authority, the track opened in 1965, five years before

Aerial view of the circuit. (Courtesy Circuit du Var)

Paul Ricard. It was substantially modernised in 2005, when it was completely resurfaced, and improved safety facilities including gravel traps and video cameras were added. 2.4km (1.5 miles) long, the circuit is flat and relatively fast. Pleasantly set in woodland, there is a 4x4 driving area next to the main track. A major project is now underway to redevelop the former leisure park adjoining it and further improve the facilities.

There are few competitive motorsport events at Le Luc, but that is pretty much the only limitation; you can hire the circuit for club events, or take advantage of the track days, passenger rides and driving courses. The range of cars on offer is exceptional; AGS, the former constructor of Formula 1 cars, is based at the circuit and offers courses in its own 650bhp V8 Cosworth-engined F1 racers.

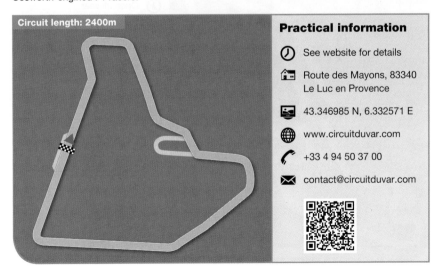

Circuit length: 2400m

Practical information

🕐 See website for details

🏠 Route des Mayons, 83340 Le Luc en Provence

🖼 43.346985 N, 6.332571 E

🌐 www.circuitduvar.com

📞 +33 4 94 50 37 00

✉ contact@circuitduvar.com

Grand Circuit du Roussillon, Rivesaltes

Close to the city and airport of Perpignan, and to the beaches of the Mediterranean, Rivesaltes is in an area you might well visit on holiday. The name may sound familiar too, as it is an 'appellation d'origine contrôlée' for a naturally sweet,

Mitjet racers, seen here during the Circuit des Remparts in Angoulême.

fortified wine which is often served as an aperitif. The Grand Circuit du Roussillon may be less well known, but it has its own claim to fame – as one of the biggest karting circuits in the world!

Many of the circuits presented in this guide have small karting tracks alongside the main track for cars, but here a single loop is used for cars, motorbikes and karts. At 1513m (1655yd), it certainly makes for a special karting experience, but bigger GT cars may struggle here and the circuit is better suited to smaller, more manoeuvrable models. It is, however, homologated by the FFSA and FFM (for cars and motorbikes respectively) and is fully equipped with timing screens, night-time lighting and a panoramic viewing terrace.

Karting events understandably lead the list of activities at the circuit; children as young as three can start in the 'Baby Kart' category, while adults contest a karting Grand Prix every month.

For enthusiasts who prefer full-size cars, you can join training sessions at the wheel of a Mitjet racer, powered by a 1300cc Yamaha motorbike engine, or bring your own car for individual tuition in car control.

Circuit length: 1513m

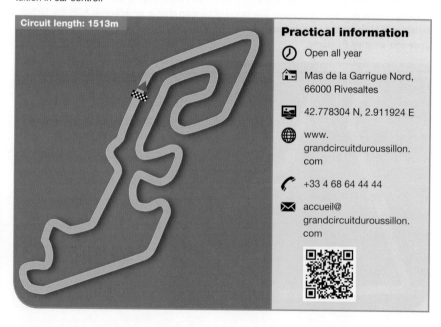

Practical information

🕐 Open all year

🏠 Mas de la Garrigue Nord, 66000 Rivesaltes

🗺 42.778304 N, 2.911924 E

🌐 www. grandcircuitduroussillon. com

📞 +33 4 68 64 44 44

✉ accueil@ grandcircuitduroussillon. com

Michelin test track, Fontange

If you've ever read a magazine report comparing different tyres, you may have wondered how the tyre manufacturers carry out their own tests. Michelin's facility at Fontange, near Salon-de-Provence, is occasionally open to the public, and gives an insight into how the company works. One of two test tracks that Michelin owns in France, Fontange was used by Kléber-Colombes (acquired by Michelin in 1981) after it sold its track nearby at Miramas to BMW.

Bibendum, the inimitable symbol of Michelin.

The main circuit is just over 3km (1.9 miles) in length, with one long straight and two banked corners, but chicanes are often added. Inside there is a smaller, very sinuous track which can be watered and used for drifting. As at the test centre at Mortefontaine north of Paris (page 228), however, the track is only one of the facilities Michelin uses here; there are also special sections to test braking, ride comfort, road noise, and resistance to aquaplaning.

In principle, the circuit at Fontange can be hired by any outside group, but it is chiefly used for events organised by car manufacturers and the motoring press. However, at least one company, Cascadevents, periodically offers driving courses on the track.

Practical information

🕐 Limited opening dates (check with organiser)

🏠 Domaine de Fontange, Chemin Chante Perdrix (RN 569), 13300 Salon-de-Provence

🗺 43.632085 N, 5.011332 E

🌐 www.michelin-engineering-and-services.com/fre/Nos-Pistes/Fontange

📞 +33 4 63 21 56 94

✉ Contact form on website

Circuit length: 3000m

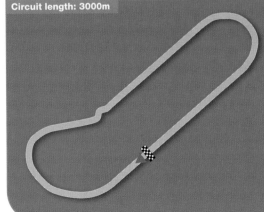

Pôle mécanique d'Alès-Cévennes

Aerial view of the circuit. (Courtesy Pôle mécanique d'Alès-Cévennes) / Toyota FT86 on track during the Passion et partage weekend.

Built on the site of an old coal mine, the modern circuit at Alès – the 'capital of the Cévennes' – is part of a small technopark housing several motorsport companies. Alongside the circuit you'll find specialist engineering companies and an importer of Caterham's cars.

The complete circuit is 2.5km (1.6 miles) in length, but can be separated into two smaller loops. It is gently sloping and varied in layout, and there are great views from the main building over the whole track. The driving schools based at the circuit naturally offer a choice of courses in high-performance GTs and Caterhams. There are plenty of opportunities to bring your own car on track, too, with monthly open days and events such as 'Passion et partage' (page 136).

As well as the main (high-speed) circuit, there's a special tarmac rally track, which can be watered to reduce grip. Deliberately narrow, it's designed to replicate all the types of corner a driver might find on a tarmac rally stage. If you're keen to try it, local companies offer rally driving courses here and at a nearby earth track.

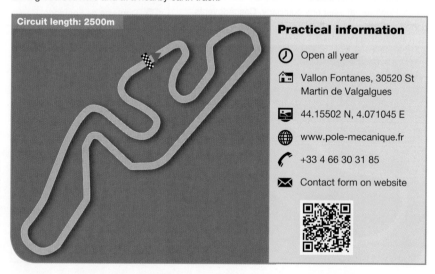

Circuit length: 2500m

Practical information

🕐 Open all year

🏠 Vallon Fontanes, 30520 St Martin de Valgalgues

📷 44.15502 N, 4.071045 E

🌐 www.pole-mecanique.fr

📞 +33 4 66 30 31 85

✉ Contact form on website

Central France & the Alps

4

Where better to begin your exploration of this part of France than in Lyon?

Once an important car manufacturing centre, Lyon was an early contributor to the historic car movement, thanks to the pioneering vision of Henri Malartre.

The museum which bears his name remains one of the most important collections of veteran cars in France. Lyon is also home to the country's second largest classic car show, Epoqu'Auto, and – in a very different register – one of the world's most advanced Formula 1 driving simulators.

As you travel through the Auvergne, Burgundy, the Alps and central France, you'll find many more automotive museums, several of them housed in fine châteaux, and displaying everything from lorries and scale models to Abarth and Matra racers. For lovers of motorsport there are many historic races and revival events, led by the Grand Prix de l'Age d'Or held at Dijon-Prenois. Track day enthusiasts can choose among more than a dozen circuits, including

Top; 1902 De Dion Bouton Populaire at the Musée Henri Malartre. (Courtesy Musée Henri Malartre) / French coachbuilders' work on show at Epoqu'Auto in Lyon.

the prestigious F1 circuit at Magny-Cours. Or, if you prefer a more leisurely pace, why not enjoy one of the classic car shows or great touring rallies like the Coupe des Alpes set in the wonderful scenery of the French Alps?

On track in the Alps.
(Courtesy Circuit du Laquais)

Contents

Museums

Shows & Tours

Market Place

Motorsport

Circuits

Musée Henri Malartre, Rochetaillée-sur-Saône

Veteran cars are displayed inside the château. / Rochet-Schneider in front of the château. (Courtesy Musée Henri Malartre)

The historic car movement in France owes a huge debt of gratitude to Henri Malartre. One of the first traders to recognise the value of breaking old cars for their parts – not just for scrap metal – he began to put aside cars of historic interest from an early stage, starting with the 1898 Rochet-Schneider you can still see now. In 1959, he bought the château at Rochetaillée-sur-Saône, 11km (7 miles) north of Lyon, to create the first automotive museum in France.

Today, you can admire over 150 cars from 1890 to 1986, as well as cycles, motorbikes and public transport vehicles from Lyon. The château itself, which dates back to the 17th century, houses the museum's exceptional collection of veteran cars, many of them unique. There are curiosities like the 1897 wicker-bodied Hugot, and cars technically advanced for their time, such as the electric-powered Mildé from 1900 or the Noël Bénet from the same year, with front-wheel

Postwar cars in the second hall, including a 1948 Wimille prototype.

![François Lecot stands beside his record-breaking Citroën Traction Avant.](image)

François Lecot stands beside his record-breaking Citroën Traction Avant.

drive and a transversely mounted engine, predating the Mini by more than half a century. The guided tours available are a great way to learn about the early years of motoring.

Across the museum's grounds, which provide ample parking for visiting car clubs, two exhibition halls house later cars, including prototypes such as the Citroën TPV from 1936 and a post-war Wimille JPW. Some of the cars have famous histories, like the Packard Caribbean which belonged to the singer Édith Piaf, or the armoured Mercedes 770 from 1942, used by Hitler himself. Special displays show the huge number of car manufacturers which once existed in Lyon and tell the story of François Lecot, a local hotelier who famously drove his Citroën Traction Avant 400,000km (250,000 miles) in 1935-36, averaging more than 1100km (700 miles) a day between Paris and Monte Carlo.

Practical information

🕐 Open every day except Monday, 9am-6pm (10am-7pm in July & August). Closed last week in January, 25 December and 1 January

🏠 645, rue du Musée, 69270 Rochetaillée-sur-Saône

🗺 45.844932 N, 4.837092 E

🌐 www.musee-malartre. com/malartre/

☎ +33 4 78 22 18 80

✉ musee-malartre@mairie-lyon.fr

Cutaway model of a Peugeot 404.

157

L'Aventure Michelin, Clermont-Ferrand

Exterior view of the museum. / The entrance hall of the museum, with Breguet XIV plane and Micheline from Madagascar. (Courtesy Michelin)

Welcome to 'Bib-City!' The Michelin Man – or Bibendum in French – is present wherever you look in Clermont-Ferrand, where Michelin has been a major employer for more than a century. Next to the Marcel Michelin stadium, L'Aventure Michelin is a brand-new museum which has already drawn more than 300,000 visitors since it opened in 2009.

Attractively designed, the museum leads visitors through ten display areas which present the story of Michelin's technical innovations. While its contribution to motoring history is well known, from the tyres used in the first motor races at the start of the 20th century to the famous Michelin X radial tyre, the company has been a pioneer in many more areas. You can see the Micheline train from the 1930s and the Breguet XIV biplane developed by the company.

Michelin is just as famous for its road maps and green and red travel guides, which sell more than ten million copies each year. On the upper floor of the museum you can learn how these have developed through research and innovation, and how Bibendum helped make Michelin the brand of the 20th century. For collectors of Michelin memorabilia an auction is held every July in nearby Royat.

Practical information

🕐 Open every day except Monday, 10am-6pm (September-June) and every day 10am-7pm in July & August. Closed 25 December and first half of January (check website)

🏠 32, rue du Clos Four, 63100 Clermont-Ferrand

🚋 Line A, Stade Marcel-Michelin

🚌 Line B, Stade Marcel-Michelin

🗺 45.790779 N, 3.105973 E

🌐 www.laventuremichelin.com

📞 +33 4 73 98 60 60

✉ Contact form on website

Innovation area in the museum. (Courtesy Michelin)

Museums

Shows & Tours

Market Place

Motorsport

Circuits

Conservatoire de la Monoplace Française, Magny-Cours

Just part of the huge collection of Ligier Formula 1 cars. / 1966 Courtois Formula 3 car with period support vehicle.

The newest museum in this guide, the Conservatoire was opened in May 2015. True to its name, it is a remarkable collection of nearly 50 single-seater French racing cars, covering Formula 1, 2 and 3, as well as the so-called 'Formules de promotion' which let up-and-coming drivers hone their skills. Informative panels guide visitors through the history of motorsport in France and the role of the circuit at Magny-Cours (page 196), for many years home to the Formula 1 Grand Prix de France.

Specific areas of the museum are dedicated to the cars of Martini, Matra (including the MS7 raced by Jackie Stewart) and Renault (with Alain Prost's RE30B from 1982 one of the stars). Visitors can also discover cars from the period when motor racing got going again after the Second World War, including a Gordini T15 from 1948 (as raced by Wimille, Trintignant and Fangio) and a unique Formula 2 Serval M101 from the following year. But it is the final room which makes the biggest impression of all: a stunning array of Ligier Formula 1 cars from 1976-1996, including nearly every model from that period, either in original condition or painstakingly restored.

Practical information

🕐 Open during major events at circuit only or by reservation for groups

🏠 58470 Magny-Cours

🗺 46.860223 N, 3.162414 E

🌐 www.circuitmagnycours.com/conservatoire-de-la_p_621.html

📞 +33 3 86 21 80 00

✉ info@circuitmagnycours.com

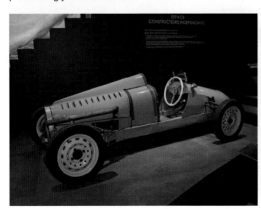

Unique Serval M101 Formula 2 racer from 1949.

Museums

Shows & Tours

Market Place

Motorsport

Circuits

Espace automobiles Matra, Romorantin-Lanthenay

Matra MS 660 driven by Jabouille and Hobbs. / An 'Art Car' before its time; the 1967 Matra M530 painted by Sonia Delaunay in front of the museum. (Both courtesy Musée Matra)

Had Matra not started out as an arms manufacturer, it may never have entered the annals of automotive history. Soon after taking over production of the René Bonnet Djet, Matra's owner, Jean-Luc Lagardère, decided to take Matra into motorsport to help sell its sports cars and improve its public image. The rest, as they say, is history: from 1965-74 Matra won 124 races, including three successive victories at Le Mans and, in 1969, the Formula 1 manufacturers' and drivers' championships. These sporting successes are celebrated in this light and airy museum, with its fabulous line-up of Matra F1 cars and sports prototypes, driven by champions such as Henri Pescarolo and Jackie Stewart. The gallery of racing engines and the exhibitions each summer devoted to different makes (not just Matra) are special treats.

The museum also marks the 1.1 million cars produced in Romorantin until 2003; 900,000 Renault Espace people carriers, successive generations of Djet, Matra 530, Bagheera and Murena sports cars, and the distinctive Rancho SUV and Renault Avantime models. There is a remarkable selection of prototypes and concept cars, like the Renault Zoom city car from 1992, and the Matra Bagheera U8 with two four-cylinder engines built around a single crankcase.

Matra V12 in the engine gallery. (Courtesy Musée Matra)

Practical information

🕐 Open every day except Tuesday (September-June) and every day in July & August (see website for hours). Closed 25 December, 1 January, and 1 May

🏠 17, rue des Capucins, 41200 Romorantin-Lanthenay

🖼 47.35852 N, 1.740093 E

🌐 www.museematra.com

📞 +33 2 54 94 55 58

✉ museematra@romorantin.fr

Fondation Berliet, Lyon

Berliet fire engine and VIL saloon displayed by the Fondation at Epoqu'Auto in Lyon. / Paul Berliet at the Salon de l'Auto in 1984.
(Courtesy Musée du Poids Lourd)

If you associate the name Berliet solely with its post-war trucks and are tempted to jump ahead, take a moment to read on. Before the Second World War, Berliet was also known for its luxury cars and was one of Lyon's most important automobile manufacturers. Although centred on Berliet, the vocation of this foundation extends to all makes of French buses and lorries, and to all the vehicles built in the region.

The offices of the Fondation are housed in the Villa Berliet, built by Marius Berliet as his family home over 100 years ago. If you're interested in automotive history, its extensive archives are open by appointment 35 hours a week, and are backed up by a comprehensive website, which attracts 7000 visits every month.

The Fondation's collection of historic vehicles is housed in Montellier (Ain) and is not open to the general public, but can be visited by groups. The Fondation also regularly loans its vehicles to other museums for temporary exhibitions. It puts on a big display each year at Epoqu'Auto, the classic car show in Lyon (page 168), where it showed a particularly fine array of Berliet's pre-war cars in 2016.

Practical information

🕐 Open by appointment, Monday to Friday (see website for details)

🏠 39, avenue Esquirol, 69003 Lyon

🚌 Line 28, Vinatier

🚋 Line T2, Ambroise Paré or Vinatier

Ⓜ Line D, Laennec

🗺 45.742067 N, 4.891856 E

🌐 www.fondationberliet.org

📞 +33 4 78 54 15 34

✉ Contact form on website

A pair of Berliet trucks on show at the Rétro Auto Forum du Var in Fréjus.

Museums

Shows & Tours

Market Place

Motorsport

Circuits

Musée Automobile de Bellenaves

Local club members celebrate Father's Day outside the museum. (Courtesy Musée Automobile de Bellenaves) / This 1927 Delahaye fire engine saw service in Vichy.

Three-quarters of an hour's drive north of Clermont-Ferrand, in a peaceful area of the French countryside, Bellenaves may seem an unlikely setting for a car museum. This friendly, informal collection owes its creation in 2000 to the enthusiastic support of the local mayor, and the village continues to provide a building to house the museum and funds a part-time employee each summer.

There is room for nearly 50 cars, most of them popular French makes from 1910 to the 1970s. Ten of them are on permanent display, but most of the cars, which belong to members of the active local club, change each season. Whenever you come, you're likely to find cars with interesting stories, like the well patinated Daimler limousine which once belonged to the British royal family, or a Peugeot 402 allegedly used by the Resistance, complete with the bullet holes to prove it! Others are rarely seen, such as the 1961 NSU Neckar in the permanent collection, or the woodie-style Simca 8 Canadienne. Their condition varies, but nearly all of the cars are in running order, and the club members take them out for special events during the year.

Practical information

🕐 Open April to October: days and hours vary by month (see website), or by appointment for groups

🏠 D43, Lieu-dit Saint-Bonnet-de-Tizon, 03330 Bellenaves

🖼 46.18555 N, 3.08903 E

🌐 museebellenaves.jimdo. com

📞 +33 4 70 58 39 73 (during opening hours) or +33 4 70 58 39 75 (other times)

✉ Contact form on website

1925 Renault NN on show. (Courtesy Musée Automobile de Bellenaves)

Musée Automobile du Château de Menetou-Salon

The current château at Menetou-Salon is a fine 19th century neo-Gothic building, but its history dates back to the 15th century, and the Princes of Arenberg, who have owned it since 1773, can trace their lineage all the way back to 501! Informative guided tours, in English and French, take visitors around the château and to the car and carriage museum.

The museum is small – just seven cars and some horse-drawn carriages – but all of the vehicles are immaculately maintained and regularly used. Prince Auguste was an early motoring enthusiast and purchased

Some cars from the collection outside the château. (Courtesy SAS le Prince d'Arenberg)

the Panhard & Levassor Type 16 on show in 1899. The current Prince continues this tradition and has taken part in the London to Brighton Run and a rally from Tierra del Fuego to Alaska. Highlights of the collection include a 1912 Turcat-Méry type LH, which has been driven twice from Paris to Moscow. It was built by the father of the French test pilot of the Concorde, André Turcat, and was amongst the very first cars to drive through the Channel Tunnel during its inauguration. There's also a stylish 1923 Hispano-Suiza H6B Berline Sport with Vanden Plas coachwork, and – the latest addition to the museum – a freshly restored 1929 Minerva six-cylinder from Antwerp.

The estate produces some of the best wine in the area, including a tasty Pinot Noir, so why not finish your visit with a wine-tasting, and maybe bring a few bottles home?

Practical information

🕐 Limited opening times in summer for individual visitors (see website), or by appointment for groups (car clubs welcome)

🏠 2, rue du Château, 18510 Menetou-Salon

🖼 47.234446 N, 2.489853 E

🌐 www.chateau-menetou-salon.com

📞 +33 2 48 64 80 54

✉ visites@chateau-menetou-salon.com

Looking down on the display of cars. (Courtesy SAS le Prince d'Arenberg)

Museums

Shows & Tours

Market Place

Motorsport

Circuits

Musée de l'Automobile de Valençay

Gangloff-bodied Bugatti 57 Stelvio from 1936 next to a 1908 Delaunay-Belleville HH6 taxi. / Much-travelled 1906 Clément-Bayard.

Like the Musée Automobile de Vendée (page 65), this museum was established by a local garage owner, Camille Guignard, who began collecting historic cars soon after World War II. It moved to Valençay in 1981 and was originally housed in the nearby château. You can buy a combination ticket to visit the château and museum, or return on a summer evening to enjoy a son et lumière spectacle or tours of the château by candlelight.

There are 60 cars on show, nearly all of them in running order and in good, but unrestored condition. French makes predominate and the museum has an important collection of pre-1914 models, such as the 1906 Clément-Bayard which has covered an amazing 400,000km (250,000 miles). There are two fine Delaunay-Belleville cars from 1908-10; one served as an officers' car alongside the 'taxis de la Marne' in 1914, the other took part in the 'Croisière Rouge' from the North Cape to the Caucasus in 1967. Later models include a magnificent Bugatti 57 Stelvio and a cutaway version of a Peugeot 403 used to train dealer mechanics. Showcases along the walls present an impressive collection of parts and accessories built up by the Guignard family.

Practical information

🕐 Open every day from mid-March to early November (see website for hours)

🏠 12, avenue de la Résistance, 36600 Valençay

🖼 47.162446 N, 1.560834 E

🌐 www.musee-auto-valencay.fr

📞 +33 2 54 00 07 74

✉ musee.automobile.de.valencay@wanadoo.fr

Some of the many French marques on show: Delage, Hotchkiss, Peugeot ...

Museums

Shows & Tours

Market Place

Motorsport

Circuits

Musée du Château de Savigny-lès-Beaune

Just part of the huge display of Abarth cars.

Some people are born collectors, and few more so in this guide than Michel Pont, who restored this château dating back to the 14th century. Altogether there are nine collections to visit, including 250 motorcycles and thousands of model cars, motorbikes and planes. As you walk through the grounds, be ready for a massive surprise as you see the display of 100 historic fighter planes from France, North America and the former Soviet bloc.

For car enthusiasts though, the collection of more than 35 Abarth cars – the biggest in Europe regularly open to the public – will be of greatest interest. There are production models like the 850 TC and 1300 Coupé, but, above all, an exceptional group of sports cars such as the 1300 OT which raced at Le Mans, a unique 2000 OT 'Coda longa' (long-tail) and a Formula 2 racer. The shelves beside the cars are lined with the cups and trophies which Michel Pont won in his successful career as an amateur racer from 1965-72. Today, his son Christophe competes in historic events and has taken over running the vineyards. Your visit certainly wouldn't be complete without trying one of the seven classed growth crus the estate produces!

Top: Motorcycles and scale models too. / Belgian F16 fighter plane in front of the château.

Practical information

🕐 Open every day throughout the year, except 25 December, and first three weeks of January (see website for hours)

🏠 Rue Général Leclerc, 21420 Savigny-lès-Beaune

🗺 47.062308 N, 4.818754 E

🌐 reception-aviation. chateau-savigny.com

📞 +33 3 80 21 55 03

✉ Contact form on website

Musée Maurice Dufresne, Azay-le-Rideau

Plus de 3 000 inventions... MUSÉE MAURICE DUFRESNE ...à l'intérieur du musée

More than 3000 inventions on display. (Courtesy Musée Maurice Dufresne)

It seems only right that this professionally run museum should be named after its founder, Maurice Dufresne. Originally a blacksmith, he devoted sixty years of his life to building up this unique collection of inventions and artefacts, which bear witness to a forgotten way of life in rural France. Covering the period from 1850-1950, its 3000 exhibits are spread through the rooms and grounds of the museum. Allow a good couple of hours to see everything, as it's easy to become engrossed in the displays. Exhibits like the weaving looms from Tours or the working models of farm machinery should be interesting to all the family, and there is even a sinister mobile guillotine from the Revolution. If you're staying in the area, why not combine time at the museum with visits to the château at Langeais or the magnificent gardens nearby, as well as a gourmet meal?

For historic transport enthusiasts there are vehicles of all sorts, from horse-drawn carriages to a 1941 electric-powered Peugeot voiturette, and even a Blériot XI monoplane. Many of the cars date from before the Second World War, and include rarities such as a 1919 Bernin-bodied Buick and a 1939 Georges Irat roadster.

The Blériot exhibition room.
(Courtesy Musée Maurice Dufresne)

Practical information

🕐 Open every day, April-October (see website for hours)

🏠 17, route de Marnay, 37190 Azay-le-Rideau

🖥 47.279048 N, 0.396373 E

🌐 www.musee-dufresne.com

📞 +33 2 47 45 36 18

✉ contact@musee-dufresne.com

Old weaving loom.

Salon de l'Automobile Miniature, Château de la Vigne, Ally

Morgan club gathering outside the château. / Looking down on the collection of model cars. (Both courtesy Bruno du Fayet de la Tour)

The original fortified castle on this site was destroyed by the English, but Bruno du Fayet de la Tour, the owner of this beautiful château, which dates back to 1480, doesn't hold a grudge! Visitors of all nationalities are welcome, both to stay in the charming guest rooms and to visit the unique exhibitions of 4000 model cars and 1000 dolls in its guardrooms.

Monsieur du Fayet de la Tour cheerfully admits that he never grew up, and since the 1980s he has assembled a wonderful collection of toys and models from more than 130 different manufacturers. All of the cars are imaginatively presented in 70 thematic showcases, set off with period catalogues and advertisements, and each season the owner adds a special temporary display. Many of the models are still in their original packaging, or come from manufacturers like JEP which have long since disappeared. It's hard to know where to begin your tour; from the cars of heads of state to the films of James Bond, from Le Mans and Formula 1 racing cars to the great marques like Rolls-Royce, Bugatti or Porsche, even a display of Ferrari F40 models in different scales – there is something here for everyone.

Practical information

🕐 Open every day 2-7pm, mid-June to mid-September, and at other times by arrangement for groups

🏠 Château de la Vigne, 15700 Ally

🖼 45.176557 N, 2.329653 E

🌐 www.chateaudelavigne.com

📞 +33 4 71 69 00 20

✉ la.vigne@wanadoo.fr or contact form on website

Original Citroën toy car from the 1920s. (Courtesy Bruno du Fayet de la Tour)

Epoqu'Auto, Lyon

The range of Follis' production can be seen in this display.

After Rétromobile in Paris (page 20), Epoqu'Auto is the second largest classic car show in France, attracting 60,000 visitors from across Europe. It's organised by a local club, Le Club des 3A (Les Amateurs d'Automobiles Anciennes), but there's nothing amateur in the way this show is run. Now nearly 40 years old, it has established an excellent reputation for the quality of its exhibits and its unpretentious atmosphere. Epoqu'Auto enjoys strong support from owners' clubs and a wide range of traders. In recent years the show has featured an auction of historic cars, many at reasonable prices, run by Osenat from Fontainebleau (page 46).

Several thematic displays provide the focal point for the show, which has backing from the FFVE (Fédération Française des Véhicules d'Époque) and, increasingly, from major French companies such as Citroën, Peugeot or Total. Highlights of recent shows have included celebrations of Salmson and Rolls-Royce and, in 2016, a fabulous display of Delahaye 135 and 235 cars, with bodywork by the leading French and Swiss coachbuilders of the day. For fans of more recent cars, there is a dedicated area for 'Youngtimers' (recent classics) too.

Remarkable Chapron and Tüscher-bodied Delahaye 135 roadsters.

The Fondation Berliet (page 161) and Musée Henri Malartre (page 156) ensure that local makes are not forgotten, with displays of lorries from Berliet and cars such as Marcadier. Motorcycles are an important part

of the show, with recent displays showcasing the bikes made by Terrot, originally from Dijon, or Follis, which produced everything from bicycles to single-seat racing cars.

Practical information

🕐 November every year

🏠 Eurexpo, avenue Louis Blériot, 69686 Chassieu

🚡 Line T3 to Vaulx-en-Velin La Soie, then bus shuttle (100), or line T5 from Grange Blanche

🖼 45.731276 N, 4.951725 E

🌐 www.epoquauto.com

📞 +33 4 72 12 14 95

✉ epoquauto@les3a.com

Top: 1932 C4G saloon part of a large area devoted to Citroën's cars. / Quirky Newscooter prototype from Voisin. / Peugeot 404, courtesy of the Daltons!

British Car Show, Nantua

Modern Lotus owners team up by the lakeside. / Elementary, my dear Watson!

It would seem that lovers of British cars are drawn inescapably towards the water; like 'Les Anglaises Ont la Côte' in Bandol (page 111), or the Swiss Classic British Car Meeting in Morges, which these events are inspired by, this show is beautifully set on the water's edge. Halfway between Lyon and Geneva, the large lake at Nantua lies in the attractive Haut-Bugey area. As well as visiting the car show, you can go swimming or take a boat trip on the lake, or tuck into the local speciality, quenelles with a crayfish sauce.

Up to 400 cars and as many as 4000 visitors attend this friendly meeting, which features a sit-down lunch and live British music. It's open to all British makes, with strong contingents of MG, Triumph, Jaguar and Lotus cars. The event has been running for twenty years now, and each year one make or model is highlighted; in 2017 the show marks the 60th anniversary of the Lotus Seven. Best of all, however, is the fact that the organisers – from the local Kiwanis association – do a fantastic job each year raising money to help sick children.

Practical information

🕐 June every year

🏠 Avenue du Lac, 01130 Nantua

🖼 46.156429 N, 5.604118 E

🌐 www.hautbugey-tourisme. com

📞 + 33 7 81 27 02 83

✉ club.kiwanis.oyonnax. nantua@gmail.com

Gathering storm clouds reflected in the bonnet of this Jaguar XK150.

Chambéry Auto Rétro

NSU Wankel Spider on one of the club stands.

The show at Chambéry is one of the final events in the calendar for enthusiasts in the French Alps. The weather may already be cold and snowy, but this surprisingly busy show is well worth a detour. Nearly 8000 visitors come to see the displays of cars, motorbikes, parts and accessories, which are spread through four well-heated halls. Live music and book-signing sessions add to its appeal.

La Manivelle ('the starting handle'), the dynamic local association which organises the event, does a great job discovering unusual cars to put on show, choosing less frequently celebrated models like the Peugeot 403, 404 and 504 pick-ups or finding period racers like a 1964 Porsche 904 GTS. There are up to 100 cars to see, covering all periods from the earliest cars, like a 1914 Dodge, through to 'Youngtimers' such as a humble first-generation VW Golf GLS. Many exhibits are proof that you don't need to attend the biggest shows in Paris or Lyon to find historically interesting models; at the last show, for example, you could see a beautifully restored 1935 Peugeot 401 CL7 Cabriolet or a Zagato-bodied Alfa Romeo TZ 'Tubolare' from 1964.

Practical information

🕐 December every year

🏠 Parc des Expositions, Avenue du Grand Ariétaz, 73000 Chambéry

🖥 45.5839826 N, 5.8977291 E

🌐 www.chambery-autoretro. com

📞 +33 6 80 04 82 62

✉ info@chambery-autoretro. com or contact form on website

Proud owner next to his Peugeot 401 Cabriolet. / Alfa Romeo TZ 'Tubolare' attracted lots of attention.

Classic Days, Magny-Cours

An eclectic mix of cars gathering for the parade lap. / Crowds watch as Jean Ragnotti leaves the pits..

It took the circuit at Magny-Cours (page 196) a couple of tries to find the winning formula for a major historic event, but with Classic Days – which celebrates its tenth anniversary in 2017 – it has hit its stride. A central location (easily reached by the A77 autoroute), enthusiastic support from many clubs and, above all, the chance to drive or watch historic cars on the celebrated Formula 1 circuit, all make this event unmissable.

At the heart of the weekend is the time on track; cars are categorised by period, from prewar racers to the '70s, and put through their paces. There are demonstration laps by many historic race cars, with highlights like the 1974 Alpine A441 or the 1976 Inaltera driven by Jean Ragnotti.

But Classic Days is much more than just a track event: throughout the weekend spectators can admire more than 1500 cars in the paddock or visit a growing range of traders selling books and artwork. On Sunday, 800 cars take to the track for a giant fund-raising parade while historic planes fly overhead. Many clubs choose the event to celebrate major model anniversaries, like the 30th birthday of the Venturi or 50 years of the Ford Mustang.

Practical information

🕐 Late April/May every year

🏠 Circuit de Magny-Cours, 58470 Magny-Cours

🖼 46.860223 N, 3.162414 E

🌐 www.classic-days.fr

📞 +33 5 55 25 27 26

✉ classicdays@classic-days.fr

Flypast of historic planes all part of the show.

Coupe des Alpes

Lake Geneva, with one of its traditional paddle steamers. / Lancia Aurelia on the road. (Courtesy Rallystory)

Also known as the Alpine Rally, the Coupe des Alpes was one of the most prestigious rallies after the Second World War. It became renowned for its challenging route over Europe's mountain passes and the high standard set by its drivers, who came back year after year to try and win the Silver and Gold Cups.

For nearly thirty years, Rallystory has organised an up-market touring event inspired by the historic rallies of old. 200 participants from a dozen or more different countries set out each year from Évian-les-Bains on Lake Geneva – where you can see the cars on show before they leave – to drive across the Alps to Cannes. They take a different route each year and climb as many as 20 passes, reaching altitudes of up to 2700m (nearly 9000ft) on summits like the Col du Galibier or la Bonette.

The Coupe des Alpes is not a regularity event and there is no classification; instead, the emphasis is on enjoying some of the most beautiful roads in Europe and lavish meals in locations like the Château du Touvet. It regularly attracts prestigious historic GTs as well as the sports cars which took part in period.

Austin-Healey emerges from between the snowy rocks. (Courtesy Rallystory)

Practical information

🕐 June every year

🏠 (Start) Place de l'Eglise, 74500 Evian-les-Bains

🖥 46.401170 N, 6.587616 E

🌐 rallystory.com

📞 +33 1 42 12 07 08

✉ contact@rallystory.com

Museums

Shows & Tours

Market Place

Motorsport

Circuits

Embouteillage de Lapalisse

Participants wait to drive through the village. / Approaching the Château de La Palice.
(Both courtesy Thierry Dubois, www.nationale7.com)

Usually when a village which is a notorious traffic bottleneck is finally bypassed, the local mayor ceremonially cuts the ribbon and the old road is soon forgotten. The villagers of Lapalisse – on the famous Nationale 7 between Moulins and Lyon – had a different idea when their bypass opened in 2006. With the encouragement of Thierry Dubois, a well-known motoring artist and champion of the Nationale 7, they decided instead to reconstruct a monumental traffic jam, made up of cars from the 1950s and early '60s.

Since then, every other year – alternating with the Bouchon de Tourves in southern France (page 113) – as many as 900 cars meet in the shadow of the village's famous 16th century château to re-enact the chaos of the past. There are plenty of popular French family cars from the period, like the Citroën 2CV and DS, or Peugeot's 403 and 404, as well as Berliet trucks and publicity vehicles from the Tour de France cycle race. Many of the drivers and passengers dress to match their cars. If you want to find out more about this famous road, you can visit the Musée Mémoire de la Nationale 7 in Piolenc, further south.

Practical information

🕐 October, biennially (even years)

🏠 L'Aire des Vérités, 03120 Lapalisse

🖳 46.246952 N, 3.611554 E

🌐 www.lapalisse-tourisme.com/146_Nationale-7-Historique.html

📞 +33 4 70 99 08 39

✉ contact@lapalissetourisme.com

Even the police are in period cars and uniforms.
(Courtesy Thierry Dubois, www.nationale7.com)

Rallye Classic Forez

'For ladies and gentlemen, and epicureans.' Such is the proud device of this well-established regularity rally, which combines driving on unspoilt country roads with the pleasures of good food and wine. Over an extended three-day weekend, nearly 100 participants cover some 700km (430 miles), including 160km (100 miles) on a series of competitive regularity stages. It's open to cars first registered before 1980, with an additional category for just five newer GTs.

Far removed from the recent brouhaha over the changes to France's administrative regions, Forez was the name given to one of the provinces of France before the Revolution; it covers parts of the modern-day 'départements' of the Loire, Haute-Loire and Puy-de-Dôme. The Classic Forez usually

Stepping back in time … beautiful poster for a recent edition of the rally. (Courtesy Classic Forez Organisation)

begins from one of the small towns near Saint-Étienne, but the rally often reaches farther afield, into beautiful neighbouring areas like the Ardèche or Cantal. The itinerary frequently includes special stages from the Monte Carlo Rally (page 128) and historic motorsport venues like the circuit at Charade (page 189) or the hillclimb at Cacharat. And between their exertions, competitors can re-fuel with freshly made mushroom omelettes or local cheeses!

Renault 8 Gordini on the road. (Courtesy Classic Forez Organisation)

Practical information

🕐 September/October every year

🏠 (Start: 2017) 42660 Saint-Genest-Malifaux

🖥 45.341074 N, 4.459255 E

🌐 classic-forez.fr

📞 +33 6 50 900 901

✉ classic-forez@orange.fr

Rallye international des cathédrales

Waving off an MGC from the cathedral at Bourges. / On the road to Mont Saint-Michel. (Both courtesy TTP Organisation)

For many motorsport enthusiasts today, the name of this rally will be a forgotten memory. But wind the clock back to the contest's heyday from 1967-73, and it was one of the longest-distance sporting rallies in Europe, its competitors starting from as far away as Denmark and covering up to 7800km (4850 miles). As they passed by cathedrals on the way, they had to send telegrams to the organisers to confirm their passage – no mobile phones or Internet then!

The modern-day touring rally, which was revived in 1996, has maintained the concept of concentration runs, made famous by the Monte Carlo Rally (page 128). Participants choose to start from one of several cathedral cities, to converge at the end of the first day for a weekend tour. Each year the organisers choose a different route, finishing in areas as far afield as Brittany or Alsace. There are stops at historic châteaux along the way but also competitive regularity sessions. These take place both on the road – sometimes following a special stage from the Monte Carlo Rally or going over a twisting Alpine pass – and at racetracks like Lohéac (page 99) or the Anneau du Rhin (page 227).

Enjoying lunch in grand surroundings. (Courtesy TTP Organisation)

Practical information

🕐 September every year

🏠 Different route each year

🌐 www.ttp-org.fr

📞 +33 6 76 70 34 21

✉ ttp.organisation@ wanadoo.fr

Salon Rétro Course, Villefranche-sur-Saône

Museums

Shows & Tours

Market Place

Motorsport

Circuits

M635CSi part of centrepiece display of BMW's competition cars. / Celebrating a special guest at the show: Sylvie Seignobeaux.

This specialised show, covering historic motorsport of all kinds, got off to a flying start in 2012. Managed by the magazine of the same name, it provides an interesting mix of displays from event organisers, racing equipment suppliers, and the cars themselves. Each year's show brings out some exceptional sporting machinery: cars such as a Citroën Visa Lotus, not seen in public for 30 years, or an ex-works Triumph TR7 V8. For BMW's centenary year, competition models from a 700S to an M635CSi were on show. Other recent exhibits have included an exceptional Matra 610 'Coupé Napoléon' prototype (shown next to a historic Matra race transporter) and a celebration of CG's 50th anniversary.

There are activities, too, including a prize-giving ceremony for French amateur racing championships and regular visits from rallying champions of the past, including Ari Vatanen, Jean-Claude Andruet and Sylvie Seignobeaux.

The exhibition centre at Villefranche-sur-Saône is close to the A6 autoroute, allowing good access from south-eastern France and Switzerland. If you're coming from further afield, Villefranche is in the heart of the Beaujolais wine area, and the show usually takes place just a couple of weeks after the Beaujolais Nouveau is uncorked.

Practical information

🕐 End November/early December every year

🏠 ParcExpo, avenue de l'Europe, 69400 Villefranche-sur-Saône

📷 45.986432 N, 4.74382 E

🌐 www.retro-course.com

📞 +33 4 79 60 03 58

✉ salon.retrocourse@free.fr or contact form on website

Matra 610 'Coupé Napoléon' prototype.

Uriage Cabriolet Classic

Chapron-bodied Citroën DS & SM (Mylord) convertibles. / Inset top: 'Matching numbers' Porsche 914 in the concours d'élégance.

I f you're planning to drive down the wonderful Route Napoléon to the Côte d'Azur, the spa resort of Uriage-les-Bains, just outside Grenoble, could make a great starting point, with its pleasant central park and two-starred Michelin restaurant, Les Terrasses. Why not savour a gourmet lunch there and then enjoy this popular open-air show, which attracts 600 or more cars and as many as 7000 spectators?

The name is misleading, as the event is not limited to convertibles; owners of all cars at least 30 years old are welcome, and additional parking space is reserved for newer, upcoming classics. Participants can opt to join a road trip in the morning, and an aperitif offered by the mayor, but the main part of the show is the lively concours d'élégance after lunch. It's an informal event, owners presenting their cars to the accompaniment of a live jazz band and hamming it up for the public. But that doesn't stop visitors getting to see some fine cars, like a splendid Rolls-Royce 20/25 Sedanca De Ville or an exceptional Citroën SM Mylord with convertible bodywork by Chapron, of which a similar model sold at auction in Paris in 2014 for almost €550,000.

Prize-winning Citroën 15-Six from 1951.

Practical information

🕐 May every year

🏠 Route de Gières, Uriage-les-Bains, Vaulnaveys-le-Haut

🖥 45.14231 N, 5.829909 E

🌐 club.vag.free.fr

📞 +33 6 17 31 79 94

✉ club.vag@free.fr

Librairie mécanique, Lyon

I f you have come this far, it will come as no surprise to read that Lyon has a thriving community of car enthusiasts. No wonder, then, that this shop selling motoring books and scale models should have built its dedicated clientele over more than half a century. Today, Stéphane Bonnier and his sister carry forward the business which their father established in 1959.

Conveniently located in a side street a few minutes' walk from the busy shopping area around the Place Bellecour, the shop is deceptively large. On the ground floor there's a good selection of scale models, together with some kits and slot racing cars. The

The shop front in the rue de l'Ancienne Préfecture. (Courtesy Stéphane Bonnier)

range of books is impressive, with nearly 5000 titles in stock, mainly focusing on cars but also covering motorbikes, aviation and militaria. The majority of the books are in French, and French makes are especially well covered. But there are some English-language titles, too, and the shop regularly supplies customers abroad, as well as attending the annual Epoqu'Auto classic car show in the city (page 168). Upstairs there are two more rooms and the owners are looking to expand into car brochures and automobilia, such as original metal plaques.

Practical information

🕐 Open Monday 2-7pm and Tuesday-Saturday 9.30am-12.30pm and 2-7pm

🏠 6, rue de l'Ancienne Préfecture, 69002 Lyon

Ⓜ Lines A or D, Bellecour (also bus interchange)

🖼 45.761038 N, 4.832393 E

🌐 www.miniatures-lyon.com

📞 +33 4 78 42 40 11

✉ Contact form on website

There's an excellent range of books on offer, as well as a wide choice of models. (Courtesy Stéphane Bonnier)

Museums   Shows & Tours   Market Place   **Motorsport**   Circuits

Chinon Classic (Grand Prix de Tours)

Looking across the river to the château at Chinon. /
Pre-war Bentleys regular visitors to this event.
(Courtesy Grand Prix de Tours)

A new name and a new location for an old favourite! For many years, Michel Loreille and his team organised a popular event in Tours, commemorating the city's Grand Prix de l'ACF. originally held there in 1923. It was won by the British driver and later land speed record-holder Henry Segrave, at the wheel of a Sunbeam.

Unfortunately, the arrival of a modern tramway made it impossible to continue with the old route around the centre of Tours, so for 2016 the organisers moved 50km (30 miles) away to the medieval city of Chinon, on the banks of the Vienne. There, the formula which made the Grand Prix de Tours so enjoyable remains the same. On Saturday, participants follow a touring rally around the châteaux and gardens of the area. The highlight of the weekend comes on Sunday, with a busy series of demonstration laps, based around the place Jeanne d'Arc. Nearly 300 competitors take part, with plenty of prewar cars and British makes like Triumph, MG and Austin-Healey well represented. Italian sports cars, American classics and the marques which were originally built in Tours such as Rolland-Pilain all add to the variety.

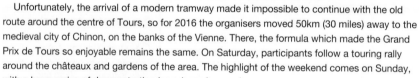

Practical information

🕐 June every year

🏠 Place Jeanne d'Arc, 37500 Chinon

📷 47.165372 N, 0.246379 E

🌐 www.grandprixdetours. com

✉ grandprixdetours@ wanadoo.fr

Waiting for the start ...

Grand Prix de l'Age d'Or, Dijon-Prenois

Maserati A6GCM in the paddock. / Simca 1000 Rallye owners gather in the club area.

Not just 'France's premier historic racing festival,' in the words of *Classic & Sports Car* magazine, the Grand Prix de l'Age d'Or is part of French motorsport history itself, dating back to 1964. After many years at Montlhéry, the race moved to Dijon in 2005 and has since been taken over by Peter Auto, the promoter of Le Mans Classic (page 88) and the Tour Auto (page 22).

For entrants, the weekend is a big-ticket event, the paddock filled with expensive transporters from the UK and Switzerland, as well as France. It attracts some of the top historic racers in Europe, who compete in races for sports prototypes of the 1970s, front- and rear-engined Grand Prix cars from the 1950s through to 1986, and for saloon cars and endurance racers from the 1960s to '80s. Fortunately, spectators can enjoy the event for much less money, and Dijon-Prenois (page 191) is an attractive location. You can sit on the terraces near the paddock or walk around to get a view of other parts of the track, like the famous climb up to the Pouas corner. There is a big club parking area to admire, too, with as many as 500 cars on show.

Practical information

🕐 June every year

🏠 Circuit de Dijon-Prenois, 21370 Prenois

🖼 47.362499 N, 4.899167 E

🌐 www.peterauto.peter.fr

📞 +33 1 42 59 73 40

✉ Contact form on website

Lotus and Cooper GP cars vie for position.

Grand Prix de France Historique, Magny-Cours

Matra F1 in the pits during an earlier event at Magny-Cours. / One of the Ligier F1 cars on show at the Conservatoire de la Monoplace Française at the circuit.

Home to 18 Formula 1 Grands Prix, the circuit at Magny-Cours (page 196) was the natural choice to welcome this ambitious new event, established with support from the FFSA (the French motorsport federation), HVM Racing and the local authorities. To this day, companies like Danielson, Oreca and Onroak are based nearby, while events like Classic Days (page 172) have drawn enthusiasts back to the track.

The Grand Prix de France Historique, however, has a much stronger focus on competition. Grouped into seven grids, the sessions on track will let fans enjoy some of the greatest racing cars from 1950 onwards, which also compete in historic races at Monaco, Spa or the Nürburgring. 50 Formula 1 cars are expected for the first edition, including front-engined F1 cars like the Maserati 250F or the rear-engined Lotus cars from the 1960s which compete in the HPGCA championship. Later F1 cars in the FIA Masters' Historic Championship will be joined by grids of Formula 2, Formula 3 and Formula Ford Historics, not forgetting GTs and sports prototypes which took part in endurance races from 1962-74.

Practical information

🕐 July biennially (first edition in 2017)

🏠 58470 Magny-Cours

🖥 46.860223 N, 3.162414 E

🌐 www. grandprixdefrancehistorique.fr

📞 +33 3 86 21 80 00

✉ info@circuitmagnycours. com

1974 Alpine A441, driven here at Magny-Cours by Jean-Charles Rédélé.

I-Way, Lyon

One of the Formula 1 simulators. / Looking down on the rally simulators.
(Both courtesy I-Way Lyon)

-Way is a motorsport experience like no other. The only centre of its kind in France, I-Way lets you enjoy some of the most sophisticated driving simulators in the world. 12 full-size simulators, six for Formula 1 (completely updated at the end of 2015) and six for rallying (based on Citroën C2 rally cars), provide full six-way movement, using highly sophisticated software based on aeronautical research. A newly added Grand Prix motorbike simulator adds to the thrills on offer.

Whichever you choose, the results are incredible. As the simulators lift you above the floor and you look across the multiple surround screens, you'll experience loads of up to 2G and sound levels of 105dB – more than the maximum allowed by many real-life circuits! No wonder that the BBC's *Top Gear* called it "the closest thing to a real racer mere mortals can get their hands on ..."

I-Way isn't cheap, but the centre offers a good range of different packages. In its first three years, would-be champions covered over 2.6 million kilometres (1.6 million miles) in 130,000 races. And whilst your stomach settles between races, you can enjoy the bar and restaurant on site.

Practical information

🕐 Open all year, reserve sessions online or by phone

🏠 4, rue Jean Marcuit, 69009 Lyon

🖥 45.7889 N, 4.813913 E

🌐 www.i-way-world.com

📞 +33 4 37 50 28 70

✉ contact@i-way.fr

Experiencing a rally simulator. (Courtesy I-Way)

Museums

Shows & Tours

Market Place

Motorsport

Circuits

Trophée Andros, Super-Besse

Jockeying for position at the corner. (Courtesy Trophée Andros/B Bade) / Adrien Tambay driving one of the cars specially developed by Mazda for the championship. (Courtesy Mazda)

For motorsport fans from countries with no tradition of racing on ice, it may seem hard to understand the passion which the Trophée Andros generates. When Max Mamers, a former competitor at Le Mans, created this championship in 1990, his ambition was to make it the Formula 1 of ice racing. 25 years later, motorsport enthusiasts and winter holidaymakers alike flock to the weekend race meetings held in ski resorts across the Alps, or at Super-Besse in the Massif Central.

The spectacle of watching the cars slither around the tight ice circuits is only part of this event's appeal. Over the years, many of the greatest names in motor racing have fought for honours in the Trophée, none more so than the former F1 champion Alain Prost, or the touring car ace, Yvan Muller, who won the championship ten times. All the cars in the Trophée run to a standard specification, with four-wheel drive and steering, 3-litre six-cylinder engines and 6-speed sequential transmissions. In 2007, however, the organisers added the first ever all-electric race; the cars' constantly evolving electric technology helps the sport present a positive environmental attitude to the public.

Practical information

🕐 December to end January every year

🏠 Super-Besse, 63610 Besse-et-Saint-Anastaise

🖥 45.505192 N, 2.855751 E

🌐 www.tropheeandros.com

📞 +33 5 55 25 03 03

✉ Contact form on website (during season)

Kicking up the snow at Val Thorens. (Courtesy Mazda)

Vichy Classic
(Grand Prix de Vichy)

Poster for the original Grand Prix in 1934.
(Courtesy Belles mécaniques en Bourbonnais)

You may be forgiven for thinking that every town in France seems to have had its Grand Prix! Vichy's turn came in 1934, when its one and only Grand Prix was won by Count Felice Trossi driving an Alfa Romeo P3. Over the past decade, the energetic local club, the Belles mécaniques en Bourbonnais, has organised this revival event, originally known as the Grand Prix de Vichy. Whilst the airstrip at Charmeil may lack the charm of some of the races held on city streets, its main straight of 1.2km (0.75 miles) lets the boldest drivers reach speeds of almost 200km/h (125mph).

The organisers do a great job attracting a varied range of entrants, lining up grids for motorbikes as well as cars. Not least amongst these are the prewar competition cars it attracts, with demonstrations by Alfa Romeo 6Cs and 8Cs and successive generations of Bugatti. Fans of more recent racing cars can enjoy demonstrations by star drivers such as Henri Pescarolo and Jacques Laffite, who drove a Ligier JS 53 at the last edition of the event. Tucked away in the paddocks you'll find many rare models, like a Ferry 'barquette' from 1957 or a British Elva from the 1960s.

Bugattis on track. (Courtesy Belles mécaniques en Bourbonnais)

Practical information

🕐 June biennially (odd years)

🏠 Aérodrome de Vichy-Charmeil, 03110 Charmeil

🚌 Shuttle from Vichy city centre to the aerodrome

🗺 46.168431 N, 3.402998 E

🌐 www.belles-mecaniques.com

✉ Contact form on website

Circuit de l'Auxois Sud, Meilly-sur-Rouvres

To some extent, the Circuit de l'Auxois Sud, 40km (25 miles) west of Dijon, exists in the shadow of its famous neighbour at Dijon-Prenois (page 191). Unlike that track, however, this circuit, which opened in 1995, was never designed with competition in mind or homologated for racing. For club events and driver training, however, it's certainly not without interest.

Built next to the aerodrome of Pouilly-Maconge, the circuit is

Ferrari and Lamborghini rides offered by GT VIP. (Courtesy GT VIP).

flat and pretty short at just 1.5km (0.9 miles). It makes up for this with its main straight of 400m (440yd), which enables drivers to build up a decent speed, and a mix of faster and slower corners, including a particularly tricky banked left-hander and a tight hairpin. It was partially resurfaced in 2013.

The detailed calendar on the circuit's website gives a good feel for the range of activities on offer, which includes numerous open days for cars and motorbikes, and courses in GT cars run by partners such as GT VIP. The track can also be reserved (at reasonable rates) for exclusive use by clubs; Alpine, BMW and Simca are among those to have enjoyed it.

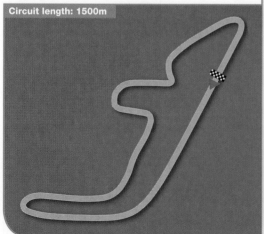

Circuit length: 1500m

Practical information

🕐 Open from end February–mid-December; summer closure in August

🏠 21320 Meilly-sur-Rouvres

🗺 47.223446 N, 4.555737 E

🌐 www.circuit-auxois-sud.fr

📞 +33 3 80 64 98 84

✉ contact@circuit-auxois-sud.fr

Circuit du Bourbonnais, Montbeugny

A few kilometres outside Moulins, this circuit opened in 2009 on the site of the city's aerodrome. Its location ensures that the track is flat, and its layout is relatively simple, but the wide run-off areas make it a safe place for track day novices to build up experience. Altogether it is 2.3km (1.4 miles) in length,

View of the track from the main building.

with six right-hand corners, two left-handers and two left-right 'S' bends. It can also be split into two smaller loops for individual training sessions.

Drifting is one of the specialities of the circuit, which can be artificially watered, and training sessions are available in a Nissan 370 Z or a bruising Chevrolet Camaro SS. If you'd prefer not to slide quite as much, Nicolas Schatz, the circuit's resident trainer, also offers classes in a DS3 Racing. A multiple French championship winner, Schatz has taken a Formula 3000 single-seater round the track in just 57.3 seconds.

A sign of the times, the circuit is developing a range of activities using electrically-powered karts and sports cars. Regular open days, karting sessions and club events complete the programme of activities at the track.

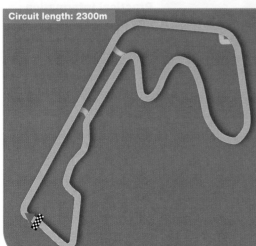

Circuit length: 2300m

Practical information

🕐 Open all year, but check calendar on website

🏠 Aérodrome de Moulins, 03340 Montbeugny

🖥 46.53722 N, 3.43 E

🌐 www.circuitdubourbonnais.com

📞 +33 4 70 34 80 02

✉ Contact form on website

Circuit de Bresse, Frontenaud

The Circuit de Bresse is one of the easiest venues to get to in this region, just 500m (550yd) from exit 9 of the A39 autoroute. Its tastefully restored Club House dates back to the 17th century, but everything else about this circuit is right up to date. It's a modern, well equipped circuit, with its own safety team and 15 individual pits. The track itself is well surfaced and provides wide run-off areas for safety. 3km (1.9 miles) in length, it's homologated by

Early Mustang coupé cornering hard.

the FFSA for speeds over 200km/h (125mph). In practice though, much of the time speeds are much lower; although flat, it's a demanding, technical circuit featuring many challenging corners, such as the 180° Anjou bend and the Autoroute hairpin.

Several schools offer courses at the track, presenting a range of modern GTs and such exotics as an Aston Martin V8 Vantage. It's also available for open days and club events; owners of Caterham, Lotus and Ford Mustangs have all enjoyed time on the track. The high-speed circuit is only one of the facilities available; you'll also find a karting track and a large road safety training area, featuring special low-grip surfaces and steep inclines.

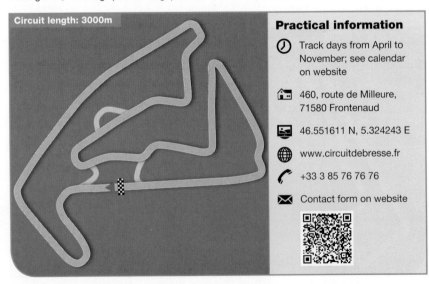

Circuit length: 3000m

Practical information

🕐 Track days from April to November; see calendar on website

🏠 460, route de Milleure, 71580 Frontenaud

📧 46.551611 N, 5.324243 E

🌐 www.circuitdebresse.fr

📞 +33 3 85 76 76 76

✉ Contact form on website

Circuit de Charade

Porsche 911s enjoying time on track. / Aerial view of the circuit. (Both courtesy Circuit de Charade)

Stirling Moss famously called it "the most beautiful circuit in the world." 800m (2600ft) above sea level, the track at Charade was built around the site of an extinct volcano and nestles deep in the countryside of the Auvergne. The original circuit was opened in 1958 and four Formula 1 Grands Prix were held here between 1965 and 1972. Sometimes known as the French Nürburgring, the modern circuit has been shortened in length to 4km (2.5 miles), but still features 18 corners and gradients of up to 9%. As challenging as it is beautiful to drive, it needs an agile car; a contemporary Lotus Elise would be just the ticket!

After threats to close it, the circuit was taken over by the regional authorities in 2012. Despite some pressure over noise levels in the area, it has re-established a programme of historic events, including the HistoRacing Festival. This attracts a great line-up of saloon and sports car racers from the 1960s and '70s. There are open track days and an informal meeting for owners of classic cars every month in summer. The circuit can be hired for club days and is unusual in offering special courses for aspiring track driving instructors.

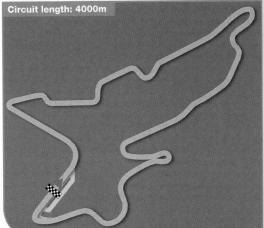

Circuit length: 4000m

Practical information

🕐 Open all year. May close in winter during adverse weather

🏠 Rond-point de Manson, 63122 Saint-Genès-Champanelle

🗺 45.747058 N, 3.023606 E

🌐 www.charade.fr

📞 +33 4 73 295 295

✉ infos@charade.fr

Museums

Shows & Tours

Market Place

Motorsport

Circuits

Circuit de La Châtre

The history of motorsport at La Châtre dates back to 1928, when the first races were held on part of the road from La Châtre to Châteauroux (now the D943). Over the next 25 years, hill climbs and races for cars, motorbikes and sidecars all took place there, before the town decided to establish a permanent track, which opened in 1956. For many years, the circuit staged rounds in the French and European Formula 3 championships. Often considered the way into Formula 1, these races saw future champions like Jean-Pierre Beltoise, Jackie Stewart and Alain Prost all compete at La Châtre.

Today this verdant circuit is home to many amateur motorsport events, some of which raise money for local charities. Among the best known are the regional slalom championships, the Slaloms du Boischaut, which culminate in a final in September. The track also holds regular mid-week open days and is available for clubs to hire; local Caterham, Porsche and Renault enthusiasts all come back often, and the twentieth anniversary of the Renault 21 Turbo was celebrated here. The driving school Euroformula offers courses at the wheel of its 210bhp Formula Renault 2000 single-seaters, lasting from a few hours to two full days. For drivers, the circuit is very short, just 1.1km (0.7 miles), and rather slow. It is, however, quite a challenging and technical track, which is best suited to smaller cars like the R8 Gordini and newer 'hot hatches.' For the slalom events, chicanes are added to the track.

Circuit length: 1100m

Practical information

🕐 Main season from March to November

🏠 Route de Bourges, 36400 La Châtre

🗺 46.5929 N, 2.006748 E

🌐 www.circuitdelachatre.fr

📞 +33 2 54 48 33 64

✉ aubrun.sassier@wanadoo.fr

Circuit de Dijon-Prenois

Some of the stars from the circuit's impressive past. / Waiting to enter the track during the Grand Prix de l'Age d'Or.

Deep in the Burgundy countryside, Dijon-Prenois is one of France's greatest circuits. In 2012, the year of its fortieth anniversary, the French magazine *Sport Auto* gave it a full five-star rating. 3.8km (2.4 miles) long, the track was designed for Formula 1 races and has many fast corners, but it's also hilly, reaching a maximum gradient of 11%. In all, it makes for a challenging drive, which is well suited to powerful cars. Indeed, the track experiences on offer at Dijon go all the way up to passenger rides in a specially adapted three-seater 700bhp Formula 1 car!

Dijon-Prenois has a rich motorsport history and staged seven French Grands Prix from 1974-84. It was here that Renault scored its first victory in Formula 1, and here again that Alain Prost won his first Grand Prix. The circuit continues to present some of the most enjoyable historic motorsport events in France, the Grand Prix de l'Age d'Or (page 181), the Coupes Moto Légende and the Dijon Motors Cup among them. It's a great track for spectators too, with improved facilities for the 2017 season and a series of informative panels telling the circuit's history all around the track.

Circuit length: 3800m

Practical information

🕐 Open all year (see calendar on website)

🏠 21370 Prenois

🖼 47.362499 N, 4.899167 E

🌐 www.circuit-dijon-prenois.com

📞 +33 3 80 35 32 22

✉ Contact form on website

Museums

Shows & Tours

Market Place

Motorsport

Circuits

Circuit d'Issoire (CEERTA) & Auverdrive

Aerial view of the circuit. / Porsche 911 GT3 RS on track. (Both courtesy CEERTA)

Half an hour's drive south from Clermont-Ferrand, the complex at Issoire is more than just a circuit. The track itself opened in 1991, and is 2.5km (1.6 miles) long. Relatively flat, it has only seven corners, but the main straight of 1000m (1100yd) gives powerful cars room enough to open up. There are regular open days and courses available in cars from a Peugeot 208 GTi or RCZ-R up to the latest supercars like a Ferrari 488GTB and a McLaren MP4-12C. Alongside the tarmac track there are dedicated areas for karting, trail bikes and four-wheel drives.

What makes the site at Issoire special, however, is the facility alongside the track, known as Auverdrive. This opened in 2009, and was conceived by the former rally driver popularly known as Tchine. There are meeting rooms, and a bar and terrace overlooking the circuit. Above all, Auverdrive houses Tchine's personal collection of 30 cars, which is open to the public a a few days each year and includes historic rally cars – like the Lancia Delta Integrale with which Miki Biasion won the Monte Carlo Rally in 1989, or the Toyota Celica which Carlos Sainz took to victory there two years later.

Practical information

🕐 See website for current dates

🏠 Z.I. de Lavaur, rue Albert de Dion, 63500 Issoire

🖥 45.535709 N, 3.261676 E

🌐 www.ceerta.com and www.auverdrive.net

📞 +33 4 73 55 56 56 (circuit) and +33 4 73 54 29 29 (Auverdrive)

✉ Contact form on each website

Circuit length: 2500m

Circuit du Laquais, Champier

Aerial view of the circuit. / Lamborghini at speed on the track. (Both courtesy Circuit du Laquais)

Claimed to be the largest track in the Rhône-Alpes region, the Circuit du Laquais is halfway between Lyon and Grenoble. The owners are sensitive to the circuit's beautiful environment and noise regulations are strictly enforced, so check online first if your car is particularly exuberant. Various configurations are possible, but the complete track, opened in 1993, is 3km (1.9 miles). It's fairly flat and there's no really long straight, but the track is nonetheless homologated by the FFSA for speeds in excess of 200km/h (125mph) and offers a good mix of slower and faster sections. The circuit's own magazine provides excellent notes on driving each part of the track.

The circuit is relatively expensive for clubs to hire, but there are frequent open days and a good range of driving courses. Le Laquais maintains its own fleet of nearly 50 cars (and 25 karts), so there's plenty of choice, from the compact Renault Clio and Mégane RS, to the latest Ford Mustang GT or McLaren 540C. During the track's winter closure, the instructors move to the ski resort at the Val d'Isère, where they offer driving courses on the ice circuit there.

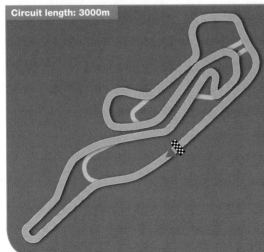

Circuit length: 3000m

Practical information

🕐 Open from mid-February to mid-December

🏠 931, route du Bailly, 38260 Champier

📷 45.466623 N, 5.296843 E

🌐 laquais-stage-de-pilotage.com

📞 +33 4 74 54 46 98

✉️ info@circuitdulaquais.com

Museums

Shows & Tours

Market Place

Motorsport

Circuits

Circuit de Lurcy-Lévis

Lurcy-Lévis is one of the fastest circuits in France, if not in Europe. Homologated by the FIA to Formula 1 standards, its main straight is wide and long (18m/59ft by 1500m/1640yd). Built in 1989, the track is regularly used by car manufacturers and racing teams for high-speed testing: standing-start acceleration and braking on the straight, and handling on the other

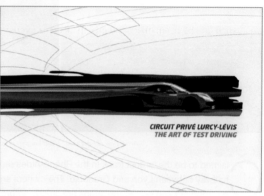

CIRCUIT PRIVÉ LURCY-LÉVIS
THE ART OF TEST DRIVING

Striking image of a Lotus. (Courtesy Circuit de Lurcy-Lévis)

sections of the track. It can be configured in five different ways, with particular layouts – from 1.1 to 4.2km (0.7 to 2.6 miles) – designed for specific measures such as deceleration testing or evaluating downforce. The entire circuit is surrounded by grass, limiting the risk of damage, despite the high speeds which are possible.

The confidentiality needed for these tests places some limits on the track's availability for private enthusiasts, and there are presently no open track days. It can, however, be rented by clubs and is used by training companies such as Euroformula, Elite Racing and Cascadevents. The variety of courses they offer lets you choose a wide range of the latest supercars, or – when space is available – test your own car to the limits.

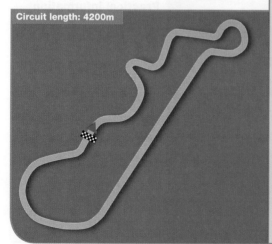

Circuit length: 4200m

Practical information

🕐 Open all year, by reservation only

🏠 Route du Circuit, 03320 Lurcy-Lévis

🖥 46.718107 N, 2.948787 E

🌐 www.circuit-lurcy-levis.com

📞 +33 4 70 67 82 29

✉ Contact form on website

Museums

Shows & Tours

Market Place

Motorsport

Circuits

Circuit de Lyon

The Circuit de Lyon is probably one of the less well known circuits in this region, but shouldn't be overlooked. The only track in the Lyon area approved by the FFSA, it's easy to reach from the city centre or the nearby airport (Lyon Saint-Exupéry). The circuit opened in 2007 and has the high level of equipment you would expect of a modern facility, with extensive lighting around the whole track allowing it to be used at night. The reception building offers a welcoming bar and a heated terrace overlooking the track.

Unusually, the circuit at Saint Laurent de Mûre is managed by a driving school, Axelera GT. Although it runs courses at the Circuit de Bresse (page 188) as well, this is its home base. Courses available here include single, dual and multi-car packages, enabling you to compare high-performance models in a demanding but safe environment. Their fleet is modern and offers plenty of choice; from a Ferrari 458 Italia and Lamborghini Gallardo LP560, to a Nissan GTR and Porsche Cayman S. The 1.7km (1.1 miles) circuit is also used by clubs and by local car dealerships for customer demonstration events.

The asphalt track is part of a bigger complex, centred on the 1200m (1300yd) karting circuit, which is open every day. You can combine a driving course with time in a kart, or come back and enjoy watching one of the competitive karting races which are held throughout the season, including a 24-hour race in June each year.

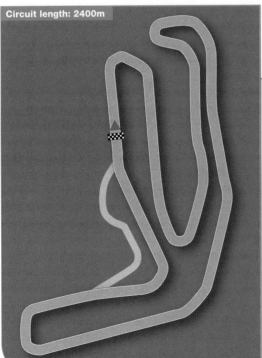

Circuit length: 2400m

Practical information

🕐 Open February to December (see website for details)

🏠 Chemin de Fournéa, 69720 Saint Laurent de Mûre

🖼 45.681937 N, 5.076042 E

🌐 www.axelera-stage-pilotage.fr

📞 +33 4 82 53 53 53

✉ Contact form on website

Museums

Shows & Tours

Market Place

Motorsport

Circuits

195

Circuit de Magny-Cours

Packed grid in this GT Tour race. / Overview of the Formula 1 circuit. (Both courtesy Circuit de Magny-Cours)

Together with Charade (page 189) and Dijon-Prenois (page 191), Magny-Cours is one of the most famous circuits in this region, and one of the most prestigious in France. Soon after it opened in 1961, it became an important motorsport venue. In the late 1980s it was completely re-designed and brought up to Formula 1 standards; from 1991 until 2008 it hosted the F1 Grand Prix de France. For 2017 the main buildings have again been completely renovated.

To this day, the 4.4km (2.7 miles) Grand Prix circuit, with its corners named after other famous racetracks of the world, is an unforgettable drive. You can take courses on the main circuit in GTs and even Formula 1 cars, but one of the best ways to experience it is by taking part in events like Classic Days (page 172), or watching participants in the Tour Auto (page 22) or Rallye de Paris (page 29) charge past.

Since 2003 enthusiasts have also been able to drive on its smaller Club circuit. At 2.5km (1.6 miles), its length compares well with many other circuits. With its tight corners before the main straight and artificially watered surface, it can be a challenging track in its own right.

Circuit length: 4400m (Grand Prix circuit)

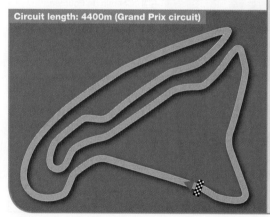

Practical information

🕐 Open all year (see calendar on website)

🏠 58470 Magny-Cours

🖼 46.860223 N, 3.162414 E

🌐 www.circuitmagnycours. com

📞 +33 3 86 21 80 00

✉ Contact form on website

Circuit de Mornay, Bonnat

Deep in the rural 'département' of the Creuse, the Circuit de Mornay is a delightful place to visit. When it compared the racetracks of France a couple of years ago, the French magazine *Sport Auto* had no hesitation in giving it top marks for its beautiful setting, the undulating and technically challenging track and the welcome of its hosts.

The author's Ford Mustang GT beside the château at Mornay

The circuit was established by Pierre Petit, a successful former racer, who was the French Formula 3 champion in 1982 and went on to achieve pole position at Le Mans in 1995. It has been designed to stretch drivers' skills, with a carefully structured ten-level training programme, inviting participants to progress from the basics of track driving to the champagne of a podium finish! The school utilises its own Formula Renault 1700 and 2000 cars, which can reach a top speed of 250km/h (155mph). The track is also used by the motoring press and manufacturers, and can be hired by clubs for members' events. The beautiful 15th century château has a large restaurant and a billiard room in which to relax after a day on track.

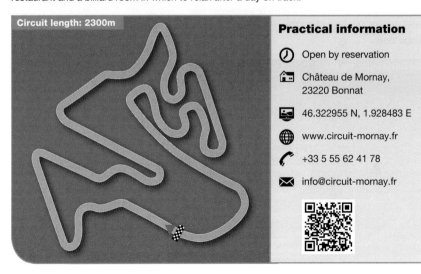

Circuit length: 2300m

Practical information

🕐 Open by reservation

🏠 Château de Mornay, 23220 Bonnat

🖼 46.322955 N, 1.928483 E

🌐 www.circuit-mornay.fr

📞 +33 5 55 62 41 78

✉ info@circuit-mornay.fr

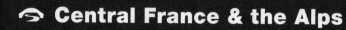

Circuit de Thurigneux

25km (16 miles) north of Lyon, the circuit at Saint Jean de Thurigneux is one of the smaller tracks in this region. Just 1.3km (0.8 miles) in length, it lacks a decent straight and has a tortuous, twisty layout, reminiscent of a rally stage. The surface is uneven, but that too contributes to the experience. The organisers have made the most of these limitations, with one theme, 'la maîtrise de la glisse' (mastering slides), the common denominator of all the activities proposed.

At its simplest level, this means a focus on safe driving and car control in low-grip conditions. You can learn the rudiments of controlling slides in specially equipped cars, safe in the knowledge that there is no risk of major damage, thanks to the grass all around the circuit.

As you move up the scale, however,

Dodge Viper, seen here at the Val de Vienne circuit.

the training cars – which include a BMW 135i and Nissan 350Z – become more powerful, and the emphasis shifts to understanding oversteer and mastering the experience of sliding for pleasure. To finish your day, you can enjoy a drive or passenger ride in the circuit's Maserati 4200GT or massively powerful Dodge Viper.

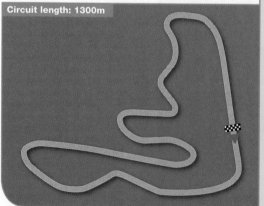

Circuit length: 1300m

Practical information

🕐 Open all year, except in August

🏠 801, chemin du Mont, 01390 Saint Jean de Thurigneux

📺 45.951057 N, 4.870978 E

🌐 www. circuitautothurigneux.fr

📞 +33 4 74 00 89 14

✉ stacs@wanadoo.fr

Vaison Piste, Torcy

Readers with long memories and an interest in rallycross might recognise the address of this circuit. Many years ago, there was a rallycross circuit on this site, and Christophe Vaison, who established this new circuit (now a conventional tarmac track) a couple of years ago, in fact competed in his first rallycross event here back in 1987. Located in the southern part of Burgundy, Vaison Piste is easily accessible from the A6 'autoroute' or by high-speed train (Le Creusot TGV station is nearby).

Panhard, one of the clubs to have visited the track; this PL17 was seen at Nogaro.

Like many tracks today, the circuit at Torcy offers driver training (with a focus on safety and eco-driving) for the general public and a range of courses and events for the enthusiast. The track is 2km (1.2 miles) in length and 10m (33ft) wide, and can be configured in two different layouts. Pits with space for 10 cars and a reception building complete the facilities available.

The circuit arranges a series of performance driving courses from March to November, whilst open track days – for cars, motorbikes and karts – are organised throughout the year. Clubs are welcome to hire the venue for their exclusive use, with recent visitors including a group of 50 classic Panhards.

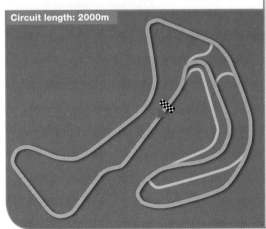

Circuit length: 2000m

Practical information

🕐 See opening dates on website

🏠 Route Centre à Centre, Zone Industrielle, 71210 Torcy

🗺 46.762528 N, 4.442545 E

🌐 vaisonpiste.com

📞 + 33 3 85 57 64 85

✉ info@vaisonpiste.com

Circuits du Val de Loire, Thenay

By its managers' own admission, this circuit is somewhat out of the ordinary. It was originally built in the early 1990s as part of the research and development centre for Hobbycar, a short-lived manufacturer of amphibious vehicles powered by engines from Peugeot-Citroën. Understandably, therefore, the circuit has no sporting heritage and has never been approved to hold competitive events. It is, however, available to

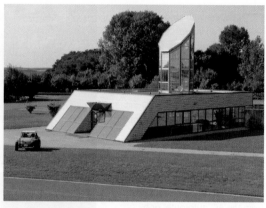

The Club House at the circuit. (Courtesy Circuits du Val de Loire)

manufacturers who wish to test or demonstrate new cars, and welcomes car clubs looking for somewhere different to meet, or stop off during a touring rally. Renault Classic and Volkswagen Beetle owners have both chosen it for their events, and it has even been featured on the popular television programme *Zéro de conduite*, similar to *Britain's Worst Driver*.

Thenay is about 2 hours' drive from Paris, close to some of the famous Loire châteaux like Blois or Chaumont. In a pleasant rural setting, the site features karting and earth tracks, and an artificial lake which was originally used to demonstrate the amphibious capabilities of the Hobbycar. Next to the 2km (1.2 miles) asphalt track, the modern Club House can be used for receptions or serve as a base to explore the region.

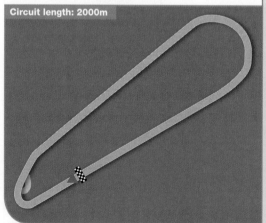

Circuit length: 2000m

Practical information

🕐 Open by reservation

🏠 Route de Contres, 41400 Thenay

🗺 47.392676 N, 1.300183 E

🌐 www.circuitsvaldeloire.fr

📞 +33 6 40 33 93 93

✉ patrick@circuitsvaldeloire.fr

North-East France

Saving the best till last? The north-east corner of France may not enjoy the balmy weather of the Mediterranean, or have the rugged coastal scenery of Brittany, but there's plenty here to make your trip an enjoyable one.

If you're coming from the Channel ports, Germany or Switzerland, many of the places in this region are an easy journey, and there are some fantastic driving roads in Alsace.

Every car enthusiast has to visit Mulhouse at least once, to tour the greatest car museum in France, the Cité de l'Automobile. The impressive Peugeot museum at Sochaux is only 45 minutes' drive away, so there's plenty to enjoy during a long weekend.

Some of the countless Bugattis on show at the Cité de l'Automobile in Mulhouse.

The old Grand Prix circuit outside Reims must be one of the most photographed motorsport locations in France, but it has a magic all of its own. If you're driving through the Champagne region, there's an interesting car museum in Reims and good classic shows throughout the year, in Reims itself and at Laon and Troyes. Closer to Paris, the famous château at Chantilly is now home to one of Europe's most prestigious concours d'élégance, a lavish late summer weekend which all the family can enjoy.

Morgans passing through the old streets of Laon. / 1903 White Rear-Entry Tonneau at Chantilly.

Contents

Cité de l'Automobile, Mulhouse

Postwar sports cars amid the famous lamp posts of the main hall, with a unique 1959 Alart in the foreground.

The entrance to the museum. (Courtesy Musée national de l'automobile collection Schlumpf Mulhouse)

f you visit just one museum in this guide, then the Cité de l'Automobile – often referred to as the Schlumpf Collection – has to be the one. Claimed to be the biggest automotive museum in the world, it houses an extraordinary collection of more than 400 cars.

The museum's history is the stuff of legend. Over twenty years, the wealthy Schlumpf brothers set out on an extraordinary buying spree, acquiring 120 Bugattis

The new outdoor demonstration and practice track.

Museums

Shows & Tours

Market Place

Motorsport

Circuits

alone. After their textile business went bust in 1976, amazed employees discovered the unbelievable treasure trove they had amassed. A huge effort ensued to save the collection, which opened in 1982 as the Musée national de l'automobile.

One of the outstanding Bugatti Royales in the Masterpieces area.

The museum is split into three main areas, covering the story of the car from its beginnings to the modern day, motor racing, and an unrivalled display of pre-war masterpieces. Each area is outstanding, with many unique cars that can only be seen here, such as the Germain Lambert collection acquired recently, or the staggering range of Formula 1 and Le Mans racers, including a 1937 Mercedes W125 and a 1957 Maserati 250F. But even these are just a taster before you see the extraordinary show of pre-war coachbuilt luxury models, the three Bugatti Royales, and further gems from Hispano-Suiza, Voisin and Rolls-Royce. If you last visited Mulhouse a few years ago, it's well worth returning to see the new entrance building and engine gallery, or watch the cars in action on the outside track, which opened in 2011.

Practical information

🕐 Open every day except 25 December: see website for hours

🏠 15, rue de l'Epée, 68100 Mulhouse

🚋 Line T1, Musée de l'Auto

🚌 Line 10, Musée de l'Auto

🖥 47.7593664 N, 7.3316288 E

🌐 www.citedelautomobile.com

📞 +33 3 89 33 23 23

Historic Formula 1 and Le Mans cars line up in the Motor Racing hall.

Museums

Shows & Tours

Market Place

Motorsport

Circuits

L'Aventure Peugeot, Sochaux

Peugeot 505 Coupé and Convertible prototypes in front of the museum. (Courtesy Peugeot) / From the origins of the car until 1904; some of the earliest cars on show.

Peugeot is the only major French manufacturer whose history can be enjoyed in a museum open full-time to the public. With its Art Nouveau décor and mosaic floors, the museum is stylishly laid out, and there's plenty to enjoy, even if you don't own a Peugeot. The displays show 150 Peugeot cars in period settings over more than a century, right up to the latest concept cars and the 908 HDi which won at Le Mans in 2009. The stars include Peugeot's first ever petrol-engined car, a Vis-à-vis from 1891, and a 1934 601D Éclipse with its innovative folding hardtop. The museum was extended in 2000 and again in 2010, allowing Peugeot more space for an impressive line-up of its competition cars, like the World Rally Championship-winning 205 T16.

The Peugeot business goes back to well before the age of the car, and there are exhibits of its cycles and household appliances, such as the pepper mills still used by many families today. Regularly changing temporary displays, a brasserie and a well-stocked shop complete the museum tour. You can also arrange to visit the nearby car plant, whilst members of the Aventure Peugeot can gain access to a wealth of archive material.

Original advertising photograph for the Peugeot 404. (Courtesy L'Aventure Peugeot)

Practical information

🕐 Open every day 10am-6pm, except 25 December and 1 January

🏠 Carrefour de l'Europe, 25600 Sochaux

🚌 Line 2 from Montbéliard train station to Musée Peugeot

🖥 47.516269 N, 6.831445 E

🌐 www.museepeugeot.com

📞 +33 3 81 99 42 03

✉ Contact form on website

Museums

Shows & Tours

Market Place

Motorsport

Circuits

Les Brigades de l'Aa, Ouve-Wirquin

Tucked away in a sleepy corner of the Pas-de-Calais, this small museum was set up by a local association 20 years ago. Housed in an old red-brick industrial building, the rather crowded collection includes about 50 cars as well as a large number of motorbikes and scooters. The range of cars on show at any time changes as the cars belonging to club members come and go, but typically includes models from the early 1900s until about 1980. Their condition varies, too, but there are nonetheless some interesting cars which are rarely seen in French collections.

The major French manufacturers are well represented; the Citroëns on show, for example, include a slightly shabby DS in the rare ministerial specification with an

Looking down on part of the collection. / From one of the last horse-drawn buggies, to relatively affordable pre-war cars.

internal division and a 1950s 2CV with the enlarged boot offered as an accessory in period. But there are also cars from Germany, like the unusual six-cylinder Opel cabriolet (which is in better condition), or from England, in the imposing form of a 1959 Princess Vanden Plas limousine. Grouped together nearby is a small collection of ex-police cars, ranging from a Renault Juvaquatre through to a Simca 1100.

Practical information

🕐 Open May-September, on Sunday and bank holidays from 10AM-6PM, and for groups by reservation

🏠 2 rue du Moulin, 62380 Ouve-Wirquin

🗺 50.659372 N, 2.155947 E

🌐 www.lesbrigadesdelaa.com

📞 + 33 6 21 20 13 80

✉ Contact form on website

At the other end of the scale: 1959 Princess Vanden Plas limousine.

Museums

Shows & Tours

Market Place

Motorsport

Circuits

Musée Automobile Le garage de mon père, Laon

CX, GS and DS models among the many Citroëns on show. / Hervé Boutelier next to some of the cars in the museum.

In just a few years, Hervé Boutelier has built up this collection of 90 cars from the 1950s to the 1990s. In 2015, it moved from the Picardy countryside to its new home in Laon, where there is more room to display the cars. It has struck a chord with many enthusiasts who know the cars on show from their childhood. Popular family cars from French manufacturers form an important part of the collection, but there are many other European, American and even Japanese makes represented, too. The cars on display are in their original, unrestored condition, but most of them are in good running order and are regularly driven.

Each car in the museum seems to have a story behind it: an authentic Ford Gran Torino from the television series *Starsky & Hutch*, a Mercedes W124 left to the museum by its showbiz owner, a Range Rover which Franz Hummel drove single-handed across Africa, or one of the last Cadillacs assembled in Switzerland. Clubs are especially welcome, and there are regular informal meetings outside the museum open to everyone.

Practical information

🕐 Opening times vary by season; check on website or Facebook

🏠 25, rue Ampère, 02000 Laon

🖥 49.580694 N, 3.645635 E

🌐 musee-auto-laon.jimdo.com

📞 +33 6 02 03 73 69

✉ Contact form on website

Record-breaking Range Rover.

Musée de l'Automobile de Lorraine, Velaine en Haye

One of just 21 Porsche 356B Carrera GTL Abarths produced. / The pride of the curator, a 1935 Reo Flying Cloud Six Doctor's Coupé.

Set in a park on the site of a former US military base just outside Nancy, this museum is little known, even among enthusiasts in France. If you are visiting it for the first time, you're likely to be all the more surprised by its airy layout and impressive display of over 100 cars. Whilst inside, your family can enjoy walks in the park, tennis, or even paintball sessions.

The cars are presented in chronological order, beginning with a De Dion Bouton from the dawn of the 20th century, and including a couple of rare Donnet models from the 1920s. French makes are strongly represented, but there are several interesting American cars too, not least the 1935 Flying Cloud Six Doctor's Coupé by Reo, named after the company's founder, Ransom Eli Olds. From the post-war period, the museum has a good range of European sports cars as well as family saloons, and an exceptional selection of Porsches, including a valuable 550 Spyder, a 904 GTS from 1963 and a rare 356B Carrera GTL Abarth. Most of the cars belong to members of the association, which has run the museum since it opened in 1970, so the selection sometimes changes.

Practical information

🕐 Open March-June and September-October on Wednesday, Saturday and Sunday from 2-6pm; July and August every day from 2-6pm

🏠 Parc de loisirs de la forêt de Haye, 54840 Velaine en Haye (off A31 autoroute, exit 17)

🖼 48.702247 N, 6.049824 E

🌐 www.musee-automobile-lorraine.fr

📞 +33 3 83 23 28 38

✉ alaacl@wanadoo.fr or contact form on website

A unique Renault 15 GTL-based convertible, built locally.

North-East France

Museums

Shows & Tours

Market Place

Motorsport

Circuits

Musée Automobile de Reims-Champagne

Bobby Alba, part of the extensive collection of rare pre-war marques. / Magnificent 1908 SCAR, built in Reims and still ready for the road.

The famous car designer Philippe Charbonneaux established this museum in 1985 to house his personal collection of cars. Although the cars he designed moved permanently to the Cité de l'Automobile in Mulhouse (page 204) in 2016, the museum retains a wide appeal, with 200 cars, motorbikes and cycles, not to mention a huge collection of 5000 miniature and toy cars. Clubs are especially welcome to tour the museum, which has ample off-road parking.

Over the past year, the museum has added many new exhibits, such as a Fournier Marcadier and a Guillet motorbike, and has enlarged its unique collection of Rumi scooters. French pre-war cars are a highlight; many of them are among a handful of survivors of marques like CIME or Michel Irat, and there is a beautifully restored 1908 SCAR Torpédo near the entrance. The SCAR was built near Reims, like the unique Radovich from 1958, based on a Peugeot 403 convertible, or the 1960 Thévenin caravan, complete with period accessories. No reference to Reims could fail to mention its place in motorsport, and the museum plans to build up its display of competition cars, which includes a 1969 Martini MW3 and a Simca-engined Geri RB10.

Thévenin caravan, built nearby in the Aube.

Practical information

🕐 Open every day except Tuesday, from 10am-noon and 2-5pm (6pm in summer); closed 25 December and from late December to mid-January (see website for details)

🏠 84, avenue Georges Clémenceau, 51100 Reims

🚌 Line 3, Boussinesq

🗺 49.2508529 N, 4.050351 E

🌐 www.musee-automobile-reims-champagne.com

📞 +33 3 26 82 83 84

✉ musee-automobile-reims-champagne@wanadoo.fr or contact form on website

Musée de la 2CV, Troisfontaines

All generations of the 2CV are represented. / As simple as it gets; the interior of an early 2CV.
(Both courtesy Pascal Irlinger/Musée de la 2CV)

Even allowing for a personal interest – the author's first car was a Citroën Dyane! – no guide to the car museums of France would be complete without this shrine to that most idiosyncratic of French popular cars, the Citroën 2CV. The 2CV and its derivatives (the Dyane, Ami and Méhari among them) remain hugely popular to this day. There are significant displays of the 2CV at the Conservatoire Citroën outside Paris (page 13) and the Citromuseum in Castellane (page 108), but this is the only museum dedicated exclusively to 'la Deuche.'

Run by an association that also organises the Fête de la 2CV in May each year, the museum displays 2CVs of all generations, from the early models of the 1950s to late-model Charlestons. In between there are many limited-edition models, like the France 3, Dolly and 007 series, as well as a special version of the 2CV designed for use by the fire brigade, and a Méhari-based ice cream van, ideal for a Mediterranean beach. The prize for the most bizarre adaptation of a 2CV, however, is a tie ... between a light plane built on top of a 2CV bodyshell, and another hiding Porsche running gear!

Practical information

🕐 Open most Saturday afternoons 2-5pm, but may change, so check in advance

🏠 Rue de la Cristallerie, Vallérysthal, 57870 Troisfontaines

📷 48.678556 N, 7.126366 E

🌐 musee2cv.free.fr

📞 +33 9 54 18 83 13

✉ info.musee2cv@gmail.com

Extraordinary tracked version of the Citroën Méhari.
(Courtesy Pascal Irlinger/Musée de la 2CV)

Museums

Shows & Tours

Market Place

Motorsport

Circuits

Musée de la Commanderie, Viâpres-le-Petit

The main building of the museum, which dates back to the 17th century.

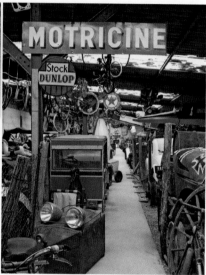

One of the impossibly crowded hallways in the museum.

As you drive through the tiny village of Viâpres-le-Petit, about 40km (25 miles) north of Troyes, you won't see a sign for this museum, which must be one of the quirkiest sites in this guide. But follow the path off the rue Grande, next to the church, and you'll reach the home of Serge Michel. In truth, this is less a museum and more a collection built up over a lifetime by one man. Imagine uncovering a succession of barn finds and you'll begin to have an idea of what awaits you.

Among the rusting piles of tractors and agricultural machinery, 50 cars gently decay. Dating from the early 20th century to the 1960s, they include a 1920 Bignan cyclecar and a one-off turbine-powered sports car from the 1950s with aluminium bodywork.

There are many military vehicles, some of them left behind by the retreating German troops during World War II. Most extraordinary of all, however, is the only remaining 'pocket submarine,' designed by a French inventor André Michel in 1936; although poorly displayed, it's a fascinating contraption. The museum is open by appointment only, but clubs are welcome to stop and picnic in the grounds.

The famous 'Pocket Submarine.'

Practical information

🕐 By appointment only, mainly during spring and summer weekends

🏠 17, rue Grande, 10380 Viâpres-le-Petit

🗺 48.561669 N, 4.041941 E

📞 +33 3 25 37 70 30

Circuit Historique de Laon

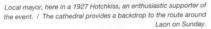

Local mayor, here in a 1927 Hotchkiss, an enthusiastic supporter of the event. / The cathedral provides a backdrop to the route around Laon on Sunday.

I f you have ever driven through the unprepossessing modern town at the bottom of Laon, you might wonder what the fuss is all about. But you'd be missing out on the lovely old city, with its medieval buildings and magnificent Gothic cathedral.

The historic setting is only one of the reasons which explain the success of this friendly event, which celebrated its 25th anniversary with a record-breaking 1000 entries in 2016. Each year, it draws entries from Belgium and the Netherlands, as well as a sizeable contingent from the UK. On Saturday, participants can join a road trip through the beautiful local countryside, with a lunch stop at a château or one of the villages, before returning to Laon to give the public the chance to admire all the cars.

The highlight of the weekend comes on Sunday, when the local authorities close the roads around the city to create a 10km (6 miles) circuit, which climbs from the modern town to the ramparts above it. There are plenty of vantage points from which to admire the cars as they go by, and each year one marque is called out, with recent honours going to Zagato, Morgan and Porsche.

Practical information

🕐 May/June very year

🏠 Mairie de Laon, place du Général Leclerc, 02000 Laon

🖼 49.565076 N, 3.620548 E

🌐 www.circuit-historique-laon.com

📞 +33 3 23 79 83 58

✉ circuit-historique-laon@orange.fr

Sunny weather for this Rolls-Royce Silver Wraith during the road trip. (Courtesy Association de la montée historique de Laon/Photo Laurenan)

Museums

Shows & Tours

Market Place

Motorsport

Circuits

Chantilly Arts & Élégance

Best of Show winners in 2016: 1938 Alfa Romeo 8C 2900B Lungo Berlinetta and DS E-Tense concept.

Held for the first time in 2014, this show has quickly established itself as a major event on the European calendar. By far the grandest concours d'élégance in France, it stands on a par with the shows at Villa d'Este or Pebble Beach. It's certainly hard to imagine a more magnificent setting than the imposing château at Chantilly, set in beautiful grounds conceived by Le Nôtre.

The event at Chantilly reinstates the sometimes-forgotten distinction between a concours d'état, in which the condition and authenticity of the cars is recognised, and a concours d'élégance, which traditionally rewarded the overall presentation of the newest and grandest cars and their no-less elegant owners. At Chantilly, visitors can enjoy both: the concours d'état

Spectacular Erdmann & Rossi-bodied Mercedes 500K from 1935.

showcases the world's most striking historic cars, broken out into categories ranging from cars of the great French or Italian coachbuilders, to those which competed in Formula 1 or the Tour de France automobile. The 'Best of Show' prize is often awarded to a top-flight pre-war car, be it Delahaye, Delage or Alfa Romeo. The concours d'élégance meanwhile features a stunning collection of modern concept cars, from manufacturers including DS, Aston Martin and

1977 Peugeot 504 rally car part of a tribute to Jean Todt's career. / Award for the best club display went to Delahaye for the first edition of the event.

Mercedes, each accompanied by models from Europe's top fashion houses.

Throughout the grounds of the château there is much more to enjoy: a display of more than 800 cars by club members, a presentation by the band of the Republican Guard, outdoor picnics, boat trips on the Grand Canal and even demonstrations of how to make Chantilly cream!

Practical information

🕐 September every year

🏠 Château de Chantilly, 60500 Chantilly

🖥 49.191574 N, 2.485351 E

🌐 www.chantillyartsetelegance.com

📞 +33 1 42 59 73 40

✉ Contact form on website

Republican Guard passing in front of the château.

Museums

Shows & Tours

Market Place

Motorsport

Circuits

Concours d'élégance, Le Touquet Paris-Plage Historique

British visitors prepare to drive their Alvis past the judges. / Proud winners in front of their strikingly painted 1935 Voisin C27 Roadster.

The elegant seaside resort of Le Touquet has long been popular with visitors from Belgium and the UK as well as France. Its grandest hotel, the Westminster – which boasts a Michelin-starred restaurant – makes a natural setting for this upmarket concours d'élégance, which raises money for leukaemia research.

Participants can join two road trips, along the coast and in the countryside inland, and enjoy a gala dinner on Saturday evening. But the highpoint for competitors and public alike is the concours d'élégance held on Sunday afternoon in front of the Westminster Hotel. Judged by the FFVE (Fédération Française des Véhicules d'Époque), entries are assessed on the basis of their historical interest, overall condition and the standard of presentation of cars and owners alike. Often introduced by a TV personality, the cars are grouped by period from the 1920s to the '70s. The concours consistently features exceptional pre-war cars from manufacturers such as Hispano-Suiza or Voisin, and more recent rarities like the Bizzarrini 5300 Strada or Chapron's Citroën SM Mylord convertible. Their owners are usually immaculately dressed to fit the period of their cars, or boldly attired to match their dashing colour schemes.

Practical information

🕐 September every year

🏠 Hôtel Westminster, Avenue du Verger, 62520 Le Touquet

🖳 50.522207 N, 1.591487 E

🌐 https://goo.gl/d1D76T

📞 +33 6 12 78 60 00

✉ philippe.charles.t@ wanadoo.fr

Participants in the road trip in front of the Hôtel Westminster.

Festival des Belles Mécaniques, Roubaix

Citroën DS convertible leads 2CV around the banked track. / Honouring Voisin and French sports cars in 2016.
(Courtesy Le Festival des Belles Mécaniques)

Parc des Sports - Vélodrome
ROUBAIX
14e Festival des Belles Mécaniques
25-26 juin 2016

Les automobiles Avions Voisin
Les sportives françaises

Roubaix
Renseignements : www.ideale-ds.eu
IDéale DS : 0 321 242 106 · Mairie de Roubaix : 0 320 664 645

The northern town of Roubaix is better known to lovers of two wheels than four, as the finishing point for the arduous Paris-Roubaix cycle race, which began in 1896 and is still held today. What better place, then, in which to hold this show than at Roubaix's historic velodrome? The condition of the original track limits its use, but 100 cars are chosen for a parade lap around it, which really brings the display of cars to life. The event is well supported by local clubs and there's a small covered display too. French makes are most strongly represented here, with a special theme chosen each year; the 60th anniversary of the Citroën DS in 2015 and a celebration of Voisin's cars in 2016, for example. It's not uncommon to see some rarer models, like the 1949 Simca Heise racer unearthed by a local dealer, and there is often a good showing of pre-war cars as well.

Roubaix's economy has suffered ever since its traditional textile industry went into decline, but it has some fine historic buildings and a remarkable public art gallery, La Piscine, housed in the town's former Olympic swimming pool, which is well worth visiting.

Practical information

🕐 June every year

🏠 Parc des Sports – Vélodrome, avenue Maxence van der Meersch, 59100 Roubaix

📷 50.679542 N, 3.206271 E

🌐 www.ideale-ds.eu/v10/

📞 +33 3 21 24 21 06

✉ contact@ideale-ds.eu

Pre-war Alvis and MG displayed by local clubs.

Museums

Shows & Tours

Market Place

Motorsport

Circuits

Festival Bugatti, Molsheim

Molsheim locals enjoying the Festival. (Courtesy Caroline Bugatti & Cyril Gautier/EBA) / Pre-production Bugatti Veyron, seen here at Chantilly.

Arguably the greatest of all French makes, Bugatti continues to stir the hearts of enthusiasts across the globe. Many Bugatti owners love nothing better than to take their cars on track, entering historic races like those at Angoulême (page 86). Although it sometimes visits the Anneau du Rhin circuit (page 227), the Festival Bugatti charts a different course, celebrating the history of the marque and the Bugatti family at a slower pace.

Over several days around 15 September (Ettore Bugatti's birthday) each year, 50 Bugattis come together from across Europe to enjoy a mix of museums, monuments and the fine driving roads of Alsace. There are visits to famous sites, like the Charterhouse in Molsheim or the Musée Lalique, and a solemn moment when the participants pay their respects at the Bugatti family tomb in Dorlisheim. The public gets to see all the cars on display in Molsheim, and what a show it is! Whether it's a Type 53 or Type 57S Atalante (both fêted in 2016), a Gangloff-bodied Type 49 limousine shown at the Paris Motor Show in 1930, a modern EB 112 prototype or the newest Veyron Supersport, visitors can admire some of the finest cars of their time.

Bugatti type 35 dans les stands Targa Florio 1925

Display of racing Bugatti models, in the Cité de l'Automobile, nearby at Mulhouse.

Practical information

🕐 September every year

🏠 Parc des Jésuites, 11, avenue de la Gare, 67120 Molsheim (public display)

🖥 48.538793 N, 7.496924 E

🌐 www.enthousiastes-bugatti-alsace.com

✉ eba.secretariat@gmail.com

Habits de lumière, Épernay

If you're looking for an excuse to visit the Champagne region and stock up on a few bottles of bubbly for Christmas, the champagne producers of Épernay have car enthusiasts like you in mind! Over a lively weekend in December, the local tourist office coordinates three days of celebrations, centred around the Avenue de Champagne, where all the great houses are based. There are tastings of food as well as champagne, exhibitions and illuminations in the streets, with a spectacular video mapping onto the façade of the Hôtel de Ville. It makes for a great weekend for all the family, attracting more than 45,000 visitors.

On Sunday morning, over 400 classic cars congregate in the Place de la République. All the cars then

Participants gather in the place de la République. (Courtesy Laurent Cornée) / Patriotic Renault 4CV heads up the avenue de Champagne.

drive up the Avenue de Champagne to the delight of the spectators, before their owners finish with a glass of fizz offered by the local producers. Although there are plenty of mainstream post-war French models, you should see some rarer cars too, such as an Iso Rivolta IR 300 or a Rosengart Super Traction. The earliest cars – like the 1903 Richard-Brasier which is a regular participant – date back more than a century.

Evening celebrations in the avenue de Champagne. (Courtesy Ville d'Épernay)

Practical information

🕐 December every year

🏠 Place de la République, 51200 Épernay

🗺 49.04341 N, 3.95699 E

🌐 habitsdelumiere.epernay.fr

📞 +33 3 26 53 33 00

✉ habits.lumiere@ville-epernay.fr

Museums / Shows & Tours / Market Place / Motorsport / Circuits

48 Heures Européennes, Troyes

Participants enjoy a break at the Château de la Motte-Tilly. (Courtesy Les 48 Heures Européennes de Troyes) / Peugeot 302 cabriolet on the streets of Troyes.

Good food and drink, a beautiful setting, and a fascinating selection of cars rarely seen elsewhere in France make this event well worth discovering. Troyes may not come to mind as readily as Reims or Épernay, but it has plenty to offer visitors. Between tours of its art museums and medieval quarter, you can enjoy a glass of champagne and local gastronomic specialities like 'andouillette.'

Up to 400 cars take part in the weekend's programme of motoring events, with road trips on Friday and Saturday calling at some of the beautiful châteaux nearby, before a gala dinner on Saturday night. On Sunday, the cars are displayed in the city centre and drive around a circuit on closed roads. In 2016, Peugeot brought along some fine cars from its museum at Sochaux (page 206), from a 1903 Type 56 and 1937 402 Eclipse, through to a 205 T16 Paris-Dakar.

What makes this show unique, however, and fully justifies its European title, is the extraordinary range of cars which come from Poland, the Czech Republic and beyond. Where else in France might you see a Polski-Fiat 508 Sport, Škoda 640 or Walter Junior from the 1930s?

Practical information

🕐 September, biennially (even years)

🏠 Boulevard Gambetta, 10000 Troyes

▤ 48.2997769 N, 4.0730578 E

🌐 www.48heures.com

✉ contact@48heures.com

Rarely-seen Škoda 640 from 1934.

Rétro Meus'auto, Lac de Madine

Peugeot 309 GTi next to other 'Youngtimers' beside the lake. / Parts and memorabilia galore!

In many ways, this long-established weekend event next to a large man-made lake is more like a huge popular festival than a simple car show. With space to picnic or camp on site and live music on Saturday night, Rétro Meus'auto has a relaxed, friendly atmosphere, which the whole family can enjoy. No wonder that it draws up to 30,000 visitors from France, Belgium and Luxembourg. With a little help from the weather, visitors can enjoy the outdoor setting for this show and wander among the numerous traders' stands and more than 3000 cars on display.

But committed car enthusiasts won't be disappointed either. Officially open to cars built before 1990, the show attracts a huge variety of classics and an increasing number of 'Youngtimers' too. Popular post-war French makes are best represented, but you might also see rarities like a left-hand drive Ford Cortina GT convertible by Crayford, an Audi 60 saloon from the 1960s or a Citroën M35 driven all the way from the Netherlands. Prizes are awarded for the best restoration (won last time by a splendid 1950 Riley RMD Drophead Coupé) and for the best restoration by an owner under 25.

Practical information

🕐 June every year

🏠 Lac de Madine, D133, 55120 Heudicourt-sous-les-Côtes

🖼 48.942231 N, 5.716462 E

🌐 www.biellesmeusiennes. com

✉ Contact form on website

Crayford Cortina GT (centre) next to Lotus Cortina and later Cortina 1600E.

Salon Champenois du Véhicule de Collection, Reims

Circus setting for this club's Peugeot lions. / Rare Génestin G7 tucked-in between the club exhibits.

Popularly known simply as the Salon de Reims, this show marks the start of the season for many classic car enthusiasts in North-East France. 2017 will see its 30th anniversary and the event goes from strength to strength, with over 30,000 visitors coming to see 600 exhibitors. In fact, the show is almost too successful; parking can sometimes be chaotic and there can be queues to get in.

Two of the show's crowded halls are given over to club stands, their organisers spurred on by a competition to create the most imaginative display around a theme like the Tour de France, the cinema or circus. There's a large central exhibit, too, which may focus on a single marque such as MG, or a period like the Great War.

The third hall, and a huge area outside, are taken up by traders in books, models and parts of all kinds – this is an especially good place to look for spares for French makes – as well as a small display of military vehicles. Before you head home, take a walk through the car park for classic cars just opposite the halls; it's almost a show in itself.

Practical information

🕐 March every year

🏠 Parc des Expositions, allée Thierry Sabine, 51100 Reims

🚌 Line 06 from Opéra (city centre)

🗺 49.2354852 N, 4.0630284 E

🌐 www.bce-reims.com/bce.htm

📞 +33 3 26 06 15 78

✉ contact@bce-reims.com

Part of the huge outdoor parts display.

Bourse d'échanges, Arras

The packed autojumble. / The city's famous belfry provides a backdrop to the event. (Courtesy Daniel Guerin)

ARRAS
DIMANCHE 19 MARS 2017
PARC DES EXPOSITIONS
40ÈME BOURSE D'ECHANGES
PIECES AUTOS, MOTOS, DOCUMENTATION, MINIATURES.

EXPOSITION D'AUTOMOBILES ET MOTOS ANCIENNES

9 h 00 - 18 h 00
ENTRÉE : 5 € - Enfants : 2 €
EMPLACEMENTS : 30 € LES 3 ml
Parking 500 Pl. gratuit pour VH anciens
1 entrée gratuite par VH de plus de 30 ars

CLUB RAVERA / 6A
Site internet : www.ravera-6a.fr
E-mail : ravera-6a@orange.fr
Tél. 03 21 48 68 71

Part classic car show and part autojumble, this event in Arras is a friendly occasion to start the year in northern France, and a short drive from the Channel for British enthusiasts. 6000 visitors attend this well-established meeting, which celebrates its 40th anniversary in 2017. Arras is an attractive city to visit; its belfry and two great squares from the 17th and 18th centuries are within walking distance of the show.

One hall is given over to a large autojumble, with 100 exhibitors (a third of them professionals), coming from Belgium as well as northern France. Prices for parts and automobilia are generally reasonable. In the second hall, there's a display of 40-50 cars, several of them brought over by clubs from southern England. One exhibitor even regularly drives his 1929 Austin Seven Mulliner to the show from south-east England! Cars on show in recent years have included a splendid 1937 Rolls-Royce 25/30 with Art Deco-style coachwork by Park Ward, as well as fine examples of the Sunbeam-Talbot 90 and Jaguar XK150. More modern rarities such as a Citroën SM Espace and a unique Gilbern prototype prove that even smaller events like this can be well worth visiting.

This Dennis lorry originally saw service in the countryside of south-east England.

Practical information

🕐 March every year

🏠 Artois Expo, 50, avenue Roger Salengro, 62223 Saint-Laurent-Blangy

🗺 50.291686 N, 2.790931 E

🌐 www.ravera-6a.fr

📞 +33 3 21 48 68 71

✉ ravera-6a@orange.fr

Museums

Shows & Tours

Market Place

Motorsport

Circuits

Circuit de Reims-Gueux

The restored pit buildings today.

The last car race was held here in 1969, but the circuit at Reims still has a unique attraction for the thousands of enthusiasts who make the pilgrimage to Gueux every year. The first races took place in 1926, but the circuit was best known for the Grand Prix de France, first run here in 1932, and the post-war endurance race, the Douze Heures Internationales de Reims. It was here that Mercedes-Benz marked its return to Grand Prix racing after the Second World War, with Fangio and Kling taking first and second places in the French Grand Prix in 1954. The drivers reached ever higher speeds on the circuit, ultimately hitting 290km/h (180mph) on the Thillois straight, and Fangio reportedly said, "At Reims you had to be mad or drunk to win."

Today, you can re-trace the 7.8km (4.9 miles) circuit, which formed a triangle around the villages of Thillois and Gueux, taking in parts of the modern-day N31, D26

Volunteers at work repainting the grandstand.
(Courtesy Ghislain Petit/Les Amis du Circuit de Gueux)

Sanesi pushes his car over the line in 1951. (Courtesy Association des Amis de Rob Roy; Copyright Rob Roy – all reproductions forbidden)

and D27 roads. But the highlight is to stop in front of the pits and the Pavillon Lambert used by the timekeepers, which have been painstakingly restored by a group of local enthusiasts over the past decade. They continue to renovate more of the buildings, including the Stands des Marques behind the pits, where the drivers could rest.

Financial and administrative challenges have made it hard to maintain a programme of revival events at Gueux, but check the association's website for news of more informal meetings to come.

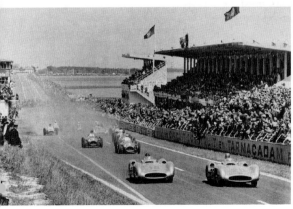

Fangio and Kling in the lead for Mercedes at the 1954 French Grand Prix. (Courtesy Mercedes-Benz Classic)

Practical information

🕐 Public road open all year

🏠 D27, 51390 Gueux

📍 49.254161 N, 3.930964 E

🌐 www.amis-du-circuit-de-gueux.fr

✉️ Contact form on website

Rallye Neige et Glace

Alpine A110 berlinettes in the Doubs. (Courtesy Tom Zaniroli/Zaniroli Classic Events)

Like so many regularity rallies in France, the origins of this event go back to a competitive rally, the Critérium Neige et Glace, first held in 1953. Fifty years later, Patrick and Viviane Zaniroli revived it as a regularity rally, and it has quickly won a reputation as a demanding but enjoyable winter event. One of its most famous participants is Henri Pescarolo, who chooses it as the only regularity event he takes part in. He is joined by 100 other entrants, who enjoy the pleasures of mastering driving on ice whilst keeping to a set average speed. A night-time stage and – for the first time in 2017 – a stage held on an ice circuit in Switzerland add to the challenge for the drivers and to the spectacle for the public.

Usually based around Malbuisson, the rally takes place in the coldest area of France, sometimes known as 'little Siberia.' Snowfall can be heavy, but the organisers work closely with the local authorities, who clear some of the roads especially for the rally. It's open to post-war cars up to 1989, later than for many events, which allows rally cars from the 1980s to take part.

Practical information

🕐 February every year

🏠 Grande Rue, 25160 Malbuisson (overnight base)

🖥 46.799683 N, 6.305052 E

🌐 www.zaniroli.com

📞 +33 4 92 82 20 00

✉ info@zaniroli.com

Lancia Stratos powers through the snow. (Courtesy Richard Bord/Zaniroli Classic Events)

Anneau du Rhin, Blitzheim

Close to Mulhouse and Colmar, and easily reached from the French and German motorway networks, the Anneau du Rhin is the longest circuit in North-East France. Set among the woods of a former hunting ground, it's an attractive and, above all, quick track, fully homologated by the FFSA. The main circuit can be arranged in several different configurations up to 4km (2.5 miles) in length, and was extended for the 2014 season, when the Tour Auto (page 22) visited it. There's also a smaller familiarisation circuit, just 1.1km (0.7 miles) long, with generous run-off areas and an easily learned layout – ideal for track day novices. Next to the track, specially designed areas let drivers practise car control, mastering skids, and even dealing with simulated punctures.

Opened in 1996, the Anneau du Rhin is a well-equipped circuit which can host up to 10,000 spectators. There's a full programme

Aerial view of the circuit. (Courtesy Anneau du Rhin)

of events each year, including single-seater championship races, club days and drifting events. Regular open days are held and there's a wide range of driving courses and passenger rides available. You can even experience the circuit as a passenger in a 1920s Bugatti Type 35!

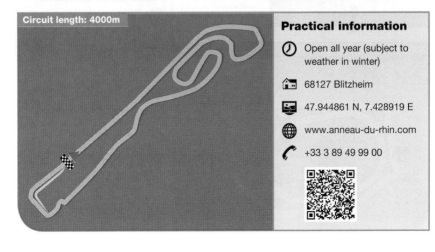

Circuit length: 4000m

Practical information

🕐 Open all year (subject to weather in winter)

🏠 68127 Blitzheim

🗺 47.944861 N, 7.428919 E

🌐 www.anneau-du-rhin.com

📞 +33 3 89 49 99 00

Museums · Shows & Tours · Market Place · Motorsport · Circuits

Centre d'Essais de Mortefontaine (CERAM)

The facility at Mortefontaine, an hour's drive north of Paris, is unique among the locations described in this guide. Originally created by Simca in 1956, to test the new Simca 1000, it passed through many hands – Chrysler, Peugeot-Citroën, Valeo and Pininfarina – before joining the UTAC group, responsible for Montlhéry (page 53), in 2008. The most important parts of the site are its 3km (1.9 miles) banked speed track, one of only four in France, and the 5.2km (3.2 miles) road circuit. Modernised in 2014, this is designed to replicate the driving conditions on a French 'route départementale,' with a mix of tight corners and faster straights. Elsewhere, there are gradients of up to 25%, a dust tunnel, and cobblestones to test ride comfort.

GT Prestige, one of the events held at Mortefontaine. (Courtesy Paris Auto Events)

Writing in the French edition of *Classic & Sports Car* magazine, François Granet described it as "the most secret circuit in Europe." Even today, the circuit is off limits most of the time, as manufacturers continue to use it for testing. On a handful of days each year, however, it's open for special events catering to top-end GT cars. UTAC's driver training arm, EFCAM, also runs occasional courses here.

The famous French pavé; a section of cobblestones leading to a saltwater ford.

Practical information

🕐 Limited public opening (check with organisers)

🏠 60128 Mortefontaine (near golf course)

🗺 49.143351 N, 2.595304 E

🌐 www.parisautoevents.com

📞 +33 3 44 54 51 51

✉ pae@utaceram.com

Circuit length: 3000m / 5200m

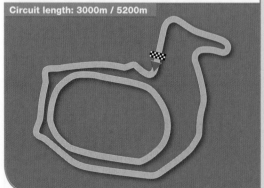

Circuit automobile du stadium d'Abbeville

Close to the Channel ports, the circuit at Abbeville was established in 1993 by Gilles Stievenart, a successful publisher of specialist motoring magazines. 2.3km (1.4 miles) long, the track has some fast sections, but is above all a technical circuit. Its layout presents a variety of challenges, which make it a good training ground where drivers can hone their skills. There are fast corners and hairpins, banked turns, and others which tighten mid-bend.

Ferrari 458 Italia, here serving as a pace car for the Grand Prix Historique in Bressuire.

You can choose from a good selection of modern GTs for the driving courses and passenger rides at Abbeville, including the latest Renault Mégane RS, Ferrari F430 and 458 Italia and several recent Porsches, from a Cayman S to a 997 GT3 RS. You can also extend your time on track with a drive on the roads nearby. One of the strengths of the circuit, however, is the opportunity to receive individual tuition at the wheel of your own car, benefiting from expert advice from the circuit's fully qualified instructors. If you want to treat a friend or partner, you can buy gift vouchers which offer a range of options, some combining time on track in different cars.

Circuit length: 2300m

Practical information

🕐 Open all year

🏠 CD 928, Route d'Hesdin, 80100 Abbeville

🖥 50.13667 N, 1.82778 E

🌐 www.stadium-automobile.fr

📞 +33 3 22 20 08 65

✉ contact.stadium@gmail.com

Circuit de Chambley

Half an hour's drive from Metz, the circuit at Chambley is next to an airstrip where well-heeled visitors can land their private planes. For enthusiasts with a more modest budget, there are plenty of more affordable ways to get on track during one of the regular open days, or the courses on offer. Francis Maillet, the circuit's director,

Aerial view of the circuit. (Courtesy Francis Maillet Compétition)

combined a successful career as a doctor and semi-professional race driver, but the emphasis today at Chambley is on training rather than competition. Many of the courses on this 3.3km (2.1 miles) track promote driving safety, and part of it can be doused in 300 litres of water an hour to simulate aquaplaning conditions.

For sports car enthusiasts, Chambley has plenty to offer, too, and magazines like *Échappement* and *Option Auto* have used it for their circuit tests. Although flat, the circuit is technically demanding, with four 'S' bends to add to the mix. The circuit is an official Renault Sport test centre, so that, as well as recent Clio and Mégane RS models, you can try a Renault Spider or work your way up to a Formula Renault single-seater.

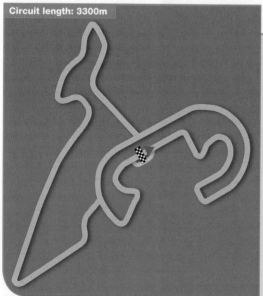

Circuit length: 3300m

Practical information

🕐 Open all year (contact circuit for details)

🏠 Site Chambley Planet'Air, 54470 Saint-Julien-lès-Gorze

🗺 49.026446 N, 5.891485 E

🌐 www.fmaillet.com

📞 +33 3 82 33 71 83

✉ Contact form on website

Circuit de Chenevières

One of the historic Alpine berlinettes, seen here at the start of the Tour Auto.

About 50km (31 miles) south-east of Nancy, Chenevières is an interesting circuit with a couple of surprises in store for visitors. Built in 2005, the track is modern and well surfaced; its main straight is long enough to allow high speeds and the circuit is homologated by the FFSA. The complete circuit is 3.5km (2.2 miles), but is notable for its flexibility, with different configurations combining parts of the main asphalt track with sections on earth and low-grip surfaces, which can be used by cars, four-wheel drives and quads. There's also a short karting circuit.

Like most circuits in this guide, Chenevières holds regular track days open to all enthusiasts and can be hired by clubs, who can take advantage of its extensive reception facilities. In June it holds a one-day meeting for classic cars, GT Legends. What makes Chenevières stand out, however, is the range of cars you can experience as a driver or passenger: in addition to the 'run of the mill' Ferrari F430 or Porsche 911, you'll discover Erik Comas' collection of historic Alpine A110 berlinettes (which are available to hire for road trips), a 1981 Rondeau prototype and even an electric Tesla Roadster.

Practical information

🕐 Open all year (contact circuit for details)

🏠 Lieu-dit Le Fays, 54122 Chenevières

🗺 48.514125 N, 6.648377 E

🌐 www.circuit-chenevieres.fr

📞 +33 3 83 72 39 29

✉ Contact form on website

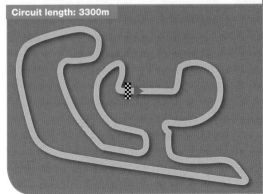

Circuit length: 3300m

Circuit de Clastres

Built on the site of a former NATO base, the circuit at Clastres opened in 2008 and was expanded just six years later. As befits such a recent circuit, it's a safe track on which to practise, with generous run-off areas all around, and is equipped with modern Alfano timing gear. Unusually, it

Lotus 340R, a fun choice for this track, here on show in Switzerland.

combines a main track of 2km (1.2 miles) and a separate drag strip of 1650m (just over a mile), which makes up for the relative shortness of the track. The strip is popular with bikers as well as car drivers; even a damp surface didn't stop the former French motorcycle racing champion Philippe Monneret hitting 284km/h (176mph) there!

Clastres is close to the A26 autoroute, which puts it in easy reach of Amiens, Reims and Lille. Track driving courses are offered there from time to time by a range of French and Belgian schools, but check with the circuit for the latest opportunities. For most of the year there are separate open days for cars and bikes, with very reasonable rates for half- and full-day sessions, and a special fundraiser for the 'Téléthon' each December. There are karting events, too, and the circuit can be hired by clubs.

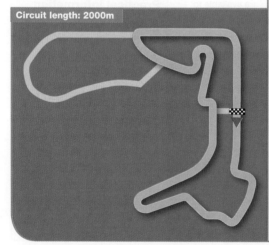

Circuit length: 2000m

Practical information

🕐 Open all year (contact circuit for details)

🏠 Pôle Mécanique 'La Clef des Champs', 02440 Clastres

🗺 49.748504 N, 3.211193 E

🌐 www.circuitclastres.com

📞 +33 3 23 63 36 51

✉ contact@circuitclastres.com

Circuit de Croix-en-Ternois

The track was completely resurfaced in 2013. (Courtesy Circuit de Croix-en-Ternois)

The track at Croix-en-Ternois is one of the older circuits in this region; its layout basically unchanged since it opened in 1973. For its 40th anniversary season, however, the track was substantially modernised and its safety features enhanced. Between corners two and six, the circuit was widened, larger run-off areas provided and a new surface laid offering improved grip. At 1.9km (1.2 miles) the track is relatively short, but sufficiently varied to make for an interesting lap. The tight corner at the end of the 600m (660yd) main straight is a good test for a car's brakes ... and its driver's judgement. In 2011 Nico Rosberg stormed around the circuit in his Formula 3 car in just 48 seconds.

Croix-en-Ternois is home to the Griffith's historic racing team and the track regularly hosts slalom, drift and racing events. There are plentiful opportunities to take driving courses with the circuit's partner, GT Academy, in cars including a Porsche Cayman R and Westfield FW300. Croix-en-Ternois is less than 100km (60 miles) from Lille or Calais, and if you plan on visiting regularly, you may want to join the circuit's club, with preferential rates and open days reserved for members.

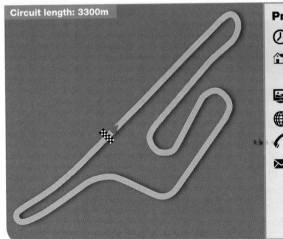

Circuit length: 3300m

Practical information

🕐 Open all year

🏠 RN39, 62130 Croix-en-Ternois

🖼 50.378611 N, 2.296667 E

🌐 www.circuitdecroix.com

📞 +33 3 21 03 30 13

✉ Contacts page on website

Circuit des Écuyers, Beuvardes

If you watch the motoring programmes on French television, you'll often see track tests here at Les Écuyers. Renault Sport, Peugeot and Citroën all use the circuit as well to test or demonstrate their sporting models. If you want to experience the track with your own car, you can opt for a regular group session or individual coaching during one of the circuit's track days, which take place a couple of times each month.

Aerial view of the circuit. (Courtesy Circuit des Écuyers)

Alternatively, the circuit's training partner, Sprint Racing, organises courses in a wide range of top-end GTs. There is a club house and terrace from which to enjoy the view over the circuit, and improved catering facilities introduced in 2014.

Les Écuyers has an attractive, naturally undulating woodland setting and wide run-off areas and gravel pits to reduce the risk of damage. The complete track is 3.5km (2.2 miles) long, but it can be divided into two smaller loops, each with its own pit area. It is fitted out with modern timing equipment, but isn't an especially fast track: as the plan of its layout shows, it's a twisty, technical circuit which is ideal for smaller cars and motorbikes.

Circuit length: 3500m

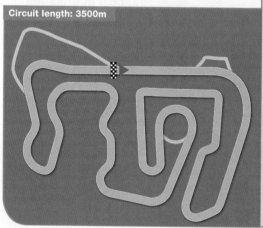

Practical information

🕐 Open all year

🏠 Ferme de Fary, 02130 Beuvardes

🗺 49.109291 N, 3.507339 E

🌐 www.circuitdesecuyers. com

📞 +33 3 23 70 98 61

✉ contact@ circuitdesecuyers.com

Circuit de Folembray

The first circuit here opened in 1975, but soon closed due to safety concerns. Henri Pescarolo acted as a technical adviser when it re-opened in 1992 and it soon built up a reputation as an enjoyable track, open to all and not just seasoned race drivers. The tarmac track can be split into two shorter sections, but in its main configuration runs to just over 2km (1.3 miles). Although comparatively short overall, there is room for a 750m (820yd) straight, and the circuit is approved by the FFSA for speeds in excess of 200km/h (125mph). Since 2016 the circuit has been under new management, with a new off-road track for four-wheel-drives under development.

Folembray is best known for its 'GTI Days' for saloon cars and 'hot hatches,' traditionally held on the second Sunday of each month. The circuit has a sophisticated video monitoring system, and these affordable track days let enthusiasts open up their engines in safety. Alternatively, you can take driving courses in top-end GTs, from Aston Martin to Porsche, through the circuit's partner, Sprint Racing. The French Lotus Club is a regular visitor, and Folembray has long been popular with British track day fans.

Top: The wooded setting of the circuit. / Supercars line up on the track under the watchful eye of the circuit's former director. (Courtesy Circuit de Folembray)

Practical information

🕐 Open all year (closed 25 December and 1 January)

🏠 Route des Hautes Avesnes, 02670 Folembray

🖥 49.54401 N, 3.299128 E

🌐 www.folembray-arena.com

📞 +33 3 23 52 01 42

✉ circuit@folembray-arena.com

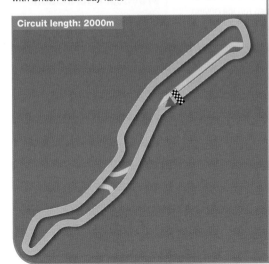

Circuit length: 2000m

Geoparc, Saint-Dié-des-Vosges

The town of Saint-Dié-des-Vosges – on the N59 between Nancy and Mulhouse – first made its mark in 2005, when the final of the Trophée Andros (page 184) was held on its brand-new ice rink. 600m (660yd) long, the rink is unique in the world for its artificial refrigeration system, which maintains a constant temperature and optimal surface quality. The Trophée

Mercedes' latest AMG GT. (Courtesy Mercedes-Benz).

Andros regularly comes back to the Vosges, guaranteeing a great show for spectators.

Soon after it opened, the Geoparc complex expanded, adding a year-round asphalt circuit for cars and motorbikes, a four-wheel drive area and a karting track. The main track can be set up in 11 different configurations, with a maximum possible length of 2.5km (1.6 miles). There are plenty of opportunities to get behind the wheel, with regular club events, open days, individual coaching sessions and training courses for both drivers and instructors. The circuit's training partner, Expert Pilot, offers an extensive selection of cars, from the compact Renault Clio RS or all-wheel-drive Ford Focus RS, to Mitjet racers and high-end sports cars like the latest Mercedes AMG GT or Ferrari 488 GTB. The instructors also run ice driving courses at Abondance in the Savoie.

Practical information

🕐 Open all year, but may close in winter during adverse weather

🏠 Rue Dieudonné Dubois, 88100 Saint-Dié-des-Vosges

🖥 48.300567 N, 6.918896 E

🌐 www.geoparc.com

📞 +33 3 29 570 570

✉ contact@geoparc.com

Circuit length: 2500m

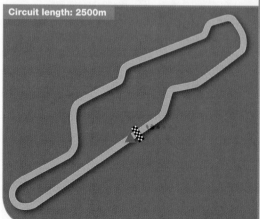

Driving in France

Driving in France should be a pleasure; away from the major cities, traffic is often light and the accident rate is much lower than in the past.

Following a few simple rules will help you to ensure that your trip is safe and uneventful.

- **Children** must be at least 10 years old to travel in the front seat
- **Drinking & driving:** the only sensible rule is not to, and in France the limit for car drivers is lower than in England & Wales or many US states, at 50mg of alcohol per 100ml of blood, or just 20mg for novice drivers during their first three years
- **Emergency services:** 112 is the European-wide number to reach fire, police and ambulance services
- **Mobile phones** may only be used with a Bluetooth connection, and even then it's much safer to pull over to make a call
- **Priority to the right** (priorité à droite): unless the signs say otherwise, drivers in built-up areas must give way to vehicles approaching from the right. Traffic entering a roundabout also has priority, unless there is a sign to give way – 'Cédez le passage' – on the approach to it
- **Seat belts** must be worn front and rear in all cars fitted with them
- **Trams:** it's forbidden to overtake a stationary tram when passengers are getting on or off
- **Valuables** should be kept out of sight when you park your car. In city traffic, it's a good idea to keep doors locked and handbags out of view
- **Young drivers** must be at least 18 years old to drive in France and hold a full (not provisional) licence

Speed Limits
Unless lower limits are signposted, speed limits in France are generally:

- **50km/h** (31mph) in **built-up areas**
- **90km/h** (56mph) on **single-carriageways**
- **110km/h** (68mph) on **dual carriageways**
- **130km/h** (81mph) on **autoroutes**

Lower limits apply when towing, in wet weather or poor visibility, and to new drivers during their first three years behind the wheel.

Your licence may be suspended immediately if you are stopped at speeds of 40km/h (25mph) or more above the limit; exceed the maximum by 50km/h (31mph) and your car could be impounded! For lesser offences, the police have the right to levy on the spot fines (up to €375), which must be paid in cash.

Radar- and GPS-based speed camera detectors of all kinds are strictly forbidden. Radar detectors should not even be carried in your car, whilst satnav devices which rely on 'Points of Interest' to warn you of speed camera locations should have this feature disabled.

Driving in Paris

At the start of 2017, the Paris authorities introduced a new requirement for all cars entering the city to display a 'CRIT'Air' sticker, based on the amount they pollute (see https://certificat-air.gouv.fr/en/). It is likely that more cities will adopt similar schemes. When driving in French cities, take special care. Look out for scooter riders everywhere. Local drivers may be more aggressive than you're used to, and often take minor parking scrapes for granted.

☑ Checklist: what to take

In France it's **compulsory** to carry the following equipment with you **in your car at all times:**

- ☐ Your **original, full driving licence,** and **passport or other official photo ID** from your country
- ☐ The **insurance certificate** and **'Green Card'** for your car, extending your insurance cover across continental Europe. Your insurer should also be able to supply you with a European Accident Statement (EAS) form to use if the worst happens
- ☐ The **registration document** for your car (the **V5C** for cars registered in the UK). If you're driving **someone else's car**, get a **letter of authorization** from the owner (or **certificate from a hire company)**
- ☐ An **emergency warning triangle**
- ☐ At least one **high-visibility reflective jacket,** which must be **carried inside the car**
- ☐ A set of **spare bulbs**
- ☐ **Two** single-use **breathalyser/alcohol tests:** although there are no fines for failing to carry these, they are still a legal requirement
- ☐ **Snow chains** are required for winter driving in **some areas** (check with the local tourist office)

If you're bringing over your own car from the UK, you'll need a set of headlamp beam converters and a 'GB' sticker or number plate showing the EU symbol. Although not obligatory, it's a good idea to keep a fire extinguisher and first aid kit in the car. Motoring assistance organisations sell convenient kits with everything you need for a trip to France, as well as European breakdown cover.

🌐 Helpful websites

Autoroutes.fr (www.autoroutes.fr):
> Comprehensive information on the French autoroute network, including current toll charges. You can also tune into Autoroute FM on 107.7 MHz for the latest traffic news.

Bison Futé (www.bison-fute.gouv.fr):
> Advice on traffic conditions during busy holiday periods and alternative routes to avoid the jams.

RAC (www.rac.co.uk/travel/driving-abroad):
> Lots more advice on driving in France.

SANEF Tolling (www.saneftolling.co.uk):
> For regular travellers from the UK to France, you can buy the 'Liber-t' toll tag to pass through autoroute toll booths across the country.

Some important road signs

The most important rule to observe in France is the notorious 'priorité à droite:' in built-up areas and whenever you see the yellow diamond sign with a black bar through it (below left), you must give way to traffic approaching from the right. When entering a town or village, the place name sign indicates the start of a 50km/h speed limit. Local drivers often fail to heed pedestrian crossings, so take care when stopping if cars are close behind you.

For more information on driving in France and throughout Europe, see *The Essential Guide to Driving in Europe*, also written by Julian Parish and published by Veloce Publishing.

Priorité à droite: priority to the right

Residential zone (20km/h speed limit)

Speed camera ahead

Motorway toll lane for cars with electronic tag

Give way

Ring road

Switch on lights

Fortnightly parking on alternate sides

Event calendar

Month		Event	Chapter / Region	Section	Page
Year-round		Vincennes en anciennes	⊕ Paris & the Ile-de-France	📷 Shows & Tours	32
Jan		Traversée de Paris en anciennes	⊕ Paris & the Ile-de-France	📷 Shows & Tours	31
...		Rallye Hivernal Classic, Vallauris	⊕ Southern France	🏁 Motorsport	137
...		Rallye Monte Carlo	⊕ Southern France	🏁 Motorsport	128
...		Rallye Monte Carlo Historique	⊕ Southern France	🏁 Motorsport	130
...		Ronde Hivernale Historique, Serre Chevalier	⊕ Southern France	🏁 Motorsport	138
...		Trophée Andros (final), Super-Besse	⊕ Central France & the Alps	🏁 Motorsport	184
Jan/Feb		Exposition Concept Cars, Paris	⊕ Paris & the Ile-de-France	📷 Shows & Tours	28
Feb		Rétromobile, Paris	⊕ Paris & the Ile-de-France	📷 Shows & Tours	20
...		Traversée de Bordeaux	⊕ Western France	📷 Shows & Tours	84
...		Salon Auto Moto Prestige et Collection, Nîmes	⊕ Southern France	📷 Shows & Tours	117
Feb		Rallye Neige et Glace	⊕ North-East France	🏁 Motorsport	226
March		Rallye de Paris GT & Classic	⊕ Paris & the Ile-de-France	📷 Shows & Tours	29
...		Coupes de Printemps, Montlhéry	⊕ Paris & the Ile-de-France	🏁 Motorsport	50
...		Avignon Motor Festival	⊕ Southern France	📷 Shows & Tours	112
...		Salon Champenois des Véhicules de Collection, Reims	⊕ North-East France	📷 Shows & Tours	222
...		Bourse d'échange d'Arras	⊕ North-East France	🏠 Market Place	223
Apr		Tour Auto Optic 2000	⊕ Paris & the Ile-de-France	📷 Shows & Tours	22
...		Youngtimers Festival, Montlhéry	⊕ Paris & the Ile-de-France	📷 Shows & Tours	33
...		Top Marques, Monaco	⊕ Southern France	📷 Shows & Tours	118
...		Tour de Corse WRC	⊕ Southern France	🏁 Motorsport	140
Apr/May		Expomobile, Chelles	⊕ Paris & the Ile-de-France	📷 Shows & Tours	27
...	Odd years	Vintage Revival, Montlhéry	⊕ Paris & the Ile-de-France	🏁 Motorsport	52
...		Corse Sud Classic Rallye	⊕ Southern France	🏁 Motorsport	133
...		Classic Days, Magny-Cours	⊕ Central France & the Alps	📷 Shows & Tours	172
May	Odd years	Rallye Dior Paris Granville	⊕ Western France	📷 Shows & Tours	78
...		Rallye International du Pays de Fougères	⊕ Western France	📷 Shows & Tours	79
...		Grand Prix de Monaco F1	⊕ Southern France	🏁 Motorsport	124
...		Grand Prix de Pau Historique	⊕ Southern France	🏁 Motorsport	126
...	Even years	Grand Prix Historique de Monaco	⊕ Southern France	🏁 Motorsport	122
...		Uriage Cabriolet Classic	⊕ Central France & the Alps	📷 Shows & Tours	178
May/Jun		Rallye Cadillac Côtes de Bordeaux	⊕ Western France	📷 Shows & Tours	76
...		Tour de Bretagne	⊕ Western France	📷 Shows & Tours	83
...		Les Anglaises ont la Côte, Bandol	⊕ Southern France	📷 Shows & Tours	111
...		Rétro Auto Forum du Var, Fréjus	⊕ Southern France	📷 Shows & Tours	116
...		Circuit Historique de Laon	⊕ North-East France	📷 Shows & Tours	213
Jun		Autodrome Heritage Festival, Montlhéry	⊕ Paris & the Ile-de-France	📷 Shows & Tours	25
...	Even years	Paris-Rambouillet en ancêtre	⊕ Paris & the Ile-de-France	📷 Shows & Tours	17
...		Rallye des Princesses	⊕ Paris & the Ile-de-France	📷 Shows & Tours	30
...		Sport et Collection, Le Vigeant	⊕ Western France	📷 Shows & Tours	82
...		Classic British Welcome, Saint-Saturnin	⊕ Western France	🏁 Motorsport	92
...		Grand Prix Historique de Bressuire	⊕ Western France	🏁 Motorsport	94
...		Le Mans 24 Hours	⊕ Western France	🏁 Motorsport	90
...		French Riviera Classic & Sport, Nice	⊕ Southern France	📷 Shows & Tours	115
...		British Car Show, Nantua	⊕ Central France & the Alps	📷 Shows & Tours	170
...		Coupe des Alpes	⊕ Central France & the Alps	📷 Shows & Tours	173

Visit **www.driveguide.guru/france/events/** for the latest events

Month		Event	Chapter / Region	Section	Page
...		Chinon Classic (Grand Prix de Tours)	⊕ Central France & the Alps	⚑ Motorsport	180
...		Grand Prix de l'Age d'Or, Dijon-Prenois	⊕ Central France & the Alps	⚑ Motorsport	181
...	Odd years	Vichy Classic (Grand Prix de Vichy)	⊕ Central France & the Alps	⚑ Motorsport	185
...		Festival des Belles Mécaniques, Roubaix	⊕ North-East France	📷 Shows & Tours	217
...		Rétro Meus'auto, Lac de Madine	⊕ North-East France	📷 Shows & Tours	221
Jun/Jul		Rétro Festival Caen	⊕ Western France	📷 Shows & Tours	80
Jul	Odd years	Elégance rétrospective automobile, Sarlat	⊕ Western France	📷 Shows & Tours	75
...		Grand Prix Rétro du Puy-Notre-Dame	⊕ Western France	⚑ Motorsport	95
...	Even years	Le Mans Classic	⊕ Western France	⚑ Motorsport	88
...		Grand Prix de France Historique, Magny-Cours	⊕ Central France & the Alps	⚑ Motorsport	182
Jul/Aug		Traversée de Paris en anciennes	⊕ Paris & the Ile-de-France	📷 Shows & Tours	31
Aug		Concours d'élégance, La Baule	⊕ Western France	📷 Shows & Tours	72
...		Course de côte (hillclimb), Étretat	⊕ Western France	⚑ Motorsport	93
...	Odd years	Bouchon de Tourves	⊕ Southern France	📷 Shows & Tours	113
Aug/Sep	Odd years	Coupe Florio Saint-Brieuc	⊕ Western France	📷 Shows & Tours	73
Sep		American Car Club de France (ACCF) Festivals	⊕ Paris & the Ile-de-France	📷 Shows & Tours	24
		Les Grandes Heures Automobiles, Montlhéry	⊕ Paris & the Ile-de-France	⚑ Motorsport	51
...		Dieppe Rétro	⊕ Western France	📷 Shows & Tours	74
...		Les Anciennes en Vallée de l'Eure Classic, Saint Aubin-sur-Gaillon	⊕ Western France	📷 Shows & Tours	71
...		Salon Auto Moto Rétro, Rouen	⊕ Western France	📷 Shows & Tours	81
...		Traversée de Bordeaux	⊕ Western France	📷 Shows & Tours	84
...		Circuit des Remparts, Angoulême	⊕ Western France	⚑ Motorsport	86
...		Rallye international des cathédrales	⊕ Central France & the Alps	📷 Shows & Tours	176
...	Even years	48 Heures Européennes, Troyes	⊕ North-East France	📷 Shows & Tours	220
...		Chantilly Arts et Élégance	⊕ North-East France	📷 Shows & Tours	214
...		Concours d'élégance, Le Touquet Paris-Plage Historique	⊕ North-East France	📷 Shows & Tours	216
...		Festival Bugatti, Molsheim	⊕ North-East France	📷 Shows & Tours	218
Sep/Oct		Rallye Paris-Deauville	⊕ Western France	📷 Shows & Tours	77
...		Les 100 Tours, Nogaro	⊕ Southern France	⚑ Motorsport	132
...		Rallye Classic Forez	⊕ Central France & the Alps	📷 Shows & Tours	175
Sep-Dec		Passion et partage, Alès	⊕ Southern France	⚑ Motorsport	136
Oct		Automédon, Le Bourget	⊕ Paris & the Ile-de-France	📷 Shows & Tours	26
...	Even years	Mondial de l'Automobile, Paris	⊕ Paris & the Ile-de-France	📷 Shows & Tours	18
...		Autobrocante, Lohéac	⊕ Western France	🏠 Market Place	85
...		Classic Festival, Nogaro	⊕ Southern France	📷 Shows & Tours	114
...		Trophée en Corse	⊕ Southern France	📷 Shows & Tours	119
...		Les Dix Mille Tours, Circuit du Castellet	⊕ Southern France	⚑ Motorsport	134
...		Tour de Corse Historique	⊕ Southern France	⚑ Motorsport	139
...	Even years	Embouteillage de Lapalisse	⊕ Central France & the Alps	📷 Shows & Tours	174
Nov		Epoqu'Auto, Lyon	⊕ Central France & the Alps	📷 Shows & Tours	168
Nov/Dec		Salon Rétro Course, Villefranche-sur-Saône	⊕ Central France & the Alps	📷 Shows & Tours	177
Dec		Bourse-expo de Cavaillon	⊕ Southern France	📷 Shows & Tours	120
...		Chambéry Auto Rétro	⊕ Central France & the Alps	📷 Shows & Tours	171
...		Habits de lumière, Épernay	⊕ North-East France	📷 Shows & Tours	219

Further reading

Press and Internet

La Vie de l'Auto: published weekly and available on subscription (see lva-auto.fr/minisite/)
News d'Anciennes (newsdanciennes.com plus Facebook): online event reports
Retrocalage (www.retrocalage.com): online listing of club events and regular newsletters

Books

The following suggestions follow the order of entries in the guide. Some titles are now out-of-print, but can be found through the booksellers in the Market Place sections of the guide.

France – general

Le Guide du Collectionneur Auto (Éditions LVA, annual)

Guide de voyages en voiture de collection: Itinéraires et hébergements en France (Bed & Historic Motors, 2017)

D Taulin-Hommell & C Courtel, *Musées automobiles de France: un siècle d'histoire* (Éditions SPAL, 2006)

L'incroyable collection: les trésors des musées et conservatoires français de l'automobile (PG médias éditions, 2006)

P Lesueur, *Concours d'élégance: Dream cars and lovely ladies* (Dalton Watson, 2011)

R Meaden, *Classic Motorsport Routes* (AA Publishing, 2007)

Paris & the Ile-de-France

T Hesse, *Mémoires de Salons* (Éditions l'Autodrome – Michel Hommell, 2016)

D Pascal & P Lesueur, *L'Aventure du Salon de l'Automobile* (Hachette, 2006)

C Courtel, *Les Grandes Heures du Tour Auto 1958-80* (Hors-série Échappement, Groupe Hommell)

S Bellu, *30 ans de design* (Festival Automobile International, 2015, English/French)

Citroën, *Le Patrimoine Citroën / Heritage Citroën* (English/French, 2015)

M-C Quef, *Citroën, un parcours architectural* (ETAI, 2009)

R Roubaudi, *L'Aventure DS, Une ambition française/A French Ambition* (Verlhac Éditions, 2013, English/French)

J-L Loubet et al, *Ile Seguin: des Renault et des hommes* (ETAI, 2nd edition 2004)

J-L Loubet et al, *Les Champs-Elysées de Renault* (ETAI, 2010)

W ('Bill') Boddy, *Montlhéry – The story of the Paris Autodrome* (Veloce Publishing)

Western France

Le Manoir de l'Automobile (Hors-série Auto Passion)

Le Musée des 24 Heures-Circuit de la Sarthe (official museum catalogue, English/French)

Automobiles et Patrimoine (APPF-Pays de Fougères, 2004)

Jean-Pierre Doury, *Sport et Collection, 15 ans de passion et de solidarité* (Éditions au fil du temps, 2009)

J Baudin, *Le Tour de Bretagne des Véhicules Anciens* (Éditions Géorama, 2014)

Automobile Club de l'Ouest, *Les 24 Heures du Mans* (ETAI, official yearbook, also in English)

G Ireland, *Le Mans Panoramic* (Veloce Publishing, 2012)

R Puyal & L Nivalle, *Le Mans Classic: Courir après la vitesse / Chasing after speed* (ETAI, 2017, English/French)

F Llorens, *Les Grands Prix de Bordeaux 1951-55* (published by the author, 2013)

J-C Fillon, *Les années circuit: L'histoire des courses automobiles à Bressuire 1950-55* (Auto-Rétro Bressuirais, 2006)

J-L Ribémon & Ray Toombs, *Deauville 1936, Un Grand Prix près des Planches* (itf Éditeur, 2010, English/French)

L'Amicale des Anciens d'Alpine, *Un siècle de compétition automobile à Dieppe* (Éditions du Palmier, 2009)

J Privat, *Rallycross de Lohéac* (Éditions l›Autodrome – Michel Hommell, 2014)

Southern France

T Dubois, *C'était la Nationale 7* (Éditions Paquet, 2012)

G Bretzel, *Grand Prix de Monaco Historique* (Somogy éditions d'art, 2008, English/French)

G Robson, *Monte Carlo Rally: The Golden Age, 1911-80* (Herridge & Sons, 2007)

M Louche, *La course de côte du Mont Ventoux 1902-1976* (Éditions Maurice Louche, 2008)

A Diviès & Bernard Le Soulan, *Si Nogaro m'était conté* (Circuit Paul Armagnac, 2001)

F Chevalier, *Circuit Paul Ricard: au cœur de la compétition auto/moto* (ETAI, 2004)

40 ans de magie de la glisse (Éditions du Circuit de Serre Chevalier, 2011)

Central France & the Alps

F Sabatès & G Blanchet, *François Lecot: 400.000 km en Traction 1935-1936* (Éditions SPE, 1998)

L'Aventure Michelin (official museum catalogue, English/French)

P Vergès, *Michelin, à la conquête de l'automobile* (ETAI, 2013)

M Chabbi, *Philippe Guédon, l'homme de l'Espace* (ETAI, 2003)

M Pfundner, *Alpine Trials & Rallies 1910 to 1973* (Veloce Publishing, 2005)

P Besqueut, *Charade, le plus beau circuit du monde 1958-2002* (Éditions du Palmier, 2003)

Y Morizot, *1972-2012 : 40 ans de passion* (Circuit Dijon-Prenois/Le Bien Public, 2012)

J-L Balleret, *Le circuit de Magny-Cours, 50 ans de passion mécanique* (La Fabrique Nevers, 2011)

North-East France

R Keller & P Garnier, *Le Musée National de l'Automobile* (Éditions du Donon, 2012)

J-M François, *Un circuit de légende : Gueux* (L'Union, 2010, English/French)

Drive Guide Guru

DriveGuide.guru is the online home of *France: The Essential Guide for Car Enthusiasts* and *The Essential Guide to Driving in Europe.* Along with author Julian Parish's blog, guide updates and news, downloads and a live calendar of automotive events in France, you'll also find social media links, videos, and information on forthcoming books from the author.

DriveGuide.guru

Home of the *Essential Guides*

facebook www.facebook.com/DriveGuideGuru

🌐 www.driveguide.guru

Also from Veloce Publishing ...

The Essential Guide to Driving in Europe

This easy to use guide helps you to prepare for your European trip, and check the information you require on the road.

With unrivalled coverage, it provides the key facts you need to drive in 50 countries across Europe – as well as general advice to help you deal with the unexpected, no matter where you are – wherever you drive in Europe, this guide gives you the facts you need for a safe and enjoyable trip.

ISBN: 978-1-845847-88-3 • Paperback • 21x14.8cm
144 pages • 448 pictures

Bonjour! Is this Italy? *and* From Crystal Palace To Red Square

Following his dismissal from a job he never should have had, Kevin Turner packs a tent, some snacks, and a suit, and sets out on a two-wheeled adventure across Europe in *Bonjour! Is this Italy? From Crystal Palace To Red Square* sees Turner jumping on his motorbike and setting out in search of further adventure.

Bonjour! Is this Italy? is also available in eBook format.
ISBN: 978-1-845845-72-8
Flowing layout
129 pictures

ISBN: 978-1-845843-99-1
Paperback • 21x14.8cm
144 pages • 129 pictures

ISBN: 978-1-845846-22-0
Paperback • 21x14.8cm
160 pages • 134 pictures

The Real Way Round

1 year, 1 bike, 1 man, 35 countries, 42,000 miles, 9 oil changes, 3 sets of tyres, and loads more ...
A pictorial diary of a once-in-a-lifetime motorcycle trip across 35 countries on a Yamaha Ténéré XT660, and a practical guide to motorcycling around the world.

ISBN: 978-1-845842-94-9 • Hardback
25x25cm • 224 pages • 692 pictures

Peking to Paris – The *Ultimate* driving adventure

Marking the 100th anniversary of the original 'Great Race', over 100 cars set out to drive the original route used by Prince Borghese in 1907.

ISBN: 978-1-845847-19-7
Flowing layout
456 pictures

---

*All prices subject to change. P&P extra.

Walking the dog – Motorway walks for drivers and dogs

How do you find great pub food, places for your kids to play, somewhere nice to walk your dog, and park a campervan, all within 5 miles of a motorway exit?

REVISED
Walking the dog
EDITION
Motorway walks
for drivers and dogs

Lezli Rees

HOW WITH GPS CO-ORDINATES

All motorway drivers will benefit from this guide to walks within 5 miles of motorway exits. The whole the UK is covered, from Exeter to Perth and Swansea to Canterbury.

Use this book to discover countryside walks for drivers, dogs and their families, with recommended family activities and suitable places to eat along the way

ISBN: 978-1-845848-86-6
Paperback • 15x10.5cm
208 pages
200 colour pictures

Also available in eBook AND App formats!

Walking the dog
Motorway walks
for drivers and dogs

eBook: ISBN 978-1-845845-52-0 • Flowing layout
200 pictures

Also available ...
Apps
Download now from
www.digital.veloce.co.uk

In partnership with the RAC

The RAC Handbook Series

This range of inexpensive, informative and, often, money-saving books and ebooks are perfect for all motorists, motorcyclists and cyclists. Whether you're looking to improve your driving skills, fix or maintain your vehicle, or simply find some beautiful scenery, we have a book for you!

Also available ...
eBooks
Download now from
www.digital.veloce.co.uk

The Essential Driver's Handbook
ISBN: 978-1-845845-32-2 • Paperback
21x14.8cm
80 pages
95 pictures

First aid for your car
ISBN: 978-1-845845-19-3 • Paperback
21x14.8cm
128 pages
137 colour pictures

Dogs on wheels
ISBN: 978-1-845843-79-3 • Paperback
21x14.8cm
80 pages
90 colour pictures

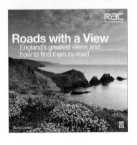

Roads with a View – England's greatest views and how to find them by road

Roads with a View is not just another travel guide. This has been written by a driver especially for fellow motorists, and provides detailed accounts of the best English roads to drive on, and the best places to drive to for that stunning front seat view. Features specially drawn maps, beautiful colour photography, and plenty of travel advice.

ISBN: 978-1-845843-50-2 • Hardback • 25x25cm
144 pages • 57 pictures

For more information on our titles, visit our websites, email info@veloce.co.uk or call +44(0)1305 260068
www.veloce.co.uk ● www.velocebooks.com ● digital.veloce.co.uk

Connect on social media   facebook www.facebook.com/VelocePublishing   @VeloceBooks

Index